Gas lamps
And
Long trousers
A story based on true events

Copyright Text © 2021 G J Collins
All Rights Reserved
.

Dedications
This book could not have been written without the major contributions of my Brother, Patrick.

Preface

Although great care has been taken writing this book, they are the memories of long ago. Some locations, dates, and events may vary with others.

About the story

Imagine living in a time before television – before head phones, laptops and the internet; and entertainment was programs such as, 'Wilfred Pickles have a go' 'Sparky and the magic piano' 'The runaway train' 'Mothers hour' 'Educating Archie with Peter Brough and Archie Andrews' 'The Navy Lark' 'Journey into Space,' brought into our homes from the wireless, powered from two accumulator batteries. When sash windows rattled from the wind, and double glazing was a thing of the future. When sitting in front of a large cast iron fire, with coal from the coal cupboard being the only source of heating. When the toilet was outside, and flushed from a chain hanging from the cistern above your head. When newspaper was cut into squares to wipe your backside on. When cockroaches scurried into the walls when the gas lamp was lit on dark evenings. When gramophone's with a seventy eight inch records played the likes of Glen Miller. When birthdays and Christmas's were celebrated around a piano, and not because of presents - but as a family.

Some people will say the nineteen forties were the good old days, when children as young as five could walk to the park without their parents, or play on the bombsites, long before the NHS was founded in 1946, and health and safety decided things like that were too dangerous to play on. When trams dominated transport, and children played hopscotch on the pavement, or marbles in the gutter, without fear of the marble bouncing into the road. Some people will say they were the good old days - but others may think differently.

This story will take you back to those years; through the eyes of a family who lived through them.

G J Collins

One
2017

It was the middle of February; Friday the 27th and I'd been in the garden for most of the day. So far I'd cut back the shrubs, cleaned out the pond, removed all the gifts in the forest bark, left by the animals in the grove, and I was now on my last job, cleaning out the weeds in the gutter

Thankfully it wasn't too cold for the time of year, and though rain clouds had been building across the sky for some time, only a few drops had fell. Apart from taking Marion to work at half eleven, I hadn't stopped, and the first roll of thunder was now telling me to call it a day.

I'd just finished filling the bags with the garden rubbish, and Dan's distinctive voice turned my head to the garden two doors away.

"Looks like it's going to pour down, James!"

"Well they did forecast it Dan," I called back. "Thunder with heavy showers, that's what they said."

"You can't have much left to do now; you've been at it all day"?"

"Just tidying up and I'm ready for a good soak mate, I stink to high Heaven. Half the gung in the gutters run down my sleeves and inside my pants. No wonder the weeds were growing in it. You wouldn't believe how much shite a gutter can hold!"

Dan suddenly dip behind the brick mustered coloured wall, and every time he spoke his head appeared just above the top row of blue bricks. "I've been putting mine off since before Christmas. Jenny saw you clearing yours this morning, and I thought that's it, now she'll want me to do ours."

I saw the flicker of lightning above the dark clouds, then the first clap of thunder rolling overhead. "That's it mate I'm in before the heavens open."

"Yeah, me too," Dan responded. "I'm off for a birthday meal with the family later; I'm seventy four this coming Saturday." Dan suddenly shot upright, arching his back with a groan. "They would've held it on Saturday, but Saturday's a busy time for most people – Seventy four!" Dan groaned again. "Sometimes I feel like I'm eighty four; too old to be digging holes; and cleaning out gutters!"

I lowered the step ladders and lay them on the path by the French doors. "You're just a few weeks older than me Dan! Wait till you ARE eighty four before you moan about being old mate."

Another clap of thunder rumbled across the sky, and I lingered only to say. "Enjoy your birthday meal mate." I grabbed the garden tools and threw them in the bunker at the side of the house. With only minutes to spare before the Heavens opened, I was inside drawing the whiff of a rotting swamp along with me.

The aromatic smell of pot-pourri, mingled instantly with the stench of gutter. And as I climbed the stairs, I noticed the squirts of air freshener in the bedroom were not winning either.

Keen to be clean, I stripped quickly and stood over the bath, squirting muscle therapy with black pepper and ginseng into the stream of water.

By one thirty I had showered, eaten the cheese and ham sandwich from the fridge; finished off the rest of the bread pudding, and was staring through the French doors at the rain bouncing off the glass.

The smell of pot-pourri had returned with a vengeance, and had it not been for the laptop failing to switch on, I would have been in my little corner, spending the rest of the afternoon tapping away on it.

I stared through the doors again, humming at my vacant expression staring back at me in the glass. I thought about watching the television, but that was something I rarely did in the day. I was behaving like a lonely retired old man, mulling around the house in my slippers, wondering how I was going to fill the time before I picked Marion up from work.

Without even realising I'd meandered to the kitchen and was making a cup of tea, staring at the biscuit tin deciding which to dunk in first: a ginger biscuit or a coconut cream.

There was still three hours to go before I picked Marion up from work. She would be asking me what I'd done all afternoon as my laptop was defunct: Then I thought about what she said not a few hours ago.

'Love! If you've got time on your hands today, will you sort out the cupboard - and tidy your wardrobe?

The draws are bulging with clothes you haven't worn for ages; and there isn't room for anything else in your wardrobe! I'm not rushing you love, but I have been asking you to do it for ages!'

In fairness the cupboard WAS a mess, and considering I'd just shoved my dirty clothes inside the washing machine, I thought it was the appropriate thing for me to do.

It didn't take long before I'd sorted out the cupboard, and stuffed all my unwanted clothes into bags for the Jewish relief. – And as Marion hadn't mentioned the top of the cupboard, I saw tidying that too was a guaranteed peaceful evening.

The moment I dragged the first box toward me, my hands were covered in particles of fine dust, which was clearly covering everything else on top of the cupboard. "Bloody hell, how long has this lot been up there?" I pulled off the lid and peered inside at the broken high heel shoes, last worn by Marion over nine years ago. "I know where they're going," I mumbled throwing the box behind me.

The holdall, relegated to the top of the wardrobe because Marion never liked the colour was still there; tucked away waiting for her to change her mind. "And I know where that's going too," I said yanking it off the wardrobe toward the box on the floor.

As the pile grew behind me, the last was a parcel in brown paper almost out of sight. Even standing on tip toe I only just managed to reach it.

At this point I was already covered in dust, and in two minds whether to shove it straight into the bin bag and be done with. Thankfully I didn't, and ripped away the brown paper instead. Wrapped inside was the red photo album I'd completely forgotten we had, filled with the memories I'd long forgotten.

I walked to the small bedroom chair, with my childhood memories coming to mind, and with a melancholy smile ousting aside my grumpiness, I turned over the first cover.

Tucked inside the pocket of cellophane was a photo of mom and dad, sitting on deckchairs squinting through dark sunglasses toward my Kodak box camera. Mom was wearing her floppy hat, a thin white blouse and summer trousers she'd bought from the clothes shop on Lady Pool road we all called - The lane. Dad had a knotted handkerchief on his head; a shirt opened fully, and light baggy trousers rolled up to his knees. The next photo was taken with us all together on the sand. And if I remembered right, it was taken by the couple with a black and white collie with long matted hair. Another was my brother Patrick, walking toward mom and dad from a puddle of seawater, with soggy green knitted trunks sagging between his legs. I smiled as I removed it from the cellophane pocket and turned it over. Scribbled in pencil were the words. 'Golden Sands holiday camp, Rhyl 1947. I was four and a quarter then. Patrick was one, and my sister, Elizabeth was seven and a half.

Dad was a great dad, and in his younger years quite handsome. I remember seeing a photo of him with his dark hair slicked back, and his chest bared posing as a boxer. Mom called him Hal; his friends called him, H; and he was Jim to his mates at work. I never could understand why he had so many names.

Because mom could suntan quicker than she could fry and egg, she always looked like a gypsy traveller in the summer. For years I never knew her name was Nellie, because dad always called her Titch - on account of her being only five foot three, even in high heels. Mom may have been small, but she was the boss. In nineteen thirty seven mom was twenty five, and an attractive petite woman. She was the typical female of the time, with short hair and a curl across her forehead. At the same time dad was twenty three and a dapper gent, with slick black hair, wide trousers and polished shoes.

Me and my Girl had just been released on the pictures, and 'The Lambeth Walk' from the film was popular at most dance halls. It was at one of the dance halls dad met mom, and he asked her to dance with him.

With so many memories coming to mind I closed my eyes; allowing me to visualise those magical moments of youth from long ago.

1946

Access to our house was up an entry to a grove of eight houses. I never considered the entry being a nuisance as the milkman, the coalman, or the dustman did. I saw the entry as the gateway to another world, where home was my sanctuary, and the toes and throes of growing into adulthood happened, without even knowing.

It was one year and four months after the Second World War ended; on a Sunday afternoon in May. Lizzie was holding my hand, walking me around our small rectangle garden; and I was pulling on her hand angrily, with a sliver of snot emerging from my left nostril.

"I want to go and see Patrick," I whined, watching some of the neighbours toing and froing from the house.

"You can't! Dad said you have to stay out here with me!"

My bottom lip quivered again, then parted from a full blown blart. "But I don't want to stay out here with you, Lizzie. I want to go in the house to see Patrick?"

"There's too many people in the house; and dad told me to keep you out here till they've all gone."

"But there won't be any food left, Lizzie. Why did Patrick have to be christened anyway? I wasn't christened!"

"Yes you were!"

"Well how come I don't remember having any cake then?"

"Because you were too young – that's why, Brat? Everyone's in the posh room, and it isn't big enough for everyone. We have to wait out here till some of the neighbours have gone, then we can go in!"

"But I want to go in *NOW*, Lizzie! It's not fair, Patrick's in the house with all the cake, and I haven't had any yet!"

*

"That was a lovely christening, Titch, Patrick looks lovely; where did you buy his christening clothes from?"

"I didn't, Annie they're Jamie's. We couldn't afford the ones on sale down the lane - and buy all the food; it was either one or the other - not both!"

"Well I wouldn't have known if you hadn't told me, Titch. I did exactly the same with Robert and Billy. Monies hard to come by as it is!"

"I know, Annie; were going to Rhyl in a few months and saving hard for it."

*

Elizabeth knelt in front of me, grasping both hands firmly - in case I escaped again. "Look Jamie, you were being a nuisance, and dad said I have to keep you outside until everyone's gone. You were crawling under the table, and jumping up and down. Mom's already told you not to jump up and down in the posh room; the floorboards under the piano move, and it's bouncing away from the wall. If you get in the way again you'll just be told off again; you're staying out here with me - and that's it!" Elizabeth stood up with her doe eyes attempting to pacify me. "Come on, we'll walk round the garden and say hello to the bees and the flowers again!"

"But I don't want to say hello to the bees again; I want to go in the house."

Elizabeth's eyes widened as they came towards me. "And, then if you want, we can go down the entry and say hello to the dragonflies as well!"

My spoilt brat faced expression faded at the thought of leaving the garden, and going down the entry with Lizzie. "Okay," I nodded while wiping the snot from my nose with the back of my hand.

"Will you stop doing that, it's filthy!! Ugh, give me your hand." Elizabeth wiped my hand with her handkerchief, and reluctantly put it inside the small pocket in her dress.

Lizzy's look of disgust didn't bother me. Dragonflies were my favourite flying things, and the ivy growing over the wall along the entry was always the perfect place to see one. Happily I walked by her side around the garden, holding her hand like a good boy should, listening to her humming to herself. My sister Elizabeth was a proper girly girl, tall and skinny with short pigtails sticking up either side of her head -

like palm trees. Sometimes she would be my sister, singing and playing with me when I was good; and sometimes she was my second mother, scolding me with a waving finger for being a little shit, and not listening to her. Looking back I was fortunate to have a sister like Elizabeth, because mom always trusted her to look after me. And I of course I could leave the confines of the garden with her, without mom saying I couldn't. Elizabeth also had a lovely singing voice too, and on occasions when she was happy made up little songs – Like the one she sang while walking me along the privet, past dad's rhubarb patch to the purple coneflowers attracting the bees.

"SHUSH, Jay–look," said Lizzie holding me back. "A bees just landed on the flower, can you see him?" she asked me quietly.

"Yes I can see him," I answered quietly back.

I felt Lizzie's hand tightening around mine, restraining me from going closer to the bee. "What's he doing, Lizzie?"

"He's collecting the nectar from the petals. That's what they need to make honey - dad told me!"

I watched closely as the bee rummaged inside the flower, oblivious to me being there. "I want to go closer, Lizzie," I said tugging her hand.

"No, we mustn't go too close or we might frighten him," she said tugging be back. "You have to give him a wave so he can see you're his friend first."

Encouraged by Elizabeth's enthusiasm I waved at the bee, growing in excitement as another bee landed on the flower next to it. "Look, there's another one, Lizzie," I said pointing bravely.

"Quick give him a wave too so he knows you won't hurt him," encouraged Elizabeth."

While I stood obediently waving at the bees I heard Lizzy singing quietly just above me.

---"One little bumblebee can you see.

---He's sitting on the flower waving at me.

---Now there's another one that makes two.

---And that little bumble bee's waving at you?"

"Did YOU see him waving at you, Jamie?" Elizabeth asked in bated excitement.

"Yes," I answered convinced the little creatures had.

*

"Hi, Lizzie, what are you doing?"

Elizabeth turned away from the flower, greeting her friend Jessica Laurence with a smile.

Although there were other kids in our grove to play with, Jessie was Lizzie's best friend, and her mom and dad were friends with my mom and dad.

"Hi, Jessie! Dad told me to keep Jamie with me until everyone's seen Patrick!"

Jessie walked along the privet from the opposite side toward Elizabeth, releasing a curious, "Oh."

"We're waving at the bees Jessie," I said releasing my boyish excitement and pointing at the flower. "You can wave at them as well if you want - can't she Lizzie?"

Elizabeth nodded, displaying her motherly importance to me and Jessie. "If she wants, Jamie!"

Jessica released a girly giggle, and waved at the Bumble bees. "So you can't come and play then if you're looking after Jamie?"

I'm taking him down the entry to wave at the dragonflies in a minute!"

"Are you allowed to take him down the entry, Lizzie?"

"Yes, I'm seven now," answered Elizabeth airing her authority. "Dad said he's leaving Jamie in my care until everyone's gone." Elizabeth suddenly straightened her back, rising from her moment of self–importance. "I'm taking Jamie down the entry to see the dragonfly in the ivy on the wall. Come with us, Jessie," Lizzie asked her again while leading me by the arm toward the gate.

Jessica hesitated, and glanced toward the front door for a sign of her mother. "Okay, but as long as I don't get my clothes dirty. Mom's banned me from playing on the bomb site in case I dirty my new clothes."

"No, only as far as the ivy, Jessie," confirmed Elizabeth.

I was four but felt like a grown up when I left the garden, striding along the path between the privet towards the entry. I was an explorer, heading toward the dragonfly's lair, pulling Elizabeth along with tiny steps.

Beyond the wall on the other side was a large pond with no fish; just pond weed and a couple of white lilies. It had been left to its own devices for years, and belonged to the creatures who lived in stagnant ponds - such as the dragonfly.

"Jaimie, stop pulling and walk properly!"

"But you're not walking fast enough, Lizzie, and I want to walk faster?"

"Yes we are;" she voiced like a head mistress. "Now stop pulling and walk next to me, or we'll turn around and go back!"

With a sour face I walked by Elizabeth's side toward the entry, listening to her and Jessie engrossing themselves in girly talk. As we reached the ivy, Elizabeth and Jessica leant against the wall opposite the ivy, continuing their giggling conversation, and I stared towards the ivy, fidgeting with impatience. I felt Elizabeth's hand tightening around mine ensuring I stayed by her side. Lizzie promised me I could wave to the dragonfly; and we were never going to do that standing this side of the entry.

"I want to go closer, Lizzie!" I said pulling her away from the wall toward the ivy opposite. My arm hurt as Elizabeth pulled me back, scolding me as mom would.

"NO, we're staying here on this side, Jamie!"

"But I can't wave to the dragonfly from this side, Lizzie," I protested.

"When a dragonfly comes, I'll take you close enough to wave to him - okay?"

Jessica moved her mouth closer to Elizabeth's ear. "Does Jamie really think bees and dragonfly's wave to him," she asked Lizzie quietly.

"Yes," Lizzie answered staunching a chuckle. "Jamie isn't grow up like us, Jessie! He doesn't know insects and a creatures can't talk. He's got a teddy bear called Teddy, and he talks to him all the time. When you turn him upside down he growls, and Jamie believes Teddy's talking to him."

"Aren't children funny, Lizzie?"

"Yes." Elizabeth exhaled in a slight sigh. "When I was young, Jessie I talked to my doll Bella all the time. I still talk to her now even though she's only a doll because I love her anyway."

"I talk to my doll Alice all the time too," said Jessica. "Mom and dad are buying me a new pram for my birthday. If you want we can take them for a walk together."

"Yes, okay," Elizabeth nodded.

Almost two thirds of the wall was overhung with ivy; and I was staring intensely at the area dangling in front of me. I could feel Elizabeth's hand slackening from her conversation with Jessica, and the moment I saw the winged creature landing on the ivy, I slipped away from hand. I was well under the foliage when I shouted to Lizzie. "LIZZIE, there's a dragonfly –and look, I can nearly reach it?"

Elizabeth's arms were around me in an instant, dragging me away with a scolding more viciously than mom would have given me. "YOU NAUGHTY

BOY, JAMIE! I'm taking you back home right NOW!"

I tried holding back, voicing by concern in wailing cry. "But the dragonfly, Lizzie?"

"I told you to stay by me, Jay, and you didn't!"

"But I only did it because you wasn't going to let me wave to the dragonfly."

Elizabeth virtually frog marched me up the entry by an arm, voicing her girly wrath upon me. "It could've bit you, Jamie and then you would've got me in big trouble."

"But I only wanted him to see me so I could wave at him, Lizzie,"

"It's a dragonfly, Jay and dragons have big teeth. They don't shake hands they bite it, and dad would've blamed me if it bit you!"

"But the dragonfly wouldn't have bit me, Lizzie; he was going to wave at me like the bees did!"

Elizabeth took no notice of me wailing, like someone falling over the edge of a cliff. I could feel her anger as she shoved me through the gate, and through the front door, yelling. "DAD! Jamie's playing up again, and I'm not looking after him anymore!"

*

Like most terraced houses in the 1940s, they were over one hundred years ago. We had no bathroom, just a zinc bath hanging from a hook on the wall outside. To the scullery was through the back living room door and into the yard. It had a single crock basin with cold running water connected to the tap by leaded pipe. The cooker was cast iron with curved legs, and the pots and pans were stored on shelves covering the wall opposite.

In the scullery was the brick copper boiler in the corner, heated from a coal fire with a cast iron door. I can just remember dad lighting the fire underneath the copper; and mom plunging the wooden dolly peg (A wooden pole with three prongs one end and a handle on the other) and agitating the clothes with it. The toilet was also outside, shared between us and the house next door.

We had two rooms down stairs. One we called the living room, and the other, the posh room. In the posh room we had the upright piano, dad had bought from one of his work mates. It was going to be burnt on their bonfire, and dad gave him two shillings to have it moved to our posh room.

We were only allowed in the posh room on special occasions - such as Christmas and birthdays, then mom would play the piano for us. It was completely out of tune, and mom would sing along as though it wasn't. Mom had a lovely voice, and before Patrick was born, she often she sang in the; New Inns, at the top of the street. Sometimes she would come home with sixpence, and sometimes it was half a crown.

"I TOLD you to be a good boy, didn't I, Cods Head?" (The term of endearment dad always called me when instilling words of warning in my ear.) "If you can't be trusted to behave for your sister, you can sit with your Auntie Mo in the corner."

My skinny arms stretched as dad hauled me up by both arms, and dropped me squarely onto Auntie Mo's lap. "Look after him for a while, Mo; he's getting bored!"

"Don't you worry about this little feller," said Mo, wrapping both arms around my waist. "We'll be just fine – *WON'T WE?*"

Auntie Mo was a big woman, twice the size of mom; and her eyes seemed to balance on her cheeks, like little ping pong balls. As her face leered toward me, my head began nodding yes without me wanting it to.

It was probably only ten minutes when mom came to the rescue, and knelt down beside the chair, but for me if felt a lot longer than that.

"Listen Jay," she said in her quiet motherly tone. "Just for a while longer you have to be a good boy, and sit nicely on your Auntie's lap. Everyone will be gone soon; AND, if you are good you can stay up a bit longer and listen to the wireless, is that okay?"

Even though I wanted to say, 'No, it wasn't okay mom,' I never did because Auntie Mo had me in a wrestlers arm lock; and with her large curls covering her head like white candyfloss, I simply nodded with a pitiful look, hoping she would change her mind.

Mom thanked Erick, Mabel and little Arthur from coming, praising Arthur for being a good boy. Arthur waved at me, and I stuck my tongue out to him, because I hadn't been.

"Now everyone's gone, I'll ask Hal to make us a nice cup of tea, Mo!"

'Mom could've asked me if I wanted some pop,' I mumbled. This was a moment of silent abandonment; where I forgot I was four and potty trained, because in sheer thoughtlessness I peed onto Auntie Mo's Sunday best.

*

"Patrick's beautiful isn't he, Mom?"

"Yes he is Elizabeth, and he's going to be big and strong like your brother - isn't he Jamie?" Mom said looking at me.

I pulled my tongue out at Elizabeth with the words - big and strong rolling proudly off the end of it.

Dad was drifting from one side of the house to the other, undecided which one of the hundred and one things mom had told him to do first.

"Titch, do you want that cup of tea now before he wakes up?"

"No, Hal, do his bottle first, he'll be waking up for it soon."

"Where's his bottle?"

"In the cupboard under the stairs, second shelf. The tin of powdered milk and Karo syrup is next to it."

Dad came from the cupboard, holding the bottle in one hand, and balancing jar and tin in the other. "So, what do I do then?"

"Hal, you've got three children now. I would have thought you'd know how to make a bottle of milk without me having to tell you, for goodness sake!"

"Of course I wouldn't," grunted dad. "You've always made up the bottles - AND I change the nappies – remember?"

Mom turned to Elizabeth, clearly agitated by dad's response – again. "All your father has to do is put two scoops of power in the bottle, add the boiling water from the kettle, add a spoonful of syrup, and shake. What is so difficult about that? It's so simple you could have done it Elizabeth."

Elizabeth positioned herself next to mom on the couch, raising both shoulders and refusing to be piggy in the middle – AGAIN!

"Here, Lizzie," said mom placing Patrick into her arms. "You take Patrick while I do his bottle. It seems your father's forgotten how to make it?" Mom yanked the bottle from dad, glowering at him with her terrier eyes. "One of these days Lizzie I might be able to go to the kitchen - without having to go outside in the cold. Your dad's been promising to build me a lean–to for so long he's probably forgotten–like he has with the milk!" Mom sauntered to the back door, and before she slammed it behind her, I saw dad give Elizabeth a crafty wink while answering. "Ah shut up you silly old cow, I'll do it when I'm ready!"

Dad went to the coal cupboard opposite the door under the stairs, and scooped a few lumps of coal onto the shovel. "Listen both of you," he said emptying the coal onto the fire. "Your mother will be tired looking after Patrick, so I want you both to behave - especially you Jamie," said dad turning his eyes to me. "You're a big boy now so no more squabbling between you and your sister – Okay both of you?"

"I only said okay because Elizabeth did. I didn't want her thinking she was better than me because I didn't say okay.

Mom returned with the bottle and lifted Patrick from Elizabeth's comforting hold. "Hal, the tin baths in the scullery filled with water. I've already put the soap flakes in, so all you have to do is put the dirty clothes in to soak. Can you do that before you put the wireless on?"

"Yes, I'll do it now!" Dad beckoned toward Elizabeth with a finger. "All your dirty clothes in a pile by the back door please. Jay, you play with your toys nice and quietly for your mom; Elizabeth will helping me to sort out the washing!"

With all the washing in the galvanized bath soaking nicely, Elizabeth returned to the living room, voicing her orders from dad. "Mom! Dad said tell Jay not to go in the kitchen, he might fall in the bath and drown!"

I objected to the way Lizzie sneered at me when she said, DROWN, and extended my tongue fully toward her.

Elizabeth simply raised her eyebrows haughtily and looked away.

"Hal, before you go to work tomorrow, will you light the fire under the copper. I'll probably have my hands full with Patrick to do it myself!"

"I'll help with the washing when I come from school in my dinner break, Mom," volunteered Elizabeth, fussing over Patrick as he drank his milk.

"And I'm going to help too Mom," I said grimacing toward Elizabeth's smug expression.

It was the hour before my bedtime, the time I always enjoyed most of all being fussed by dad. Now there was someone else sharing my moment of happiness; and something I would learn to contend with.

*

Mom and Elizabeth were together on the couch as usual, with Patrick now filling the space between them. I was snuggling on dads lap, taking sips from his mug of tea cautiously - in case I wet the bed again.

Our radio was a Bush Dac90, and while the flames were dancing above the hot coals, I was listening in contentment to, Variety Bandbox, with Philip Slessor presenting. Although I never understood half what they said on the wireless, Lizzie always laughed when, mom and dad laughed, and laughed with them. The wireless was my way into another world, creating visions in a young boys mind. There was, 'Beyond our Ken - and Round the Horn,' with Kenneth Horn. 'Rays a Laugh, with Ted Ray', and the line I always eagerly awaited, 'My name is, Nigel-by the Smyth's- with a hyphen, owner of this emporium.' And of course on a weekend, 'Educating Archie, with Peter Brough and Archie Andrews.' Archie was the puppet, and Peter was the ventriloquist. On the wireless the show was a major success because you couldn't see Brough's mouth moving. It would become a major flaw when transferring to television, because then the whole world could see it moving.

Every now and then the signal faded, and dad suddenly looked across the chair at mom. "We never exchanged the accumulators on Saturday, did we, Titch? With the Christening and everything I completely forgot!"

"It's not going to go off is it Dad?" I said, looking up drowsily into his eyes."

"No Son, it should be okay for another hour or so!"

That was all I needed to hear. My world of selfish happiness was going to continue for the next hour. After that it wouldn't have bothered if it blew up because, I'd be asleep so that was okay!

"If you put the accumulators in the pram Dad, I can take them to the shop and get full ones after school," said Elizabeth, offering almost immediately. "I'll ask Jessie to come and help me push the pram back up the road."

"Now that's two things to be done before I go to work!" commented dad.

Mom thanked her caring daughter by tapping her arm while answering, "Thank you Elizabeth; are you sure Jessie will go with you? I don't want you being on your own hauling those things up the road, pram or no pram; they're far too heavy."

"Yes, she went with me to the coal yard on Friday, and she helped me push the pram up the hill."

"When does the coalman deliver, Titch?" Dad asked.

"Tuesday, Hal!"

"Good, Tell him to leave two bags this time, I'll leave the money on the mantle–piece. Thanks to you Lizzie we'll just have enough until then."

Up our grove the coalman always came once every other Tuesday. The milkman came every day. The dustmen came on Friday's; and the rent man came for the seven shillings and six pence on Wednesday.

I never liked any conversation that included Elizabeth, without including me; especially when she was being thanked for something, and I wasn't. Selfishly like the brat I was, I slid from the chair and stood in front of mom, protesting the unfairness of being excluded. "I want to go with Lizzie and Jessie to the shop as well, Mom?"

Elizabeth's head swivelled toward me with her eyes widening. "NO you can't you little brat! Jamie can't come, Mom," Elizabeth continued her protesting. "He wouldn't do as he was told for me today, and last Friday when we were going to the shops he ran into the horse road again. I'm not getting into trouble if he runs off into the horse road again, Mom!"

"But I didn't run into the horse road on purpose Mom - Lizzy pushed me. I'm going so there?" I retaliated.

"Well you can't, ferret! I pushed you because you kept running off; I'm not taking you, so there to you! I'm not taking him Mom, I can't watch him, and push the pram!"

Mom hummed, agreeing with Elizabeth. "Your sisters right Jamie. She'll have her hands full pushing the pram up the street."

"But Jessie won't be pushing the pram; I can hold her hand, Mom."

"Those accumulators are heavy, Mom. And Jessie will be helping me push the pram. He's not going with us and that's it," voiced Elizabeth adamantly.

Titch rose from the couch, and tucked the blanket neatly around Patrick. "Elizabeth, I'll have to sort out the washing, I can't leave it to your father. The whites have to be soaked separately with blue whitener, and he's probably thrown them all in the bath together again. Hal, can you make sure the fire under the copper is ready to light in the morning," said Titch firing her words toward dad.

Dad heaved a sigh. "Give me a minute to tune in the wireless, Titch and I'll make sure!"

"Can I sit next to Lizzie then and hold Patrick," I moaned feigning a tear.

"If you're good you can. Elizabeth, make sure Jaimie doesn't get too close to Patrick, he hasn't long been asleep, and I don't want him being woken up."

"Okay Mom I'll make sure he doesn't!"

I waited until mom and dad left the living room, and climbed on the couch, stretching myself across Lizzie's legs to reach Patrick.

"Jamie, sit down please. Mom said you're not to get too close."

"I'm not getting too close, I can't see Patrick from here; I want to sit next to him!"

"Well sit quietly then - and no poking his face like did last time or I'll tell mom."

So, there was I, sitting next to my baby brother, watching him stretch and contort his face like I did with Rupert, my rubber monkey; and all I wanted to do was hold him like my sister.

"I want to hold him now," I said, reaching awkwardly toward Patrick.

"Jamie, move your arm and sit still; or I'll tell mom you're trying to wake him up on purpose!"

"But you're holding him - why can't I?"

"Because I'm seven and you're only four - That's why, brat!"

I scrambled off the couch, riled into a temper by being called a brat, and unable to have what I wanted. "I'm telling dad you're being nasty to me, and called me a brat."

"Good, tell dad then - see if I care!"

"I will!"

"Good!"

I stood by the back door, staring at Elizabeth in childish defiance. "I'm telling dad you left me in entry to play with Jessie; and when I waved at the dragonfly it nearly bit my finger."

"Good because dad will stop me from taking you anywhere. You'll be locked in the garden on your own while I'm playing with my friends in the grove."

"GOOD, I don't care!"

"Well that's okay then because I don't care either!"

"And I don't care."

"GOOD!"

"GOOD!"

I may have only been a child, but I did know the difference between childishness, and stubborn foolishness. One may have given me the sweet revenge I wanted. But in doing so I was creating a punishment of my own doing. Thoughtfully, I walked toward the couch, filled with the pangs of deep remorse.

"Is he still asleep?"

"Yes, now go back to the chair and listen to the wireless like a good boy!"

"Okay!" As I half waddled toward the chair and climbed into it, Elizabeth called to me softly. "I'm joining the Brownies next week, Jamie. Mom and dad said I could so I might not have the time to play with you then!"

In ignorance I looked at Lizzie, asking her, "What's the Brownies?"

"It's somewhere children my age go. Some girls in my class are already Brownies. Mom and dad said if I like it they'll buy me the uniform too."

I half looked across to my sister, and for the first time I felt the age gap between us becoming even wider. I stared at the fire with the sound of the gas–lamp hissing between the wireless - and I wanted to join the Brownies too!

"Lizzie, I want to join the Brownies as well. I can go with you, dad will let me!"

Elizabeth chuckled as Patrick stirred on her lap. "You can't join the Brownies silly. It's for girls, Jamie, not boys. And anyway you're too young, you have to be seven to join, and I'm seven!"

"So what can I do then?" I said sulking into a mood.

"Ask dad if you can join the cubs when you're older."

"How much older?"

Elizabeth sought the difference between her fingers, counting silently. "About a year and a half I think?"

I slunk even further into the chair, ignoring the wireless fading in and out from the failing accumulators. "A year and a half, how long is that?"

"Not long. Anyway you'll have Patrick to play with when he gets older?"

"But what if Patrick doesn't want to wave at the bees with me; or go down the entry to see the dragonfly? Who will I go with then?"

Patrick had been stirring on Elizabeth's lap for a few minutes, drawing her attention away from me. I just sat there on the chair feeling deserted, and the moment mom and dad came through the back door Patrick began screaming; and my concerns were shoved even further aside

Mom lifted Patrick and sat with him on the couch next to Elizabeth. "Just in time aren't we," said, mom making herself comfortable. "Hal, bottle please?"

Elizabeth suddenly left the couch, and almost ran to the back door,*

"Where are you off to?" Dad asked her.

"To the toilet Dad, I need a wee."

"I think next door are using it. Run up the stairs, the buckets on the landing empty."

Elizabeth ran to the stairs door, and closed it with her feet thumping on the treads to the ceiling.

"Who's turned the wireless off?" Dad asked scrutinising the dials for tampering.

"It went off on its own, Dad." I said truthfully.

"That means the accumulators have died."

"Hal, on your way back from work tomorrow, can you pick us some more Karo syrup from the shops. There's just enough to make two more bottles."

"Yes, Titch," responded Hal irritated by the request. "Anything else before I walk through the door?"

"There's no need to be like that, Hal. The number 38 tram stops right outside the shops."

"I know it does Titch, so does the 39; but it seems you only run out of something when I walk through the door?"

"Elizabeth, if I give you the money, will you pop in the shop on your way home from school, and get the Karo for me?"

"Yes Mom."

"Thank you." Titch turned her head toward Hal with her words snapping at his heels like a terrier's tiny teeth. "Now you don't have to put yourself out coming home, Hal?"

"Good, and if we bought two jars not one while he's feeding every two hours, we wouldn't run out, would we, Titch?"

"Perhaps if you stopped being a tightwad, Hal, and put your hand in your pocket more often I would buy two jars!"

"I've been working an extra half day since you became pregnant. My hands are in my pockets more often than out."

"Good, and don't forget Elizabeth's joining the Brownies, Hal, and she'll need a uniform?"

"And I want to join the Cubs Dad," I voiced innocently.

Two
1947

Monday January 21st and the first snowflakes of winter landed on the windowsill.

Dad was already on the tram going to work; and mom was preparing Lizzie's corn-beef sandwiches for school on the table, next to the coal cupboard.

Because Elizabeth went to 'Upper Highgate Street School, not far from the Alhambra picture house, I had this vision of her traveling to a beautiful place, surrounded by trees; and a park where people walked together hand in hand. The vision remained with me for many years before reality intervened.

Patrick was in his cot fast asleep, and I was in front of the black leaded cast iron range, with a blanket wrapped around me. The mantle over the range was edged with a red velvet cloth edged in gold trim. At times such this, I often wondered what else, other than dads watch, a pair of glasses, and a silver cigarette lighter was up there - beyond my reach. I saw a lump of hot burning coal fall onto the hearth and bounce just inches from the rug.

"Mom, the coals going to burn the rug again!"

"Stay where you are, Jaimie and don't touch it," called mom, finishing Elizabeth's sandwiches. Without a second thought that the burning lump could have set fire to the house, mom reached for the tweezers on the hearth, and neatly placed the burning lump back onto to the fire. "Jamie, upstairs and get ready please, you're not sitting in front of the fire all morning?"

"But it's cold up stairs Mom!"

"Yes, and it'll be cold down here too when the fire goes out." Mom hurried Elizabeth along with little movements of her hand. "I've put an extra sandwich in your lunch today love. Don't throw it away if you don't eat it; bring it back. We can't waste food with the price they're charging."

"Okay Mom!"

"Can't you put some more coal on the fire so it doesn't go out, Mom?" I whined.

"No, it's wash day today, Jay and were already burning coal under the copper. I've a dozen nappies to boil today and we can't have two fires burning at once. Now go upstairs and get ready please. And put two jumpers on!"

"If you think we're running short of coal Mom. I can take my pram to the coal yard if you want?"

"You can't take your pram to fetch coal, Lizzie, it's made for carrying dolls, not things like coal."

"It'll be okay Mom. I'll take everything out and I can take dad's newspaper to cover the inside."

"Well, if you're sure Lizzie! If you damage the springs we won't be able to buy you a new one - well not for a while anyway?"

"It's a big dolls pram, Mom. I've pushed Jaimie around in it lots of times."

"Yes she has Mom, and I didn't want to. She kept on putting a bottle in my mouth: and she was going to smack me if I didn't stop crying!"

"Well you are a baby, Jay because you're always crying - so there!"

"Lizzie said I'm a baby, and I'm not Mom?"

"Of course you're not son, now stop crying because I've a lot to do today. Thank you Elizabeth," said, mom ushering Elizabeth toward the door. "It will be a big help if you can do that for me."

"Jamie can help you with the washing Mom; that'll keep him warm," said Lizzie more like an adult than a child.

"But I don't want to help mom with the washing, Lizzie," I answered stifling the need to cry. "It's too hard!"

"Don't listen to him, Mom. I was helping you around the house when I was four. All he wants to do is play with his stupid toys."

With the urge to cry becoming too great, I succumbed and let out a piercing yell "I'm going to tell dad what you said, Lizzie, and he'll tell you off!"

"No he won't, because I'll tell him you were idle, and you didn't want to help mom; then you'll be in trouble!"

"Mom," I cried, "Lizzie said she's going to get me in trouble with dad."

"Elizabeth will you stop winding up your brother? And you Jamie can stop your crying; I want you to keep an eye on Patrick while I'm in the scullery. Elizabeth get yourself off to school now or you'll be late."

I stood with a satisfying look, sneering and pulling my tongue out at Lizzie

"Spoilt brat! You'll be starting school next year, so you won't be lying around doing nothing then." Elizabeth threw the satchel over her shoulder and kissed mom on the cheek. "I'll fetch the coal, then help with the washing when I come home, Mom."

"Thank you love, you're a good girl."

The moment Elizabeth opened the front door the cold whipped in around her. "It's really snowing now Mom," called Elizabeth, looking skyward.

I rushed toward the door squeezing myself between Lizzie and the doorframe. "Move, I can't see the snowflakes Lizzie!"

"Elizabeth turned to me with a snowflake beginning to melt on her glove. "There, you can see one now," she said, shoving the glove in my face.

"*MOM!*" I wailed.

"What is it NOW, Jamie; can't you see I'm busy with Patrick?"

"Lizzie's just put snow on my face!"

"Well come away from the door then?"

"Mom, can we build a snowman if it gets deep enough?" called Elizabeth.

"I'm hoping it won't last long enough to build one, love: Now off you go please you're letting the cold in."

Elizabeth slammed the door in my face, and I rushed to the window, wishing I was walking along the other side of the privet with her.

During the following two hours the flakes had grown denser, covering the tops of the privet like layers of ice cream. "Can I help Lizzie build the snowman Mom?"

"If you're a good boy you can!"

"What if Lizzie says I can't?"

"If you're a good boy I will tell her you can help her."

"I'm getting ready to build the snowman now!" I called rushing to the stairs door.

"Don't go throwing your clothes all over the bedroom floor please Jay, there isn't enough room in there as it is."

"I won't!"

"And don't you go messing about on Elizabeth's side. She knows where everything is and she'll know if you've touched anything."

"I won't Mom!"

"Well don't - or instead of helping her build the snowman, you'll be watching her through the window. Oh, and while you're up there bring your dirty underpants down for washing, instead of shoving them under the bed?"

"Okay," I called climbing the stairs as quickly as I could. The bucket on the landing was half full with wee, which dad normally emptied before he went to work, but today he hadn't. "Mom," I yelled down.

"What Jaimie?"

"Dad didn't empty the bucket!"

"Well it'll have to wait until your father gets home."

Every now and then, the window sashes in the bedroom rattled from the wind, and wisps of cold air filtered through the gaps between them. I picked up a piece of folded cardboard from the floor by the skirting, and placed it with another on the small table. They were the pieces of cardboard dad wedged between them to stop them rattling in the night.

There was only two bedrooms in our house, one was mom and dad's, the other was shared between, Elizabeth, me - and now Patrick. It was never a problem while we were all young, but before Elizabeth had reached her seventh birthday, dad had put a large brown curtain around her bed for her privacy. It was always going to be a source of curiosity for some who was only four years old.

 . I had mastered putting on a jumper, even though it was either back to front, or inside out, by the age of three. Today I only realised my second jumper was both after I'd pulled it over my head.

Most of my day was spent watching the snow falling, curious as to why the snowflakes were falling as black dots in the sky, and only became white as they floated to the ground.

"Jamie," came mom's voice from behind. "Take your nose away from the window and help please, I need to you to feed Patrick for me while I'm in the scullery!"

"Okay," I said, drawing myself away from winter's glorious presence.

Mom settled me on the couch, and placed Patrick in my arms. "Give him half the bottle, then wind him before giving him the rest, and don't go teasing him or making him cry because I'll be listening!"

"Okay, Mom."

"I'll pop back in ten minutes to see how you are."

"I know what to do Mom, I've fed him before?"

"Right then. You can help me put the clothes on the clothes horse later on. And for being so good, you can play outside in the snow tomorrow - if it's still snowing!"

"Awe, great, Mom." I was four; and learning how to get the things I wanted very quickly came at a price. One was doing as I was told without arguing. The other was feeding Patrick with a smug look on my face. Of course I realised I was never going to get everything completely right like Elizabeth, but she was seven and going to school. She had already learnt being good was more rewarding than being bad!

*

"Thanks for coming with me Jessie!"

"That's okay, Lizzie, you came with me last week didn't you?"

"I see you've got your new hat and scarf on, Jessie; they're better than mine," said Elizabeth, noticing the fur around Jessie's hat, and the densely knitted woollen scarf.

"Yes, they cost mom a shilling from the lane." (Ladypool Road)

"I'll put the coal in the pram, Jessie, you just help me push it up the hill."

"Alright."

"I hope Robert doesn't get in too much trouble with his mom and dad - as well as being caned, Jessie? It wasn't him who peed over the toilet wall in the playground; Arthur Edwards and David Lawson did!"

"I know he didn't, Lizzie, but he was in the toilets with them; that's why Mr Holarson caned him, as well as Arthur, and David in front of the whole school at Tuesday's assembly. I think it was really disgusting, and I don't know why they did it!"

"I do, Jessie, it was Arthur who started it. He bet David his Craven A cigarette packet he couldn't pee higher than him against wall, and David bet Arthur his Robin cigarette packet he could. Alice - Julie, and Rebecca were on the other side, feeding the rabbits in the hutch when the wee came over. Alice ran to Miss Adams and told her, and she sent them to the headmaster."

"I don't know why boys collect cigarette packets, Jessie; I think it's stupid!" Elizabeth held the pram tightly as the front wheels slid sideways over fresh snow toward the gutter. "I've never seen anyone caned at school before, Jessie."

"Me neither, Lizzie."

"I'm never going to be caned," said Elizabeth steering the pram into the lines made by footsteps in the snow.

"I think only boys are caned, Lizzie; girls are hit on the hands with rulers!"

A few weary and agitated people were already queuing at the coal-yard, with prams and carts moving steadily forward each time someone came out. Elizabeth reached into the pram for the Birmingham Daily Gazette, preparing to line the pram. "The time when you didn't come with me, a woman came out the yard and a wheel fell off her pram, Jessie."

"What did she do?"

"The coal man gave her a carrier bag."

"What! She put the coal from the pram in a carrier bag?"

"Not all of it, Jessie; the coal man said would have to come back for the rest. He said if she didn't want the pram he would put it inside for the rag and bone man."

All the way down Edward road, children were out in abundance; some were diving through the snow like penguins, and some were throwing snowballs at each other across the road. They were all perfectly safe, with only a few cars parked against the curb under mounds of snow. Several snowballs suddenly flew randomly across the road, splattering against the prams in front of Elizabeth. She nudged Jessie's arm as the woman suddenly left her pram, and walked brazenly toward the boys who'd thrown them.

"You do that again you little sods and I'll come and box your ears." The woman raised a threatening man sized fist towards the boys, continuing angrily. "If you want to throw snowballs at something, then throw them at your own front doors, and see how your parents like it!" The woman looked formidable with her large cheeks glowing red from the cold, and her hair engulfed beneath a pattern green and red scarf, curling around her head and neck like a poisonous snake. The tweed coat she wore was the length of her boots, pulled tightly around her waist by the belt.

The boys ran erratically down the road, half turning and hurling rude obscenities towards her instead of snowballs.

"Cheeky little sods," said the woman aloud. "It's bad enough me traipsing in the snow lugging coal on a pram; without little sods like that pelting me with snowballs."

Elizabeth and Jessie's stifled giggling was cut short when, Mrs Andrews from number 42 left the coal yard, with only a few lumps of coal in her pram, and two shovels of slack. Her message of doom and gloom passed from mouth to mouth, and the winter suddenly became much colder.

---"They're running out of coal. It's the weather, I bet the horses can't get through because of the snow!"

---"We've not much left in the coalhouse, and he's only allowing everyone a small amount?"

---"I'll have to cut down on the coal we're burning for a bit; just to see how we get on."

---"I'll have to start washing the clothes in the tin bath, and not light the fire under the copper."

As if the curse of winter had been listening, it was snowing again, with flakes falling larger than the last. Elizabeth pulled her knitted hat further over her ears as the temperature suddenly dropped two degrees.

"Next," called the voice from within the yard. The coal-man's mouth curled at the half size pram, lined with newspaper instead of a dolls blanket.

"Sixpence worth please," said Elizabeth, half smiling at the imposing figure, clad in a thick leather apron, large leather gloves, a peak cap, and string tied around the bottom of his baggy trousers.

"You can only have what you're allowed young lady," responded the coalman, sliding his shovel into the coal and slack, pausing to feel the weight. "That'll be a Joey please?"

Elizabeth glanced at the coalman's outstretched hand, then looked up toward his dark brown eyes. Carefully Elizabeth removed her left glove revealing the silver sixpenny piece in the palm of her hand. "Is this enough," she asked.

The coalman's left eyebrow curled upward. "A Joey is four-pence; I can see your history lessons don't include the value of old money!"

Elizabeth placed the sixpenny piece into the coalman's hand, answering with a respectful, "Thank you."

"And thank you young lady," he said, placing two one penny coins into Elizabeth's hand. "And tell your parents unless I get a delivery of coal soon, I'll have to ration the coal even more. Tell them to be careful how much they burn for a while, okay!"

"Okay," Elizabeth answered shyly.

"And tell them to send someone older with a bigger pram next time?"

Elizabeth nodded then pushed the pram out through the coal yard gates with Jessie's help. "I didn't like the coalman for saying that, Jessie. If mom could've gone she would've. She's got Patrick to look after, as well as Jaimie; and dad's always working. It's alright for him, he's not going to run out of coal because he's the coalman."

"My mom won't be happy when I tell her the coal yard's running out of coal, Lizzie. The house doesn't get warm when we do have a fire!"

"I know, ours doesn't either," Elizabeth responded.

A few minutes went by before Jessie asked the question, most children would have asked in circumstances such as this. "Are you telling your mom the coalman only charged you four pence, instead of sixpence? You can buy a lot of sweets with tuppence, Lizzie!"

"But that would be stealing Jessie. And what if your mom asked you to get some coal, and the coalman only charged you four pence. What would you do?"

"I think I would give her the change Lizzie; mom always knows when I'm lying because I get a rash around my neck."

"AND you can go to prison for stealing, Jessie."

"I know!"

*

A blast of freezing cold air engulfed the living room as the front door suddenly opened.

"Dads home Mom," called Elizabeth.

"You're an hour late coming home Hal," mom said shivering at the blast of cold air.

"Have YOU seen it out there Titch, it's snowing a blizzard. The conductor said if the snow doesn't let up before morning, they'll be taking the trams off."

When mom was concerned about anything important, her voice always rose an octave higher; and it was in her voice as she emerged from the cupboard under the stairs. "Taking the trams off? If they do that, Hal, how will you get to work?"

"I'll have to walk to work and back won't I!" said dad solving the problem instantly.

Like the caring daughter she was, Elizabeth held dad's bag - while he took off his coat, opened the door again and shook off the snow.

"HAL, the cold!" Mom shouted.

Dad closed the door quickly, and threw his coat over the hook on the front door.

While Elizabeth was helping dad with his boots, I was playing with teddy on the carpet in front of the fire, quite happy to let Lizzy do so. Sometimes when Elizabeth voiced her concern I raised my eyes, because sometimes she sounded like mom.

"But you can't walk to work in the snow Dad, your work is miles away," said Elizabeth. "It'll take you ages - AND you might freeze! What if you freeze?"

"If your father says he's going to walk to work in the snow, Elizabeth, then he'll walk in the snow. Stop fussing over him and make him a nice cup of tea. Hal stop being a martyr to your family and sit by the fire. I'VE been in the brew house all day washing and wringing out clothes. I can't sit by the fire when there's mouths to be fed. At least being late means you've missed all the washing steaming in front of the fire."

"Who's being the martyr now Titch?"

"We've made a snowman in the garden dad, did you see it?"

"No Son. I'll see it in the morning, WHEN I go to work!"

"So you're determined to go then, even though nothing will be running?" said Titch.

"Well that's a silly question to ask, Titch! If I don't go I don't get paid; and if the snow continues the way it is, we'll be burning coal in the scullery and the living room none stop!"

"Dad, the coalman told me to tell you if he doesn't have a delivery of coal soon, he'll be rationing the coal."

"That's great," dad sighed. "The way it's snowing that's a certainty."

"Are we going to freeze, Dad?" I asked foolishly.

Elizabeth marched across the living room carrying dad's boots, and put them in the small cupboard above the coal cupboard. "Of course dad's not going to let us freeze – stupid," she said marching back.

"Mom, Lizzie's just called me stupid again."

"Of course you're not Son," said mom patting my head. "Sit on the chair and I'll bring your tea."

"They sacked Arthur Mallow on Friday, Titch," said Hal, shoving his hands in front of the fire.

"For what?"

"For being late."

"For being late? That was a bit harsh wasn't it, Hal. It must've been for something more than that; they won't just sack someone for being late?"

"No, he'd been late three times before I was told."

"Have you ever been late Dad?" Elizabeth asked inquisitively.

"Your fathers never been late going to work, Elizabeth. Even when the bombs were dropping you were never late; were you Hal?"

Hal settled back in the chair, thawing out nicely from the coal fire's heat. "No, and neither were you, Titch!"

Elizabeth tilted the teapot and poured the tea through the gauze strainer. "So you went to work when the bombs were dropping as well, Mom?"

"Yes Elizabeth: I worked in the same factory as your dad, only in a different section. Your dad was a welder, and I was a riveter."

Elizabeth's curiosity grew as she handed dad the cup of tea. "Is that where you met mom, at the factory, Dad?"

"No, I knew your mother long before she worked in the factory, Elizabeth. She lived in the house behind me."

"We were practically neighbours," mom added.

"So when did you get married?" asked the all enquiring daughter.

"We got married in Nineteen thirty seven, two years before you were born, Elizabeth."

"And what about me!" I said willing myself into the conversation.

"We had you six years after we were married, Jay."

"Why was Lizzie born first? Mom?" I voiced in pure ignorance. "Why couldn't I be borne first?"

Elizabeth's hand flicked me as she turned to place the teapot on the table. "Because you wasn't, so stop asking mom silly questions."

I flinched as though I'd been hit with a cricket bat, shedding my crocodile tears on teddy's shoulder. "Ouch, that hurt, Lizzie. Mom, Lizzie Just hit me on the arm."

Elizabeth scoffed at my reaction showing no sympathy at all. "Stop crying like a baby, Jaimie, I never hit you, I just touched you that's all - Mom, I never hit him on the arm, I only touched him!"

The moment mom's eyes turned to me, my mouth contorted, and more floods of tears erupted from my eyes.

"Jaimie your disturbing Patrick now," said mom quietly. "What are you crying for?"

I had now gotten myself into such a state, my bottom lip was quivering as the words, "Because Lizzie asked you a question, and she said I couldn't," came out in short bursts.

"That's silly now, of course you can ask me something. Elizabeth stop tormenting your brother; I'm sure you enjoy winding him up. Now, Son what do you want to ask me?" said mom giving me her full attention.

With everyone's eyes on me, I dragged teddy toward the arm of the chair and sat against it, gawping like the codfish dad often called me. "I'm not telling you; I'm telling teddy instead!"

Elizabeth had settled herself at the table, her head resting on one hand, and turning the pages of the: Calling all Girls, magazine with the other. "Dad, Mr Robson our teacher has been telling us why we had blackouts in the war. He said when the German planes were flying over at night, if someone hadn't closed their curtains and they saw the light, they could drop their bombs on them."

"Oh yes!" dad responded.

"Yes, he said in the blitz the Germans bombed anything that was lit up. That's why everyone closed their curtains. Amie, who sits next to me asked me why it was called the blitz, but I didn't know either. I was going to put my hand up and ask Mr Robson, but Amie ask me not to in case everyone in the class already knew, and we didn't. She said we would've looked stupid!"

Mom suddenly craned her neck toward Elizabeth. "Well next time your teacher says something you don't know, Elizabeth, stick your hand up. I'll bet everyone else in the class didn't know either!"

"Listen to your mother Elizabeth, you'll never learn anything by being afraid to ask. And blitz is the German word for lightning. I would say it was the perfect word to describe the amount of bombs they dropped on us."

Mom suddenly ejected a loud, "Ah! That reminds me, Elizabeth. You've been using that bombsite as a short cut to your friend, Jessie when I asked you not to."

"Mom, half kids in the area play on the bombsite!"

"Yes, maybe they do, Elizabeth; but the only thing holding the houses up either side are those lumps of wood, and if you ask me they don't look safe at all."

"The lumps of wood are called trusses, Titch," intervened dad. "They're shoring up the sides of the houses, and are more than strong enough to do that!"

"Maybe they are, Hal, but a bombsite's no place for children to play - or walk over. With the snow covering the rubble it's an accident waiting to happen. The last thing we want is Elizabeth, or anyone else for that matter falling and breaking something - Do we Hal?"

Dad heaved a heavy sigh as yet again mom displayed more common sense than he did. "Elizabeth, your mother's right. A bombsites no place for anyone to be on. Just promise her you won't be on it again - before we enter into an argument."

My eyes turned to dad, as his voice growled like the voice box in my teddy bear.

"Elizabeth, I'm waiting for an answer?"

"Okay I promise," said Elizabeth with droll reply. "But don't blame me if I'm late home because I had to go the long way round, Mom!"

There followed a contented silence while dad fiddled with the radio; Mom meandered to and fro from the cupboard under the stairs; Lizzie absorbed herself in her: Calling all Girls, magazine; and I snuggled against teddy, watching the flames dancing between the coals in the fire.

The peaceful interlude ended the moment Lizzie finished reading her magazine. "When you said you walked to work when the bombs were dropping, Dad, why wasn't you fighting the Germans like Jessie Roberts dad did?" Elizabeth questioned innocently. "She said, that's why he always walks with a limp, because when he was in the war some metal went into his leg?"

"The ministry of defence wouldn't let your father join up, Elizabeth," said mom, recalling the memories still vivid in her mind. "You tried twice didn't you, Hal; and they refused you. They said your father was more important as a welder making equipment for the soldiers to fight with. You was an Arp Warden though, wasn't you Hal?"

"Yes - most of us were in the factory. We worked in rota so we all took part without the factory stopping."

"What's an ARP warden, Dad?" I asked before Elizabeth could.

Dad emptied the cup until only the strains of tea leaves remained. "We made sure houses were blacked out when the sirens sounded son, so the planes couldn't see any light when they flew over. When the bombs started dropping we led everyone toward the air raid shelters, then helped in rescuing anyone trapped in the houses that were hit."

I slunk across the arm of the chair, understanding nothing of what dad had said. Lizzie's eyes were scrutinising me for any weakness, so I just sniffed and pretended I couldn't see her.

."The teacher said because all the men were fighting the Germans, the women had to work in the factories. Did you work in a factory, Mom?" asked Elizabeth.

"Of course I did, I was a riveter."

"I wanted to ask mom what a riveter was, but Lizzie kept looking at me, so I didn't and let her ask instead.

"What's a riveter?"

"You wouldn't understand if I told you Lizzie. It's someone I hope you'll never be."

"I'd be really scared if it was happening now," said Elizabeth.

"And me," I cried out. "I can be scared as well as Lizzie Mom!"

"And you wouldn't be on your own, either of you," said mom. "Now no more talk of bombs dropping, and be happy they aren't anymore."

*

Mom was knitting Patricks swimming trunks in blue cotton wool for our holiday in: Golden Sands Holiday Camp Rhyl. Dad was reclining in his chair, listening to the wireless while reading the Gazette, Elizabeth was at the table creating some work of art for the Brownies. And I was squashed between dad and the arm of the chair, enjoying the whole family ambiance in my pyjamas reading the, Beano annual.

A knock came on the back door, interrupting the moment of family serenity.

"I'll go," said Elizabeth being closest to the door.

Elizabeth pulled the curtain across the door, and drew back the bolts top and bottom. Auntie Hazel's voice instantly floated into the living room on a draught of freezing air, and the door was slammed shut.

"Was that Hazel, Elizabeth?" asked dad.

"Yes, she said the pipe in the toilet was beginning to freeze because the paraffin lamp had gone out. She said she's filled it now, but it's our turn next time to fill the lamp."

"Hal, I thought you said the paraffin in the lamp would last another two days?"

"It should've done, somebody's been turning it up full?"

"It wasn't turned up full, when I used it yesterday: Hal."

"Well somebody must have; it couldn't run out that quick on low like it should've been. The pipe probably needs more rag around it - I'll do it tomorrow!"

"Ah well! It's a good job I nagged you into putting more rags round the leaded pipe in the scullery, or we wouldn't have any water either?"

"Err, excuse me! If you remember, Titch I lagged the kitchen pipe before you even asked!"

"See how your father gets riled up when he doesn't like hearing the truth!"

"What will we do when we want a poo Dad?" I asked, purely from the fact I required one as we spoke.

"In the bucket like we did last year when it froze up Jamie, and that goes for us all. Till then just tell your mother or me when you've used it, and we'll flush it down with a bucket of water."

"And what about at night Dad?" Elizabeth asked

"Same as always Elizabeth. Use the bucket when you have to, and I'll empty it in the morning. Titch, you better make sure the spare buckets always empty in the scullery - just in case!"

"There was only a few sheets of newspaper left on the string this morning, Dad. Do you want me to cut up the paper when you've finished reading it?"

"Yes please Lizzie, and don't make them too big this time; they're to wipe your backsides on not paper the walls."

I instantly rolled around on the chair laughing and pointing at Lizzie in my childish way. "Ahh that was funny Dad - wasn't it Mom?"

"I don't know why you're laughing Jay, you don't even know how to wipe your bum. Mom has to do it for you!"

"Elizabeth! Enough of that please," voiced mom in disgust.

Mom put the knitting to one side and walked to the window. The snow was falling like feathers in the gas lamps ambient light, settling gently in abundance on the snow covered ground. "I've never known it snow as long as this, Hal. It's been on and off for three weeks, and no sign of stopping."

Dad hummed while he placed a lump of coal from scuttle, onto the fire. "Two of the welders never turned up to work today. If they take the trams off again, a lot more will be struggling to get there. The snow we all cleared for the milkman and coalman is almost a foot deep again. If keeps snowing the way it is the horses won't be able to pull the carts, then we'll all be in trouble."

"What about you Dad?" asked Elizabeth. "You won't be able to go to work if the snow gets too deep either?"

Mom returned to her knitting, shunning the idea of dad staying at home. "Elizabeth, nothing will stop your dad from going to work. If it ever gets to that stage it'll mean the whole world has stopped going to work too!"

Three

"You can stop the wriggling Jamie. If you're going to Hancock's with me, you've got to put your scarf on."

"But I don't like my scarf, Lizzie, it rubs my neck; and anyway it's only at the top of the road."

"My scarf rubs my neck - but I'm still wearing it because it's freezing outside."

"Well don't pull it tight then or I won't be able to breathe?"

"Mom, is that all you want from the shop, a jar of malt?"

"At the moment Lizzie. Edward's boy Tommy fetched some shopping for me on his sledge yesterday. It was worth giving him a halfpenny to do it. The one thing I wanted and forgot was the jar of malt. Thank goodness it's stopped snowing for a bit," said mom placing the thru penny bit into Elizabeth's pocket. "Make sure it's the Virol malt – and not the other sort?"

The instant I walked through the door the cold air entered my lungs. Although I never said it, I was grateful Elizabeth had ignored my whinging, and wrapped the scarf around my neck. By sheer coincidence, Alice from opposite was also going to Hancock's, and we all walked down the entry together.

"What are you going to the shop for?" Alice asked tightening the scarf around her neck.

"Virol malt," Lizzie responded.

"I'm going for a box of matches, and a packet of twist for dad. He smokes park drive, but he likes smoking twist in his pipe more I think."

Everything was white, nothing was left uncovered from the snowy white stuff; apart from the bits around the chimneys spewing out dark grey smoke, which seemed to hang in the air before dispersing.

"Hand Jamie!" voiced Lizzie reaching for my hand.

I avoided my sister's hand by shoving mine inside my coat pockets.

"Hold my hand - NOW PLEASE?"

"But I want to walk on my own, Lizzie," I protested.

Elizabeth stood holding out her gloved hand in front of me, determined not to go any further if I didn't. "Hand - Now Jamie!"

"I'm glad I haven't got a younger brother, Lizzie," said Alice creating a snobbish glance in my direction.

"Philips a boy like me - and he's your brother," I said, creating a snobbish look of my own.

"I know, but Philips a year older than me - and he doesn't have to hold my hand."

Reluctantly I held Lizzies hand, following the footprints in the snow along entry. I looked to the top of the wall capped by thick snow, and could just see the ivy peeping through. It was going to be a very long time before I could wave at the dragonflies again.

We were halfway up the road and the milkman appeared, steering the horse between the narrow pathways, cleared by snow shovels. He was already two hours late, and several woman standing at their doors were openly grateful he had come at all.

"Three bottles please Norman," I heard one say, struggling from the door towards the cart with the empties.

"Leave them there Mavis, you almost came a cropper then," came the milkman's commanding voice.

"I don't know how you're doing it coming out in this?" she said inching her way back to her door.

"Aye, it's the worst snowfall I've seen, and I've seen a few. Let's hope it doesn't go on too long – eh Laddie!"

The horse clearly understood him, rocking his head from side to side.

"Now I've got some milk, would you like a cup of tea, Norman, you look perished?"

"No thanks, Mavis, I've had three already. If I have another one I'll be writing my name in the snow."

Mavis tutted harshly then very carefully shuffled to the horse. "And how's Laddie, she said patting the horses neck. "Are you feeling the cold like me?"

The horse remained still with his head inside the nose bag strapped around his neck. Every now and then he snorted, clearing the hay from his nose.

"He'd rather be in his stable, that's for sure, Mavis; wouldn't you old man!" Norman dragged the crate of sterilised milk from the cart, and made his way toward the entry, making a strange whistle before disappearing. The horse began to pull the milk cart down the road, then stopped at the next entry, waiting for his master to return.

*

The small bell jingled over the door as we walked into Hancock's; and I followed Lizzie's and Alice's example by stamping my feet on the rubber mat. Two boys from Tindle Street School were in the shop, and Lizzie recognised them instantly as Stuart and Peter croft. Anxiously she led me away from them toward far end of the shop, where the jars of, Virol Malt were on the bottom shelf. Alice had made her way toward the tobacco behind the counter, waiting to be served.

After spending a moment looking for the right jar, Lizzie walked me slowly toward to the counter, next to Alice.

The two brothers were now by the shop door, giggling and pushing each other in unruly play.

"Hey, watch the sign please? If you want to mess around like that, do it outside – not in the shop," voiced Mr Hancock.

The sign next to the door was propped up on three legs, displaying a man and woman sitting on a striped couch. At their feet was and a dog with the words (Why be irritated? Light up an 'Old Gold'. Apple and honey helps guard from Cigarette Dryness)

Mr Hancock lent over the counter with irritation voicing his anger. "Hey, that's enough I said! If you want to muck around do it outside and not in my shop!"

Unintimidated by the waving finger, the boys pushed each other through the door, laughing and jeering at the grocer through the large glass window. They seem to have gone, until several minutes later a barrage of snowballs thudded against the glass.

Mr Hancock raised the counter flap to the catch on the wall, and walked briskly through the door. He stood for several minutes, then walked in with the door closing slowly behind him. "Cheeky so and so's. If they was one of mine they'd have my hand I can tell you. Now what can I do for you?" he said lowering the flap without a second thought.

"A box of matches and a packet of twist please," said Alice politely.

"Certainly young lady, I hope it's not for you?"

Alice chuckled. "No! It's for dad."

"Just this jar of malt please Mr Hancock," said Lizzie in the same politeness.

"And is this jar of malt for you young man," asked Mr Hancock.

"No, it's for my brother; he's just a baby - not big like me!"

"There, now why can't all my customers behave and talk politely like you three?"

I left the shop holding Elizabeth's hand, chuffed at being called polite. I wasn't sure what polite actually meant, only that it was a nice word to be called.

"Can I carry the malt, Lizzie? I won't drop it promise."

"Yes, but hold it tight - and walk slowly next to me!"

The milkman was still three entries away from ours, and apart from Stuart and Peter on the opposite side of the road, hiding in the opening of the builders yard, we were the only ones braving the snow.

Two snowballs suddenly flew in front of us and splattered against the houses.

Before Lizzie could dash in front of me, two more snowballs followed, one hitting my legs, the other striking me in the face, spinning me round and ousting the jar of malt from my hand into the snow.

All I could see through my snow covered eyes was my sister, running toward the boys with her fists flaying wildly, and her voice screaming. "YOU COWARDS YOU'VE JUST HIT MY BROTHER. GO ON HIT ME IF YOU DARE AND I'LL SCRATCH YOUR EYES OUT!"

Peter hit her across the arms scoffing at her words, and Elizabeth left two claw marks across his left cheek. Then I heard the milkman's voice calling warningly from the milk cart.

"HEY, what's going on over there?"

"Those two boys are being really horrible," Alice shouted. "They were throwing snowballs at Jaimie, and he dropped the jar of malt!"

"Leave her Pete, were already in trouble!"

Peter began to run too, issuing more warnings as he did. "There's plenty of time to get you back before we start School," he cursed with threating gestures.

Elizabeth ran after them for a short distance, with her eyes wide and fuelled with anger. "Well you better be quick then, Peter Croft. Because I'm going to your school and tell the headmaster. When he knows what you did in Mr Hancock's shop, you'll both be caned in front of the whole school. THEN I'LL TELL YOUR MATES WHAT COWARDS YOU ARE, FOR HURTING A DEFENCLESS FOUR YEAR OLD BOY," she shouted as Peter ran down the road.

"Are you alright?" asked the milkman kindly.

"Yes, thank you!"

"You did well tackling those two, I've had dealings with them before, and they're not to be taken lightly."

"They don't scare me, they're just bullies!"

"Even so young lady they're not to be messed with." The milkman reached down and retrieved the jar of malt from the snow, thankfully unbroken and placed it in my hand. "I think you're a lucky boy having a sister who defends you like that! I know a lot of girls who wouldn't have done something as brave as that."

I think Alice was grateful to my sister too; and I held onto Lizzie's hand the rest of the way home -

without being asked. Even though we often had disagreements, I never knew till then what a great sister I had!

Four
1948

"Dad," called Elizabeth the moment he walked through the door. "Brown Owl has given us this assignment to do on a famous place. She said it had to be in our own words and the winner would receive a badge."

"And?" answered dad while hanging his coat on the door, and retrieving his newspaper from one of the pockets.

"Well, the Lickey Hills is a famous place – isn't it?"

"And I suppose by going there, you'd have all the information you wanted for your assignment?"

"It's a lovely badge Dad, I've seen one."

Dad slumped into his chair, waiting for the tea to stew in the teapot.

"Were supposed to be saving for our holiday in Rhyl, Hal; we've still got school clothes to buy for Jaimie, and that's only a few months away!"

Dad raised his eyes from the newspaper. "How much have we got saved?"

"Not enough to go to the Lickey's and buy clothes for Jaimie, Hal!"

"I've got one shilling and sixpence saved," responded Lizzie.

"You're going to need a lot more than that for a day at the Lickeys - and a week by the sea, Lizzie!"

I clambering from the chair tugging at mom's dress. "I've got tuppence in my tin, Mom; and dad hasn't given me my penny to put in this week yet?"

"And what about our holiday, Jaimie? If you're going to spend your money at the Lickey hills, where are you going to get the money for Golden Sands?"

"But, Mom!"

Dad turned his eyes from the newspaper, cautious not to over-rule mom. "Your mom's right, but it's not just about the money going the Lickey Hills. It means walking all the way to Bristol road, then waiting for the tram; and then there's the journey back."

"Well I don't mind walking to Bristol Road, Dad," said Elizabeth. "I've walked it before, and I was only three then!"

"And I did Dad," I voiced

"No you didn't – You was a baby, and dad pushed you in the pram, Jamie."

"But I don't need the pram now; look I can walk faster than anyone." I raced around the room with a look of sheer determination etched on my face.

"Jamie, be careful please, you're going to knock something over."

"No I won't I can run faster." I suddenly disappeared between the table legs, and the small plant pot spun dispersing its contents over the floor.

"Now look what you've done, Jamie?" voiced mom. "You've hurt yourself now; sit on the chair and behave before you wreck the place!"

I wasn't lying on the floor crying because I'd hurt myself. I was crying because Lizzie was smirking at me. And when she said to dad, "Can't I just go with you then Dad." I was standing to attention, crying harder than I had ever cried before.

Elizabeth simply huffed at my tearful display. "He hasn't hurt himself really you know, Dad; he's just crying for attention!"

"No I'm not!" convincing myself I meant it.

"Yes you are, you're just a little brat!"

"Mom, if I can't go to the Lickey's, Lizzie can't go either!"

Mom vented her agitation by tutting aloud. "Lizzie, will you stop annoying your brother and clear the mess off the floor. Jay sit on the chair and be quiet like a good boy. Hal, if we take everything with us, all we'll need is the money for the tram."

"Jaimie's not going to walk all the way to the Bristol Road and back, Titch, he'll want picking up!"

I instantly leapt from the chair, eyes wide and not a tear in them. "I can Dad, I can walk to the moon if I wanted!"

Elizabeth ejected a huffing laugh. "No one can walk to the moon, idiot. It's up in the air, not on the ground!"

"Lizzie, is that floor cleaned yet?"

"Just doing it, Mom!"

"Can we go to the Lickey Hills - pleeeese?" I said again pestering mom for the answer I wanted.

"We'll have to wait and see how things are. We'd need to have a hot dry day if we do go Hal, Patrick's been having one chesty cold after another lately. We wouldn't want him to have another before we go on holiday!"

"Mom, why do we have to go on holiday to Golden Sands? Maybe we could go somewhere not so expensive. Then we wouldn't have to worry about not having enough money?"

"We're going to Golden Sands because Dr Cronian advised us to, Lizzie. He said the sea air there would good for Patrick's chest."

"Have YOU been anywhere else Mom?" Elizabeth asked.

"Yes, I went to Blackpool with my mom and dad when I was seven."

"Urrg, Blackpool, but that's just a big dirty puddle," I said pretending to vomit. "Why didn't you go to Rhyl like we are?"

"Blackpool is a big seaside resort. Jaimie, not a big dirty puddle. The prom is longer than it is to your Auntie, Mo's. There's a big fairground, and shops where you can buy anything you want. AND not only has it got three piers, it has a big tower with a circus underneath. I only went there once because it was so expensive; after that I only went on day trips to the seaside."

"Is that why WE don't go to Blackpool, Mom, because it's so expensive?"

"Yes, Lizzie – and because the air in Rhyl is better for Patrick."

"Dad, can we see the sea from our caravan this time?" Lizzie asked.

"I'm not sure about that, Lizzie; anyway all the caravans on Golden sands are only a few minutes from the sea."

"Yes I know, but I couldn't hear the waves rolling the pebbles the last time. The ones right next to the sea would have!"

"I don't know, all we've got is a number; it might be one of those on the sea front, but it doesn't matter if it isn't. It's the weather you should be worrying about, Lizzie, not how close to the sea we are!"

Elizabeth folded her assignment paper neatly under her arm, and walked to the stairs door. "I'm going to put my nighty on, Mom."

"Lizzie, about your assignment?"

"That's alright, Mom! If we can't go to the Lickey's, I'll think of somewhere else to write about!"

Dad listened to Lizzie climbing the stairs, then sat for a moment, looking down thoughtfully at the newspaper. "Perhaps I can do a few extra shifts at work, Titch! I think we should go to the Lickey's, I'd like Lizzie to do well in the brownies!"

"Yes, she's a good girl, Hal, and she's always helping me with the washing."

"And she said it was a lovely badge!"

*

It was a Sunday in May, just before dinner when Lizzie came running into the house, talking so quickly I couldn't understand her.

"Dad, quick the Boys Brigade are forming in Vincent Street; the brownies, the cubs, the scouts, the G L B, everyone are assembling behind them!"

Dad quickly grasped Patrick from mom's arms, telling her in a hurried voice. "Come on, Titch, this'll be something to watch!"

"And what about the dinner, who's going to look after that?"

"Just turn everything off, Titch, the dinners not going to spoil over a few minutes. We've all seen them parading before except Patrick. His little eyes will pop out when they go marching past, drums beating and bugles playing."

"Well if the dinners spoilt, Hal; it won't be because I didn't warn you."

"Come on Dad, hurry up, they were nearly ready when I left?"

*

As we walked past the police station I could hear the steady drum beat of a base drum. Everyone was heading toward Vincent Street, and we just joined the flow of excited children, dragging their flagging parents along, as I was dragging mine. We arrived just in time to see the drum major raising the mace, and the parade began. The rapid beats of the snare drums followed, beating together in unison; Patrick was bouncing up and down on dad's shoulders, screaming in fear and joy. Lizzie was wending her way through the crowd toward Jessie, walking with her mom and dad; and I was jumping up and down as the bugles sounded, thrilled by the whole spectacle of different uniforms marching in step behind one another. The Sunday dinner was ruined, as mom said it would be, but that didn't matter. "Dad!" I shouted above the throng of bugles and drums. "One day I want to be in the parade!"

Five

"How much money have you got, Jamie?"

"These many," I answered, counting the three copper coins for the umpteenth time.

"Do you want me to look after them for you, just in case there's a hole in your pocket?"

"No, I can look after them myself."

"Okay, but don't go crying to mom if you lose them, and you've got no money to spend in the arcade!"

"I won't," I answered placing them into my pocket carefully. Those three pennies were my entrance to a world a million miles away from Edward Road.

"Are we ready then?" Dad called placing the pack over his shoulder.

Mom checked the bag for nappies, milk bottle and rusks for the umpteenth time. "Yes, ready," she said with confidence.

Other than the few wisps of white cloud straggling the sky, Mom and dad had thankfully chosen a warm summer's day for our outing to the Lickey Hills.

"Where are you going?" called Tommy, leaning over the gate.

"We're going to the Lickey's on the tram, Tommy,"

"Oh! We went there two weeks ago and it rained." We're going on holiday to Blackpool soon, hope it stays like this and doesn't rain, Lizzie!"

"We're going to Rhyl in a few weeks," said Elizabeth quietly. "I hope it doesn't rain either."

I carried on next to mom toward the entry, pondering over the world of Blackpool mom had spoken about.

Halfway along the entry my eyes caught the movement of a dragonfly in the ivy.

Instead of waving I just smiled, preferring my hand to be touching the three pennies tucked inside my pocket.

"What's this? Going somewhere nice are we?"

I turned smartly to the policeman as we walked past the entrance of the station "We're going to the Lickey Hills on the tram," I said breathing excitedly.

"Are you now!" responded the man in uniform, following me with his eyes only.

"Yes, and were going to Rhyl by the seaside soon. And we'll see the sea from our caravan window this time," I continued inhaling my excitement.

"Well you've certainly picked a nice day for the Lickey Hills, haven't you? In weather like this wish I was coming with you?"

"You can if you want. He can, can't he Dad?" I said tugging dad's arm.

"I would think the policeman had more important things to do, Son!"

"But!"

Elizabeth squeezed my arm, hurrying me along past the police station. "Shut up, Jamie you're embarrassing mom and dad."

"I only said he could come if he wanted to, Lizzie."

"Policemen don't go on picnics, they arrest people, Jay. Now stop telling everybody they can come, or there won't be any room on the tram for us."

From then on I never said a word. Patrick was making all the noise as dad jiggled him in his arms, talking to him in a foreign language.

It was a good three quarters of an hours walk to the Bristol Road from the entry. Our walk took us past the police station, and down past Rogers coal yard on the right. The shop where accumulators for the wireless were charged was on the left. George Street was next, then Mary Street, Hallam Street; and down toward Jakeman Road. Cannon Hill Road, (which led to Cannon Hill Park.) was on the left, and Calthorpe Park on the right.

Compared to the slow moving traffic of Mosely road, which had horse and carts, and the occasional black Austin car rambling beside a tram, Bristol Road belonged in a different era, than the one at the top of Edward road. It was a road divided by trams rumbling along the tramlines both ways. And so many cars it seemed as though every car in Birmingham was travelling past my eyes. My heart was pumping from fear and excitement as dad led us along the pavement, toward the people queuing at the stop for the, 742 to the Lickey's

Patrick had learned to hobble around three months ago, and mom and dad had been aiding his learning by walking him along by a harness under his arms. I think dad was thankful they had put Patrick in the harness while waiting for the tram.

"How long before the tram comes, Dad?" I asked forcing my impatience to be aired above the noise of the traffic.

"Not long, Son," said dad, flexing the arm he'd carried Patrick with.

"How long is long, Mom?" I asked, probing for a more definitive response.

"About five minutes if it's on time," said the woman in front, turning her head with a large hat toward me.

I shied away from the woman's peering eyes, circled with black mascara, leaving mom to say thank you for me.

"Thank you!"

"You're welcome, love; he's just like my son and doesn't yet know how to be patient."

Mom laughed, "Yes, all children are exactly the same!" said Mom, nodding her head toward Patrick.

"Ahh, and how old is he?" she said lowering her head a little toward Patrick.

"He's thirteen months old now."

"Thirteen months old and standing next to his Daddy. What a good little boy you are!"

"Mom - Dad, the trams coming!" voiced Elizabeth, excitedly.

Dad took up his rightful position in from of us all. "Right, no one move till I do!"

The 742 clanged to a halt in front of me, displaying her streamline beauty to my awestruck eyes. Dad carried Patrick - and mom helped me onto the platform with Elizabeth in toe. The bottom deck was almost full, so dad led us up the winding iron stairs to the upper deck.

I was looking eagerly between mom and dad to the seats at the front, sighing inwardly when I saw they were taken. With a heavy heart I settled into a seat by the window next to dad, while Elizabeth sat next to mom in front with Patrick on her lap.

The trams mechanical warning sounded, and with a slight jolt we began to move. After a few minutes the conductor appeared, calling "Fare please."

"Two adults and two children to the Lickey's please," said dad."

The conductor glanced at Patrick sitting on mom's lap, then pulled two tickets from one roll, and two tickets from another further along the reel. "That's two tuppence - and two ha'penny tickets – five-pence please," he said punching small ragged holes at the end of each one with a clipper.

Dad placed the sixpenny bit into the conductor's hand, and in return received a penny change. With the four tickets punched our day to the Lickeys was official.

Thankfully, I rested my head against the glass window, watching the inner world of Birmingham passing by. Between each stop the tram rambled along between a steady fifteen to twenty miles an hour, swaying gently from side to side along the un–even track. The sound of the trams electric motor was fluctuating between speeds; and the undecipherable voices converging around me was all part of the trams magic. For a four year old boy with a head full of dreams, the magic was real.

Longbridge Island! The place where reality suddenly ended and the magic of youth began. From here on the trams electric motor whirled like a spinning top, driving the elegant slim–line machine along at forty miles an hour along the central track. The Horse Chestnut trees either side were now whizzing by, and in my mind's eye, I saw piers stretching out into the sea, and sandy beaches lined with people on deckchairs, clutching cornets with ice scream, melting in the heat of a summer's sun.

"Are you alright Son?"

My head turned away from the window, nodding dreamily. Of course I was alright, I was on the fairy–tale flying machine, whisking me toward a place where steep hill walks replaced streets; and the bilberry thrived amidst the heady smell of Scots pines, Douglas firs, Larches and spruce, all growing within carpets of bluebells and buttercups. And within this natural potion of happiness - where children climbed hills not walls, was the fair -and a shop selling pink candyfloss on sticks. The arcade was the place where a farthing activated one arm bandits; and machines lowering shiny silver grabs into a mound of soft toys. It wasn't just the thrill of going to the Lickey's that would remain with me for life; it was being taken there on a machine destined to be unlike any other. And for a young four year old boy who sat on that tram with his family, it was priceless.

Six
Rhyl

"Come on, Titch hurry up; it's already half past six and we need to be at the pickup point before the charabanc gets there."

"What time is pickup time?"

"Quarter past seven, Titch."

"The pickups before Park Hill school on the other side of the horse-road, we should have plenty of time, Hal."

"Well, you know what I always say?"

"Better to be where you're going half an hour early, than a minute late!" said Lizzie and mom almost together.

Mom took dad to one side, talking so I couldn't hear. "It's Lizzie's birthday on the Monday we come back, Hal; with all this running around, she probably thinks we've forgotten, seeing as it hasn't been mentioned!"

"Well getting her what she wanted is out of the question now! We'll sort something out when we get back. Right, off we go before you think of something else we've missed!"

"Hal, stop rushing me, I know we're missing something?"

"There's only one thing missing I can see, Titch!"

"Oh, and what's that, Hal?"

"The scullery sink, Titch."

"Ha, ha, your father thinks remarks like that are funny. Ask him if he's packed his razor? The one he left on top of the shelf so he wouldn't forget it?"

"Oh blast, I forgot I'd put it there!"

"It's alright, Hal, don't you worry yourself; I've packed it for you. Are you okay carrying that bag Lizzie?" Mom asked, eying up the bulging bag slung over Elizabeth's shoulder

"Yes I'm okay, Mom!"

Hearing the key turning in the rim lock was the best sound ever. It meant our holiday had begun, and we were saying goodbye to the grove for a whole week.

"Are you sure we don't need the pushchair, Hal?"

"Titch, even if we really needed it, we couldn't carry it with all this lot. Anyway we'll only need it to the 50 bus stop. When we get to Golden Sands we can hire one for the week."

Normally a tram, or bus from Town would have been along by now, but for some reason or other this morning they were both running fifteen minutes late.

"One should have come by now, Hal?"

"Yes, I know," answered dad, looking at his watch again.

Another five minutes past before dad's voice called thankfully. "The bus is coming!"

"Lizzie, the bus is coming!" I said tugging Lizzie's arm.

"Yes I know Jamie, you don't have to tell me - I can see it too!"

Hal was heaving the cases onto the bus before the wheels had stopped rolling, then he jumped down helping Titch onto the platform with Patrick in her arms. "Come on quickly you two, up you get," he said with one hand holding the pole, and the other hauling me and Lizzie up from the pavement.

"Sorry about the delay," said the conductor helping dad with the cases under the stairs. "A wagon shed its load of vegetables heading for the market. I've never seen so many cabbages and swede rolling along the road. It wasn't gathering up the good ones and putting them back in the boxes that took the time, it was shovelling up the ones squashed that took the time."

Hal offered the conductor a consoling smile, then glanced at his watch again. It was five minutes past seven; only ten minutes before the charabanc was due to arrive at the pickup point.

*

"We've missed the pickup, Hal!"

"Yes we have; that fifteen minutes made the difference between us being here in plenty of time. We should have left earlier – like I wanted!"

"Okay, Hal, let's not spend the holiday listening to you preaching on your soap- box – as well as being broke?"

"Does this mean we can't go, Dad," asked Elizabeth.

"What! We aren't going on holiday?" My hands were grasping Lizzie's coat, tugging at it until my fingers turned white. "Lizzie, I want to go on holiday, I've been saving my money!"

"Jay, shut up. Does it mean we can't go, Dad?"

"No! We've missed the Charabanc, Lizzie so we'll have to go by train. It just means your mother and I won't have much money left after paying for the fare!"

"You can have some of my spending money, Dad if that will help?"

"No thank you Lizzie; we'll be fine, it just means being careful with the money."

"And doing without the things we could have done," said mom.

I didn't care if Lizzie gave dad all her money. She wasn't having any of mine. My fingers released her coat, and curled around the pennies in my pocket.

*

New Street Station, and my little heart was pounding as I stood on the platform close to dad. I knew what a train was and looked like from picture books, but I had never seen one for real. Dad's arm was around me, ensuring I didn't step another foot closer the edge, with mom's warning voice from behind.

"Hal, not too close to the edge; you know what he's like!"

I didn't know what mom meant by that, but if I could have taken another step, I would have. The glass roof above me was an awesome sight, arching over the entire station. The glass panes were so dense with smoke and grime, the only light coming through was from the broken – or the missing. A voice from the Tannoy suddenly announced. *"The train now coming through platform two, is the Northbound express. Please keep well back from the edge of the platform- Thank you."*

Dad held my hand even tighter, pointing across the central platform to the furthest in the station. In a voice of bated excitement he said. "There's an express train coming through!"

"An express train? What's an express train?"

"Just keep your eyes looking over there, Jaimie, watch and listen?"

I did so, and in the distant I heard the sound of a trains whistle sounding several times. I could feel platform beneath my feet vibrating gently, and then the muffled sound of rumbling, coming closer with every beat of my heart. Then like some fire-eating dragon, the train suddenly thundered through the station, belching out white steam and smoke. Its tender was glowing like a furnace, dragging the coaches and the whistles sound along with it, until it too had faded as quickly as it came. I couldn't even feel dads hand tugging me; I just wanted stand on the platform in boyish awe, reliving every second of this brief encounter with a dragon, over and over again. My eyes followed the plumes of smoke, rising toward the stations arched glass roof, adding to the soot and grime already imbedded in the glass panes.

*

It was another ten minutes before the voice in the speaker announced again. *"The train now arriving at platform five is the twelve forty five to Rhyl, changing at Chester."*

Dad suddenly ushered me toward Elizabeth, ordering me to hold her hand. "Okay, has everyone got everything; we don't want to leave anything behind?"

My heartbeats increased again, as the train rumbled slowly toward me, expelling spurts of deafening white steam as it slowed. Without thinking, I was waving at the train drivers black coated face; and with a smile exposing pure white teeth against black, he waved back at me. The instant the train came to a halt at the end of the station, the carriage porter was opening the carriage doors. Lizzie quickly grasped my hand from dad, and ushered me toward the one nearest.

"Lizzie, don't let go of Jaimie until he's sitting beside you," said dad struggling through the door with the cases. "Titch, you grab the seat in front of Elizabeth - I'll find a place for these!"

Up to this point, I was obeying every order spoken to me by Lizzie; even when I asked her if I could have my comic now, and she said not until we were all settled and the train was moving! If she had said I couldn't have something at home, I would have been standing to attention, bawling with an open mouth for the whole grove to hear – and would have carried on until I had my own way – but I wasn't at home; and I wasn't in a tram going to the Lickey's; I was on a train, looking out of the window, lulled into contentment from the sights and smells of the station.

The train porter released two short blasts from his whistle, and the carriage suddenly jerked. "Look Lizzie, were moving – Dad," I said squirming around in my seat. "We're moving!"

"Yes, now sit down in your seat and be a good boy?"

"Can I have my comic now – please, Lizzie?"

"Here!" she said, thrusting the beano into my hands. "And don't move till we get to Chester, or I'll tell dad!" Lizzie settled herself beside me, and eased out the, Polly Pigtails magazine from her satchel. "Mom, it's my birthday next week; I don't mind if you can't buy me the clothes for Alice, she can wait until Christmas!"

Greyish smoke was bellowing past the window as the train picked up speed, creating the clickety clack sounds of the wheels rolling over the expansion joints. Within ten minutes, the comic was draping across my lap, and I was asleep, rocked into my world of dreams from the sound.

*

Due to faulty signals along the way, our train from Birmingham arrived almost an hour late at Chester. Although we had three quarters of an hour to be at the connecting platform, after missing the charabanc in Birmingham, dad was in no mood to be held up by anything now.

"Hal, I think Patrick need his nappy changing!"

Dad voiced his frustration as Patrick vocally released his. "Can't it wait till we're on the train, Titch?"

"It's too long to wait, Hal; he's already got nappy rash, that's why he's crying!"

"Dad! Lizzie just said I'm not walking fast enough on purpose," I said, bawling as loud as Patrick.

"He is Dad, he keeps dragging his feet to slow me down!"

Dad's face said it all. After missing the charabanc by minutes; and having to spend most of the holiday money on train tickets; now the clouds were shedding their burden to add to the misery.

"How far is it to Rhyl now Dad?" I asked as Lizzie dragged me under the platform canopy.

"I hope the weather's not going to be like this all week, Hal? Stuck inside a caravan all week?"

"If we'd left the house half an hour earlier like I wanted, it wouldn't have mattered! We would have had the money to spend keeping everyone happy."

"Dad – how far is it to Rhyl now?"

"The train will be here anytime now, Hal. Hold Patrick while I make sure we've got everything?" Mom fussed around the luggage, preparing to board the train once it arrived. "Hopefully, Hal, it might have stopped raining by the time we get there, and you'll have stopped being so grumpy?"

"DAD – how far is it to Rhyl now?"

*

The moment we left the train station, a young boy suddenly ran toward us, pulling a four wheel cart by the rope around his waist.

"Where are you going to?" he asked.

"Golden sands holiday camp," said dad.

"The buses here are slow - and they're always full! "It's only a two mile walk from here, I can take your cases on my cart for thru pence!"

Dad mulled over it for a moment. "What do you think, Titch?

"And if you go by taxi it'll cost you more than the bus," the boy added.

"Even if the busses aren't full, like the lad said, Hal. It'll be a nightmare carting all this lot on and off it, I'd rather walk to the camp, than stand on the platform watching over the cases."

Dad was nodding his head. "Well it's stopped raining, so it looks like you've got the job mate!"

The lad couldn't have been more than nine years old, yet he was handling the cases with the strength and enthusiasm of a grownup.

"So how long are you staying for then?" began the chatter in an accent.

"We're staying for a whole week," I answered before Lizzie could.

"Oh right! Well I hope it'll be better than last week because it rained every day."

"It's not going to rain everyday – is it, Dad?" I asked without thinking.

"I sincerely hope not!" said dad, aware of the lightness in his wallet.

Lizzie was walked steadily next to the boy, intrigued by his grown up manner. "So how long have you been doing this then?" She asked him.

"I was going to ask him that!" I said quietly, rattled by Lizzie asking him first.

"A couple of years before my brother did! Then we made him a cart so he could do it too."

"Your brother does this as well - how old is he?"

"He's a year and a half younger than me. That's him over there," he said pointing to the lad hauling the cart laden with cases as he was. "OI, Bagsy, how are you doing," he yelled to him.

"Okay, Ash, this is my sixth one today!"

"Good, I'll meet you by Jonkers café later!"

A thumbs up from across the road followed.

*

The approach to Golden Sands was up a long concrete slope, next the railway bridge. Just before the slope was the gift shop, with multi coloured buckets, spades, kites, and blow up beach-balls, all dangling from string either side of the doorway. The slope curled to the right at the top and became, The Beach Road, with a huge sign. Golden Sands Holiday Camp spanning the road on metal legs. Our first stop was the camp office for dad to sign in, and given the keys to the caravan. The second was the hire shop, and a pushchair for Patrick hired for the week. My eyes turned swiftly to the four wheel bike, steered by a grownup, and a happy girl next to him waving as the beautiful contraption past us.

"Dad – Dad - look? Can we go on one of them?"

Dad's eyes flashed to the prices chalked in on the hire board; Tandem bikes – Half an hour one shilling. Two hours one shilling and sixpence.

"What number are we, Hal?"

"ONE-SIX-EIGHT," said dad, glancing at the key tag. The woman said to follow the path on the left around the site; according to the site map, ours should be just past some trees and a farm gate."

While we were walking around the site, my eyes were absorbing all there was to see. Caravans were in rows on concrete bases, with grass between each one. And flying above were the seagulls, releasing their shrill like calls in an orchestra of different tones. In the midlands, Magpies, Crows, Rooks and pigeons dominated the sky. Here on the edge of the land, with fields behind me, and the sea in front, seagulls dominated the sky, with at least one perching either on the roof of a caravan, on top of the camps electricity poles, or on the pole with two speakers, like the ones on a gramophone.

Mom began to feel optimistic as we reached 165, because the last five caravans had been very nice indeed. As we walked past the farm gate toward the trees, we stopped between caravans 167, and 169. "Hal, where's 168?"

I saw dad glancing at the key tag in confusion, then walking toward someone working on a caravan wearing the blue and yellow camp logo. There was a look on dad's face I'd seen many times from being naughty, and automatically I said, "It wasn't me dad, I haven't done anything!"

"Hal, what is it, have they given us the wrong key?"

"No, Titch, they've given us the right key; apparently our caravan's been moved to a pitch further on past those trees."

With optimism turning to apprehension, we walked past the trees, and daubed in white paint on a dented galvanised dustbin were the numbers, 168.

"Dad, where's the caravan?" Lizzie asked.

"There isn't one, Lizzie, this is where we are supposed to be staying."

"But it's a charabanc, Dad!"

"Yes it is, Lizzie, which is probably why it was so cheap!" voiced mom, grasping the key from dad. Mom strode past me, saying as she did in a calm voice. "Come on then, no point standing here looking at it; let's get inside and unpacked before we turn around and go back home?"

The charabanc may have looked like something from a scrapyard, propped up with bricks under the axels, but inside it was a plush hotel, with everything you could want for a holiday by the sea. The remaining Saturday was spent unpacking, and walking around the site with mom dad, making note of where everything was. Between the sea-view caravans was the pathway, leading down onto the pebble beach.

The beach was the only place we had yet to visit, and my little heart was pumping for joy when dad finally said, "Come on then, let's go and see what the beach looks like!"

Huge concrete blocks almost as tall as myself were evenly spaced along the beach. I would have asked dad what they were for. But that would have made me look ignorant in front of Lizzie, so I waited for her to ask dad instead.

The waves were gentle, rolling over the pebbles with the sound of marbles being fumbled in a bag. Dad suddenly took off his socks and shoes, and strode toward the waves, "Come then, who's going to be first in the sea?"

Without dad repeating himself, I was racing against Elizabeth, struggling to remove my socks and shoes before she removed hers. "Mom, I can't undo my laces," I whinged with my eyes on Lizzie.

"Well go and tell your dad then; I'm holding Patrick!"

"Dad!" I shouted, hobbling to the water's edge. "I can't undo my laces!"

Dad paddled back, and slowly removed my socks and shoes, throwing them one by one onto the pebbles behind. "Hurry up Dad, Lizzie's going to say hello to the sea before I do!"

"Son, you'd already be paddling if you'd kept your feet still."

"Beat you!" called Lizzie running past me into the waves, then dancing and kicking the water just to make me feel even more miserable.

"DAD! Lizzie's saying hello to the sea before me!"

"Well you can say hello to the sea before Lizzie tomorrow - if you're a good boy!"

"Dad said I can say hello to the sea first tomorrow!" I shouted, pulling my tongue out toward Elizabeth.

Dad suddenly waded back onto the dry pebbles, while opening arms to Patrick. "Well Just look at you then? Who's a clever little boy?"

Mom had taken off Patrick's socks and shoes, and was walking him toward the waves with his feet just touching the pebbles. "He wants to come and paddle with you, Hal!"

"Does he now?" Dad eased Patrick from mom, and supported him gently toward the waves. Patrick was laughing and chuckling, with his little legs flicking seawater onto his face.

"Aww, look at him, Dad? Look at him, Mom?" called Lizzie, paddling quickly toward Patrick. "His legs are splashing water everywhere; who's a big boy then - who's a big boy then?"

I sauntered back toward mom, and sat next to her on dad's coat.

"What's the matter, Jaimie? Why aren't you paddling like Lizzie and Patrick?"

"I don't want to, Mom; I want to go back to the charabanc!"

*

Rhyl was the: Hide de High, holiday resort of nineteen forty eight; and the pavilion was the camps place of entertainment. The fish and chip shop was just before the pavilion's entrance, wafting the smell from the fryers to the noses passing by. Above the doors, 'Golden Sands Camp' was spelt out-in large wording; and higher than the pitched roof, the union jack flag was flapping in the wind on a sturdy flagpole. As we walked in we were instantly greeted by a team member of the camp, donned in black trousers, blue waist coat, and yellow tie, introducing us to an atmosphere of overwhelming joy. Seats surrounding the wooden blocked dance floor were filling quickly; and mom led us hastily toward the chairs still vacant at the edge of the dance floor. On the stage a team member stood between the gramophone, and the table where the seventy eight records were stored individually in compartments.

"Welcome everyone to, Golden Sands Pavilion; I am Christine, the camps entertainment manager. We have dancing here every-night until Thursday for the grown-ups, and on Friday it is, Discovery Time for the children. If anyone here under the age of Ninety has a talent," a ripple of laughter followed. "And would like to share their talent with us on the stage, put you names down in reception tomorrow. Now have a lovely time, and I will leave you in the capable hands of Julie here. If anyone has a particular record they would like to dance to tonight, please tell Julie – if she has it, she will play it – Thank you!" The music of Glen Millers: In the Mood, blasted through the speakers as Christine walked off.

"Come on, Titch, we haven't danced to this for ages," said dad, grasping mom's arm.

"Hal, I've got Patrick, and it's already been a long day!"

"Go on Mom, I can look after Patrick, go and have a dance with dad!"

"Are you sure, Lizzie?"

"Yes, now go on! It's your holiday too, Mom!"

Mom lifted Patrick into Lizzie's arms, easing her conscience by saying, "We'll get you some pop and crisps in a bit."

I'd only ever seen mom and dad dancing once, and that was in the posh room, dancing to the record on the gramophone. But I think they must have been messing about then, because it wasn't anything like they were dancing now.

*

The Sunday began with the voice from the speakers calling. *"Good morning campers, it's going to be a beautiful day today. If anyone at Golden Sands has a birthday this week, please come and tell us, and we announce it across the camp. And the first to be wished a happy birthday is Jennifer Roberts. Jennifer is six today, so come on everyone, all join in and sing happy birthday with us?"* Almost everyone did, and their exuberant voices of – '*Happy birthday to you, happy birthday to you, happy birthday dear Jennifer Roberts, happy birthday to you,"* joined in with the voices from speakers.

In the afternoon, after fish and chips in the charabanc, we got ready to go to the beach. Mom was squeezing Patrick into the blue bathing costume she'd spent two weeks knitting. Dad was tying the string around my trunks with a shoelace knot. And Lizzie was easing herself into the mauve coloured bathing costume.

Without any of us noticing, a wasp had entered through the open door, and landed under the top of Lizzie's costume.

"DAD! A WASPS JUST STUNG ME!"

Dad instantly flicked the wasp to the floor, grasped it with his handkerchief and threw it outside.

Lizzie was behaving hysterically, and I wasn't sure whether to cry with her or not!

"It's alright, it's alright," said mom, tugging down her costume.

"It's stinging Mom, it's really stinging!"

"I know love! Hal, see if anyone's left anything in the cupboards?"

Dad opened every cupboard quickly. "Just a half box of matches - and a packet of salt, Titch."

Mom grasped the packet of salt from dad, tipped a small heap into the sink, and mixed it with water from the dripping tap into a paste. "This'll make it better," said mom, covering the small red swelling with the mixture.

I was standing quietly, resisting the urge to cry too. I remembered Lizzie, warning me not touching the bees in case they stung me. I may not have listened to anything she said then, but I certainly listened to her after that.

"Are we going to the beach now?"

"In a minute love, in a minute, just be a little bit patient will you?"

And I was patient, because everything Lizzie had warned me about had just happened to her.

*

Even though it was a lovely day, not many people were on the beach. Lizzie's wasp sting had stopped stinging, and she was running in and out of the water, releasing girly giggles with me. The sea had gone out far enough to expose the sand, and dad had created a seawater hole for Patrick to sit in. Mom had settled herself on dad's coat, watching in contentment while the seagulls flew around her, waiting for signs of food. "Hal," called mom reaching for dad's camera, "look at Patrick?"

Lizzie and me looked too, and my brother was wobbling across the sand unaided, with his never been worn before green knitted bathing costume, bulging with seawater and sagging to the sand.

The whole week went by too quickly. And our journey back home to Birmingham was in the Charabanc we had missed.

Seven

"In 1948, I went to school for the first time. The teachers then were strict, and corporal punishment was the answer to unruly behaviour. No pupil was spared a slap on the head, or the threat of the cane - not even pupils five years old were exempt.

"Will all the new children come forward please?" called Mrs Watson extending both hands in the air. "That's it, all come forward so you can hear me shouting. Moms and Dads, can you remain on the other side of the gates please?"

I felt moms hand let go mine, and instinctively I grasped it back, looking at her like a puppy dog who'd just had his favourite toy taken away from him.

"It's alright Jamie; remember what I said, and do as the teacher says." Mom lent toward me, pointing at the girls and boy's shuffling apprehensively toward Mrs Watson. "They're all just as scared as you are. See the little boy there?" she said turning her finger the boy with short curly hair and dark rim glasses. "See, he's looking at you!"

Mom nudged me from behind. "Give him a wave, maybe he's looking for a friend to start his first day at school with too!"

Instinctively I gave him scanty wave; and surprisingly he gave a scanty wave back.

"There's half a spam sandwich in your bag for lunch, now give your little brother a kiss."

As I leaned toward the pushchair, Patrick grasped my tie and pulled it to the left again. My head came out without administering the kiss, and I felt moms hand release me.

"Go on off you go, Jamie, and be a good boy for Mommy?"

I know mom had a tear as I walked away. She was saying good bye to her little boy, who had grown into a little man before her eyes.

"Alright children, all face the front and look at me. No looking at your moms and dads please," she called pointing to those desperately hanging on to the last glimpse of their parent's faces.

"Boys to the right," she called waving her hand to the right. "Girls to the left," she said waving her hand to the left.

I was just behind my newly discovered friend in the line. "What's your name?" I asked tapping his shoulder.

"William, but you can call me Willy. What's yours?"

"Jamie - are you scared like me?" I whispered to him.

"Yeah," he answered. "I didn't want to come; and Toby was standing by the door crying."

"Is Toby your brother?" I asked"

"No, he's my dog. My brother is Jack. He always cries when we leave him in the house.

"Your brother does?"

"No, Toby does! Have you got dog?"

"No," I answered. "I've got a brother and sister though!"

My new friend suddenly turned his head fully, forgetting where he was. "I haven't got a sister!"

"Keep your eyes to the front please," came Mrs Watson's voice with her eyes looking down at my new friend Willy. "And no talking in line." Mrs Watson led us through the double doors into an assembly hall, and I had never seen so many children in one place, all sitting cross legged on the wooden floor facing the stage.

Mrs Watson led us to the back row, reassuring us newcomers with words of kindness. "This is your first assembly and I want you all to sit quietly with the other children. No talking and listen to the headmaster, Mr Holarson!"

My eyes roamed along the line of teachers on the stage, all sitting on chairs, then followed Mr Holarson's slow march across the stage to the middle and stood facing everyone.

"To those who have only just joined us, welcome Tindle Street School," he announced in a loud voice. "I am Mr Holarson the schools headmaster. Behind me is, Mr Segmore, my deputy head, Mr Edwards, is the arts, and handicraft teacher, and Mrs Arnold is our teacher for music and scripture. To the new infants here, your teacher is Mrs Watson," he said pointing to our teacher against the wall. "If there is anything you need to know, do not be afraid to raise your hand and ask her. She is here to teach you, and guide you through your first year here at Tindle Street. Now," he said standing with his hands behind him. "I will begin morning assembly by saying; Good morning children -To which you will reply, Good morning Mr Holarson. – Good morning Children," Mr Holarson said again.

Nerves halted my greeting, and I only joined in when the others began. "Good morning Mr Holarson."

"Now the new children have been introduced to our teachers, Mrs Watson will you lead them to their class room?"

Mrs Watson nodded, and ushered us through the assembly doors. Before the doors closed, I heard Mr Holarson's voice calling. "We will begin by singing – Oh God our help in ages past."

I'd heard the hymn before, because Lizzie sang it at the Methodist church. I only ever thought hymns were sung in a church, and I was confused to hear children singing it in a school too.

Mrs Watson led us fledglings along the corridors to our classroom. Even before I walked through the classroom door, my heart was pounding, for this was going to be my second home for a long time, and the thought of that filled my stomach with fear and trepidation.

"Aright everyone, take a cushion from the side and sit down please. You can sit by someone you know if you wish! If not I am sure you will make friends with them very quickly."

Amidst the chattering of excitement and uncertainty, I quickly sat on my chosen cushion at the back, saving the place next to me for Willy.

"Willy – sit next to me!"

He smiled and said, "Thanks."

I smiled back, contented by him feeling just as nervous as I was.

"Now hands up those who can spell their names," asked Mrs Watson.

Three girls, and one boy put their hands up.

"Come on, up you get!" Mrs Watson handed the first girl a piece of chalk. "See if you can write your name on the chalk board, for us all to see?"

The girl wrote, 'Lucy' in an unclear attempt.

"Very good, Lucy, a clap for Lucy everyone!"

Willy and I were glancing at each other, breathing sighs of relief when the other three children wrote their names, all in squiggles that could not be deciphered by Mrs Watson.

"Now I will ask each one your name, and write it on the chalkboard; beginning with - you!" said Mrs Watson, pointing at the boy on the front row."

The girl sitting shyly in front of me to the left, wiggled her pigtails when asked her name. I saw her mouth moving only, and Mrs Watson asked her again.

"I'm sorry I couldn't quite hear! Speak up so we can all hear you?"

"Alice!"

"Alice is a lovely name," said Mrs Watson, writing her name on the chalkboard.

I saw the puddle of wee forming around Alice's cushion, and her eyes looked slowly toward me. I just stared ahead pretending I hadn't noticed.

Just before ten o-clock, two school monitors came with crates of milk on a trolley, one was a girl, and one was a boy. After sliding the crates onto the floor, they both stood by the door.

Mrs Watson glanced at the clock above the door, announcing. "Children, it is almost ten o-clock. If you need to use the toilets the monitors will escort you to them. Those who do not, remain seated while I place the shells, in front of the cushions."

"What are the shells for?" I asked Willy, following behind the monitor to the toilets.

"I don't know." Willy tapped the shoulder of the boy in front of him. "Hey, do you know what the shells are for?"

The boy half turned. "My brother was in this class, when he started. He said he had a shell for catching the crumbs from his sandwich!"

When I came back, Lucy -who had remained seated, looked as though she was about to cry. She acknowledged the involuntary smile forming on my lips, and felt I had made another friend.

*

At home we drank sterilised milk only, which came in a tall bottle, narrowing at the top and sealed with a tin cap crimped to the neck of the bottle. It was the only milk I'd ever tasted; and when the small bottle of pasteurised milk was placed in front of me, I wasn't sure whether it was to drink or not. I looked around, watching a few poking the straw into the silver cap, and followed their example. I had never tasted anything like it. It was smooth and creamy, like ice cream that hadn't been frozen.

"Right children, remain sitting quietly while the monitor takes your empty bottles to the crates. Hands up who would like to be classroom monitor for the day, emptying the shells into the bin and putting them away?"

Almost every child in the class put their hands up, including me and Willy, all calling, "Me-Miss-Me," with enthusiasm lifting our bottoms from the cushions.

Mrs Watson pointed to Riley, the boy with the longest arms, and I slunk back airing my disappointment quietly. "Aww, I wanted to do that!" Of course there would be many times when I could, and I found kneeling on the cushion for extra height was the advantage.

"Now children the next twenty minutes is your rest period. During this time you may rest your heads on your arms quietly. Sleep if you wish, it will not be questioned." Mrs Watson's eyes turned to Robert's arm raising apprehensively. "Yes Robert?"

"I only slept a little bit last night, because my little brother kept crying – he's only two months old and mom told me to keep awake and pay attention; if she knows I went to sleep in class I'll be in trouble." Robert rolled his eyes around the classroom for some comfort.

"To anyone else feeling like Robert, your parents are fully aware this time period is important. The first year at school is the first stage of your education. It can be a heavy burden placed on some of you; and it is important we guide you through your early learning years slowly. Your rest periods are for recharging your batteries, allowing your brains to absorb everything I teach you. So, for the next twenty minutes I don't want to hear a sound from anyone. Begin your rest period?"

Within minutes I heard the sound of snoring from someone a few rows away. It was a sound I never imagined I would hear in a school classroom, and my fears of going to school were quashed right there and then.

.

Eight
1949

Christmas Eve was the special event of the year in our house. In a few hours Santa Clause would be making his yearly visit, dropping down the chimney, with not even a soot coated footprint left on the rug.

The handmade coloured chains, Elizabeth and myself had spent hours making were tied to the gaslight, draped and secured with drawing pins to the four corners of the room. Ball shaped decorations hung like coloured wasps nests in between the chains, and in between those were tiny stars, revolving on thread with every movement of air beneath them.

The fire suddenly belched out a plume of black smoke, engulfing everything in front of the cast iron fireplace.

Mom grasped Patrick and made toward the back door, calling. "Lizzie open the front door before we all choke."

Dad flew from the chair with his newspaper in both hand, wafting the acrid smoke toward the half open door.

"Can't you do something about the smoke, perhaps it wants sweeping, I can't remember when it was last done, Hal?" voiced mom.

"Titch, we haven't had strong wind like this for ages, and when it does it blows the smoke down the chimney."

Mom continued wafting the smoke away from Patrick, while commenting again. "There must be some way we can stop it, Hal? It's not good breathing down smoke whenever the wind blows. Patricks been having one chesty cough after another."

"We can, but it means not having a fire when there's a gale, Titch!"

Mom gave a sigh at the option. "And then it'll blow down the chimney anyway, and we'll all be sitting in the cold."

"It's either one way or the other Titch," said dad.

"Or having it swept, Hal!"

"Urgg, I can't breathe Dad," I said with my hand across my mouth.

"Put your pyjama top over your mouth then, Son, it'll be gone in a minute."

"I still can't breathe!"

Dad fanned the smoke vigorously with the newspaper, only for it to be fanned back in again by the gale–force wind, spinning the stars until they were blurs of silver.

A few minutes passed before the air cleared, and all returned to normality.

"I think we should have the chimney swept after Christmas, Hal."

"Sweeping the chimney means spending money! And it won't stop the smoke blowing back down the chimney, Titch."

"Dad," I uttered

"What Son?"

"What if Father Christmas can't get down our chimney because of the soot. He might take all our presents to Josh's house instead?"

"And why would he do that?" responded dad.

"Because I was playing marbles in the gutter with Toby, and the chimney sweep man's brush was sticking out of Josh's chimney."

Lizzie gave me a curious sideways look. "Well I never saw a chimney sweeps brush sticking out of Josh's chimney!"

"NO, because you was at Brownies when it was sticking out."

Elizabeth released a thoughtful "Hmm!"

"Dad, Lizzie just went, hmm. She thinks I'm lying!"

"No she doesn't."

"She does Dad, she's just jealous because she didn't see the chimney sweep brush sticking out of the chimney like I did."

"Lizzie, tell your brother you don't think he's lying?"

"WHY would I be jealous of HIM, Dad? When we had ours swept a long time ago, the chimney sweep man said to wait outside, and tell him when I saw the brush poking out of the chimney."

"Well I don't remember the chimney sweep man sweeping our chimney. MOM, I think Lizzie's lying!"

"Yes we did Son, sometime last year."

"Well why didn't I see him then, Mom?"

"Because you was at school, Jamie. I asked Lizzie to take Patrick into the garden so the soot wouldn't go down his chest."

Lizzie turned from mom and smirked at me. "Now stop moaning and being a brat, you're annoying mom and dad, Jamie. Father Christmas doesn't come to children who moan, and annoy their mom' and dad's!"

With a face sourer than a lemon, I wormed my way back onto dad's chair. I was hoping the chimney wasn't too caked with soot, and prevent Santa from dropping down it with a sack over his shoulder.

The cuckoo appeared on the flimsy spring, calling out the hour from the clock, then swiftly vanished behind the little door again.

"What time are we going to bed?" I asked looking at the big hand moving slowly past six, o-clock.

"I've peeled the sprouts the carrots and potatoes and put them in water, Hal."

"I don't like sprouts or carrots, Mom."

"I know you don't, Jamie, but everyone else does!"

"Are you making your special Yorkshire pudding, Dad?" Elizabeth asked enthused by the first full Sunday dinner since last year.

"Oh yes, Lizzie, big as the plate."

"I like your Yorkshire pudding, Dad," I said raising my voice above Lizzie's "Are you making your special gravy as well?"

"As much as you want, Jamie, and thick enough to stand a spoon in."

"Hmm, lovely," I said. "What time are we going to bed?"

"Hal, when is Erick bringing the turkey?" Titch enquired, ignoring the sounds of an inpatient boy.

"He said about half nine in the morning, Titch!"

"It wouldn't have bothered me if we had goose again this year."

"We have goose every year Titch. This year were having turkey!"

"But you've never chopped the head off a turkey, Hal. Are you sure you'll be able to do it?"

"No reason why not, anyway Erick' next doors helping me; he did it to his turkey last year."

"What time are we going to bed?"

"Soon, Son, now listen to the wireless; the carols will be on soon."

"Come on, Patrick, that's it walk to mommy."

Patrick walked over the rug from the couch toward mom's open arms, widening his eyes with the smile of a Cheshire cat across his face.

"He's talking really good now isn't he mom," said Elizabeth holding her hands out too.

"Yes, Lizzie and tomorrows his second Christmas. Who's a big boy then, and what's Father Christmas going to bring you this year I wonder?"

"You want a Teddy bear don't you Patrick, just like Jamie's," said Elizabeth holding out her hands.

Patrick swayed from side to side, unsure of who to go too first, Lizzie or mom.

"I'm glad you managed to get the, you know what, from the shops Hal?"

"What's the, you know what, Mom?" I asked with my ears pricking. "What's the, you know what, Dad?" I repeated again.

"Nothing for you to worry about Son!"

Hal suddenly released a quietening. "Shush, listen – Carol singers." Hal turned down the wireless to low, allowing the voices of; Oh come all ye faithful to permeate the wooden door. The singing stopped and after a moment of whispering, they rose again to, 'Hark the herald angels sing Glory to the new borne King.'

"Oh, I love this one." Elizabeth quickly left the couch and stood by the door, singing along with the voices on the other side.

The living room was suddenly a place of joyful music, with mom's beautiful voice joining in with Elizabeth.

The carol songs ended abruptly with ("Christmas is a coming and the goose is getting fat. Will you please put a penny in the old man's hat! If you haven't got a penny, a ha'penny will do. If you haven't got a ha'penny," (they all blew a loud raspberry) "To you!"

"Here, Lizzie give them this," said dad handing her a ha-penny.

Elizabeth opened the door to the ramshackle choir of one small girl, concealed inside a big woolly hat, long woolly scarf and thick coat. And a small boy hiding under a balaclava, scarf and jacket. Behind them was, Bethany Archer who sang next to her at the church harvest festival. She was wearing a pink knitted hat, a heavy coat and a large pink scarf wrapped twice around her neck.

Gratefully Elizabeth handed the ha-penny coin to Bethany. "Hello, Beth, I didn't know it was you singing."

"I came to keep an eye on these two," she said, shrugging her shoulders.

"Are they your brother and sister?" Lizzie asked.

"Yes, they begged me to take them carol singing. We've done pretty well too. Have you been carol singing, Lizzie?"

"No, not this year I haven't!"

"Oh! You have a really nice voice, you should have?"

"I would have, but Jaimie wouldn't come, and my other friend Silvia's got a cold; I wasn't going to go on my own."

"You can come with us now if you want, we've still got half an hour?"

"No it's alright, thanks anyway!"

"Oh, well I hope you have a nice Christmas, Lizzie?"

"And I hope you do too, Bethany."

"Happy Christmas," voiced the two little singers."

"Thank you," answered Elizabeth closing the door gently.

Elizabeth returned to her seat on the couch, saying in a wishful voice. "I wish I could've gone carol singing this year, Mom! I love singing carols."

"I know you do Lizzie," answered mom. "That's why you like singing in the Church. I don't know why you didn't join up with Bethany, or even some of the girls from church. The Methodist Church is only along Mosely road, you could have met them there. You get on with them don't you?"

Elizabeth grasped Patrick's hands pulling him toward her eyes. "Yes, but I only mix with them when I'm at church, Mom!"

"Right then," said, Hal turning up the volume on the wireless. "You can sing along with the carols for half an hour."

"Will you sing with me, Mom?"

"Of course I'll sing with you, Lizzie," Mom thought for a moment, then said, "Tell you what - Hal, go and light the fire in the posh room, coal or no coal, it's almost Christmas. I'll play the piano, then we'll have a proper sing song!"

"But what about Father Christmas, Dad?" I said without understanding the true meaning of Christmas is not always about presents.

"If father Christmas comes while were singing, Jamie, he can sing along with us. I think he might like that, don't you Lizzie?"

"Yes I do, Dad. I bet no one's asked him to sing with them before?"

"Well I want to sing with him first then?" I said aspiring to be Santa's special child.

In the posh room, the flames were now dancing above the coals crimson embers. Mom was still on the piano, bouncing the stringed instrument on the rotten floorboards, with her head rocking, and the dulcet tones of, 'Here comes Santa Claus,' - and, 'Let it snow let it snow let it snow,' sung in unison between her and Elizabeth. I had decided singing was not my forte, and decided to sit on the couch with Patrick on my lap, watching dad putting a few more baubles on the little Christmas tree, standing proudly in the middle of the drop leafed table. The feeling of inner warmth was overwhelming my naivety; and it was one of those moments when time stood still, capturing and storing the moment in my memory forever - Like a photograph in an album.

*

"The sun had barely breached the horizon, and I was out of bed, staring in wonder at my pillowcase bulging with presents. Elizabeth was still asleep behind the curtain dad had put up to give her privacy. Curiously I glanced at her pillowcase, resting against the wall at the side of the curtain.

"Lizzie," I called just above a whisper. "Father Christmas's been."

Lizzie answered me with a yawning mumble. "Go away Jamie, it's not morning yet."

"But Father Christmas's been – Look, he's left lots of presents in your pillowcase?"

"Good - now go back to sleep, Jamie."

I grasped the curtain and pulled a little so I could peep behind it.

"Jamie close the curtain or I'll shout dad!"

"But look, Lizzie! Father Christmas has been. Don't you want to even look?"

"No! Go and open your presents and leave me alone!"

"But I want to open them with you, Lizzie," I said waiting solemnly by the curtain for Lizzie to respond.

"Jamie, why are you being a pain, you never wanted me to open my presents with you last year."

'No I didn't,' I thought. Last year I'd opened every present before Elizabeth had even opened her eyes. And then I sat surrounded by Christmas paper, watching with envy while she opened hers, screaming with delighted surprise to each one.

"Lizzieee - pleeeese!"

"Right, but you open yours properly, and read who they're from before you rip all the paper off them."

"Okay, Lizzie." - Now I said okay, but I couldn't understand the reason why. The presents were from Father Christmas, everyone knew that; why would I want to know who they were from? Eagerly I waited for Elizabeth to appear from behind the curtain, willing her to hurry with sighs of impatience.

Elizabeth pulled back the curtain with one of the blankets wrapped around her, glancing toward the window rattling with the wind. The snow had built up on the window sill, and Jack Frost had paid us a visit in the night, creating beautiful designs on the glass. "Don't get rushing and opening everything all at once, take your time and look at the presents properly."

The door opened slowly, and dads head poked through. "Merry Christmas?"

"Merry Christmas, Dad," answered Elizabeth.

"LOOK DAD, Father Christmas's been. We don't know what he's brought us because we haven't opened anything yet. Have we, Lizzie?"

"NO," responded Elizabeth, drawing the blanket even tighter around her.

"Good, if you want to wait for half an hour your mom will be up with Patrick! I'll have the fire lit then, and you can open your presents by the fire while I'm making breakfast."

"Is that a Christmas breakfast, Dad?" Elizabeth asked.

"Yes, your mom's been thrifty with the rationing book, Lizzie, so eggs bacon and beans are on the menu!"

"And fried bread," drooled Lizzie.

"And fried bread," said dad.

"Oh, that's great, thanks Dad!"

The door closed and I dropped to the floor, pushing myself against the wall with my legs raised and arms folded. "Awww, we've got to wait for another half an hour?"

"Yes, so stop moaning, Jamie. You can open yours if you like but I'm opening mine by the fire; my hands and feet are freezing."

The draught from the window was blowing like a gale down my neck, and reluctantly I climbed onto my bed and slid beneath the blankets, drawing myself into a tight ball. I knew Elizabeth was right, she was always right. And yes of course it was going to be better, opening presents in front of a roaring fire, and not in the presence of a wintery blast; but I could have opened mine in less than five minutes, then gone down stairs and sat in front of the fire.

*

"Merry Christmas," called Erick walking in through the back door wearing his Father Christmas hat.

"Merry Christmas, Erick," we all called back.

"There's a turkey out here waiting to be chopped and plucked, Hal. Mine's already done and in the oven."

Dad walked to the back door, half turning his head toward Elizabeth and me. "Lizzie, hold on to your brother, this is not for either of you to see."

"What about breakfast, Dad," I voiced.

"I'll make breakfast when the turkeys ready for the oven, Jamie."

The door had only been closed for a minute, and the curiosity of seeing the turkey was overpowering the urge to open my presents. I slid from the chair and ran to the back door, ignoring mom's voice warning me not to.

"Jamie come away from the door, please; your dad's told you not to go outside. Elizabeth get Jamie away from the door please."

Elizabeth released an inconvenient sigh, and strutted toward the door like a school mistress about to admonish me.

"Get away from the door, NOW!" she said gripping my arm tightly. "You're not doing as you're told again?"

"NO - I want to see what's happing to the turkey, Lizzie." I pulled my arm free, and squeezed through the door before she could grasp me again. I stepped into the yard just as Erick's knife severed the turkey's head; and instantly the headless turkey flew from Erick's grasp toward me. I screamed in horror as it suddenly swerved past me into the toilet, with Erick still clutching the turkey's head, and dad running beside him.

"Jamie go into the house now!" Dad called closing the toilet door behind him.

I never gave dad the option of asking me twice, because I'd walked through the back door into the living room, and was on the chair staring ahead white as a sheet.

"Elizabeth, what's wrong with Jamie?" Mom asked.

"The turkey ran past him without its head. It serves him right, Mom for not doing what you and dad told him to do."

"Did you see it too, Lizzie?"

"I saw the turkeys head in Erick's hand and looked away."

Mom patted the cushion next to Patrick. "Jay come here!"

I did so without a whimper of stubbornness.

"Jamie, when your dad told you not to follow him outside, it wasn't because he was being spiteful. You ignored what he told you not to do, and you saw something you shouldn't have! It's frightened you hasn't it?"

I nodded because it had.

"Well next time when you're told not to do something you'll listen, and not do it - won't you?"

"Yes, Mom!"

"Would the turkey have known it hadn't got its head, Mom?" Elizabeth asked.

"No, the turkey was dead, Lizzie, it wouldn't have known anything."

"But it was running, Mom; why was it running if it was dead?"

It was the question I wanted to ask, mom, and hoped her answer to Lizzie would be enough to prevent me from having another nightmare.

"The turkey wouldn't have known it was running, Lizzie. It wouldn't have known anything. Now the kindest thing you can do is thank the turkey for making our Christmas special. And enjoy the gift he has given us by not wasting it - right Jamie," said mom patting my hand.

"Yes, Mom – And can we open our presents now, please?"

*

It was half past eight Christmas morning; and by now almost every child would have had their breakfast, and opened their presents. I was still walking round bored, waiting for dad to come in from the back yard.

Lizzie was also showing her impatience, asking with a sigh. "How long's dad going to be, Mom?"

"Not long now love," mom answered bouncing Patrick on her knee.

I walked past my pillowcase of presents, and stood looking through the living room window, wondering what Father Christmas was doing now.

"Okay, turkey all done and stuffed," said dad coming through the back door.

"Can we open our presents now, Mom?"

"Yes, Jaimie. Hal turn the wireless on before you make breakfast, John Masefield's Christmas box of delights will be on!"

Instantly the room was alive with carols, played by Victor Hely–Hutchinson's Symphony; and the smell of bacon and eggs, were now overriding the smell of burning coal.

*

"Dad, look, I've had a pink buggy for Bella," said Lizzie as dad came through the back door. "It's just what I wanted."

"And look what I've got Dad," I said quickly assembling the circular tracks for the clockwork train.

Dad Hummed aloud. "You must have been a very good boy for Father Christmas to leave you a train set, Jamie."

"Yes I know; and Patricks been a good boy too Dad," I said reaching toward Patrick, sitting on the rug between moms legs. "Look, he's got a teddy bear just like mine." I snatched the bear from him and held it above me so he couldn't reach it.

"Jamie," shouted mom, "Stop being spiteful and give Patrick his teddy! Hal is that breakfast ready yet?"

"Finishing it now, Titch!"

"Good, I'm starving," I said throwing Patrick's teddy into the air and catching it again.

"Jaimie, I've told you to give, Patrick his teddy back!"

"In a minute mom, I'm just playing with it!"

"Lizzie, give Patrick Jamie's train-set to play with; I'm sure Jamie won't mind, seeing as he's playing with his brother's teddy!"

I shoved the teddy into Patrick's arms, and stood like a guard between him and my presents from Santa. During a lifetime of memories one thing will not be forgotten, and that is sitting cross legged in front of the Christmas fire; with Lizzie and me either side of Patrick, our fry up on our laps, and carol's on the wireless. Unbeknown to us, it was the last time we would all be together for a long time.

Nine
1950

October was really cold, and smoke was belching out almost every the chimney in the grove. We were all huddled around the coal fire, which seemed to take a long time to get going. I was in my usual position, sitting cross legged on the rug in front of the fire, mom had Patrick on her lap, cuddling him with a blanket around him, and Lizzie was wearing jumper, with a scarf around her neck.

"Dad, I'm freezing," I said, watching the flames struggling to heat the coal.

"Hal, I told you to light the fire earlier; why is it taking so long? You know Patrick's not been well."

Dad went to the front door, lifted his big heavy coat from the hook in frustration, and wrapped it around me like a cloak. "The coal's damp, Titch, that's why it's taking so long to warm up!"

"I've told you to always make sure the coal cupboard's full. You know coal coming straight from the coalhouse is always damp!"

"The coal cupboard's full now isn't it?"

"Yes, I know it is, but it wasn't this morning was it, Hal?"

Dad grabbed his newspaper, pulled out the whole middle sheet, and placed it over the front of the fire. Instantly the sheet was drawn inward from the downdraught, and the flames behind drawn upward creating a rushing sound. The middle of the sheet began smouldering and dad pulled away the newspaper before it burst into flame. "It's heating up now," dad said, crumpling the newspaper into a ball.

Even though the fire was now giving off precious heat, dad thought one more covering with newspaper was needed. This time however dad failed to pull away the smouldering newspaper quickly enough, and the whole sheet ignited, with the flaming pieces drawn up the chimney. This I remember happening to dad several times before without a problem

About ten minutes later, Edward from three doors up opposite was banging on the door, shouting for dad.

"Hal, I think your chimney's on fire mate!!"

Dad went outside to the gate with Edward, Lizzie and I followed, drawn into the cold only from curiosity. Flames and sparks were being ejected from the chimney amidst plumes of soot laden smoke.

Dad hurried back into the house, talking to all of us in quick bursts. "The chimney's on fire, Titch, I'll go to the phone box up the road and call for the fire brigade!"

Mom was off the couch like a spring, lifting Patrick to his feet. "This is all we need right now, Hal, The house is going to be freezing!"

Edward quickly grasped dads arm by the door. "I'll go and ring for the fire brigade, Hal, you take everyone across to my house. You can stay there while fire brigade tackle fire, and it's safe to come back."

"Thanks, Ed! I really appreciate it. Jaimie go with your mom to Ed's house. Lizzie you stay here and help me drag everything across to the wall!"

"Dad, I won't be able to lift anything heavy!"

"I know you won't, Lizzie, I'll drag the couch against the wall, and lift the chairs onto it, you just carry what you can into the posh room."

"Hal, does Mabel know we're coming to hers," said mom grasping Patrick's hand.

"I saw Ed going to his house before racing off down the entry, he would have told Mabel so stop worrying!"

"Stop worrying you say!" Mom was on the verge of tears as she glanced toward the chimney. "The floor's going to be under water with black slime when we get back, Hal! It's going to take us days to dry the house; never mind cleaning everything covered in soot!"

"And if it is, we'll clean it all up; just like the Rowlands did when their chimney caught fire?"

"Is the house going to burn down, Mom?" I asked innocently.

"No, Jaimie the house isn't going to burn down, let's just do as your dad said!"

*

Within the space of and hour, the fire engine's hose was spurting water up the chimney, and the whole grove was in their gardens, watching the plumes of fire- steam and smoke diminishing.

I don't know how much dad paid for the fire brigade to come, but I think he gave them a ten shilling note. And mom was right when she said it would take days for the living room to be back to normal.

Ten
1951

A few months before Christmas, Patrick had become really poorly. He was taken to Hilltop hospital in Bromsgrove, and confirmed he had TB. This Christmas would be our first without Patrick, and the atmosphere of jollity I normally enjoyed on Christmas morning was sombre. Even Lizzie, who always displayed her joy when opening presents was quiet. Just after breakfast Chalky White, one of dad's friends from work arrived in his car.

"Merry Christmas, Jim, merry Christmas everyone!"

"Merry Christmas, Chalky," said mom, who had been on the verge of tears since I woke up.

Chalky stood pensive by the door, choosing his words carefully. "Any news on the little man?"

"No, we won't know anything till we get there!"

"Dad, are we taking Patricks present with us," asked Lizzie.

"I don't know, I'm not sure if there's room in the car,"

"How big is the present, Jim?"

Dad reached behind the couch for the box, containing a metal wind up race track. "This big Chalky!"

"Well it's going to be a tight squeeze in the back for three, but if you can get it between your legs and the front seats, we can take it Jim; we can't have Father Christmas forgetting the little man can we?"

"Thank you, Chalky," said mom, looking tired and strained. "I don't know what we would have done without you today?"

The roads were all deserted and the shops were all shut as we travelled to Hill croft hospital in Bromsgrove. I was squeezed in between mom and Lizzie, and dad was sitting in the front passenger seat, having little conversations with Chalky. It had just begun to rain as we left Edward Road, and for most of the journey I was held in fascination, peering between dad and Chalky to the car's front screen the wipers, changing speed each time the gears were changed. Whenever we stopped, so did the wipers, when the cars slowed down, so did the wipers, when the engine revved faster, so did the wipers, speeding back a forth across the screen with spurts of rushing air.

Three months ago a brick cobbled road was being overlaid with tarmac. I was one of the children there watching with dad and mom on our way to the lane, looking for cheap clothes for me. Mom always said the smell of molten tar was good for the chest, but whenever I inhaled the smell it made me cough. I always believed people who coughed were more likely to be healthier than those who didn't. Standing in awe at the huge steam roller, rolling back and forth, squashing the tarmac with its huge front roller, filled and weighted down with water was a sight to behold. The fire heating up the boiler was aglow from burning coal, with smoke belching from the chimney in short puffs. A piston was spinning the small wheel, connecting the drive wheel by a belt of leather to the roller. It was a huge clanging monster, rolling back and forth at a snail's pace, changing directions from spinning the steering wheel wildly with a knob. The reason why the vision of this was recalled inside the car, squashed between mom and Lizzie was because Chalky was the steering the car with hardly any movement to the wheel at all.

"Thanks for taking us mate, especially as its Christmas morning, I'll give you the money for the petrol!"

"It's fine, I don't mind Jim! The mother in-law lives not too far from Bromsgrove, and she's having Christmas dinner with us, that's why I said yes when you asked me. I'm just sorry I can't wait and bring you back."

"Dad, why are we taking Patrick's present from Santa with us. Isn't he coming home with us today," I voiced severing my hypnotic stare from the wipers?"

"No not today, Son!"

"But I wanted to show him my new game, Dad!"

"You can show him when he comes home!"

"But I might lose some pieces, then we won't be able to play it!"

"Jaimie shut up," said Lizzie, nudging my side. "If you're worried about losing pieces, put it back in the box until Patrick comes home - then you won't lose the pieces!"

"But then I won't be able to play with it, Lizzie - Mom if I put it back in the box I won't be able to play with my Christmas present from Santa!"

Mom remained silent staring ahead. She was holding back the tears I was too wrapped up in self-pity to notice.

"I think this rains in for the day, Jim," said Chalky looking at the clouds. "It wouldn't surprise me if we had a bit of thunder later!"

Lizzie turned her concerns to mom, asking her quietly. "How longs Patrick going to be in hospital for?"

"Were not sure at the moment, Elizabeth. We have to wait and see what the specialists say."

"So he might not be coming home for a few days then?"

"No, I think it's going to be longer than a few days, Lizzie."

"Jim, how are you getting back home?" Chalky asked.

"Getting home isn't important right now," answered mom before dad could. "Patrick might not be allowed to have his present, because of infection; but it's what he asked Santa for. We just wanted to make sure it was already there when he was well enough to have it. We had to come, Chalky, even though it meant having to walk to the hospital and back. We promised we would come and see him on Christmas day; and to let him know Santa hadn't forgotten him!"

I nudged Lizzies arm discreetly. "Why would Santa forget Patrick? Is it because he's been naughty, Lizzie?"

"No it isn't, it's because he's poorly; now just sit still and stop mithering!"

I did sit still, I sat still for the rest of the journey, not really understanding why I had to.

"How long do you think you'll you be at the hospital, Jim?" Chalky asked turning into the entrance of the hospital

"I'm not sure; the first time was about an hour and a half - wasn't it, Titch?"

"About that, and Mo, my sister looked after Jaimie and Lizzie for us! They're with us today because we promised Patrick they'd see him on Christmas day. They're very strict on infection, but we're hoping they can come into the ward and see him for a few minutes with us!"

"Does that mean we might not see Patrick today, Mom?" Lizzie asked.

"I'm hoping that's not the case, Lizzie!"

I nudged Lizzies arm again. "Aren't we going to see Patrick then?"

Lizzie dug her elbow into my side, releasing a quiet, "Shush!"

*

Chalky waved to us as we walked from the car toward the entrance of Hill croft. I was walking as closely as I could next to Lizzie sharing her pink umbrella; and mom had her arm around dad sharing his.

In the hospital, Lizzie and I remained in the waiting room, while mom and dad asked if we could see Patrick too. Unfortunately the answer was no; and it must have been an hour and a half before they came back. Thinking back now, Lizzie made that hour and a half seem like five minutes, playing little games and singing songs I could sing along with. Mom was crying when she walked in the waiting room; and before I could say is Pat's alright, dad! Dad gave me one of his stern looks. I was only a little bit upset when Dad replied to Lizzie's question - "Is everything alright with Patrick, Dad?"

It must have been the tranquillity of the hospital surroundings, encouraging me to keep any thoughts to myself.

As we left the hospital, the umbrellas were up and doing very little to keep us dry. It was going to be a good two and a half hours walk back to Edward Road, and just something else for mom and dad to worry about.

We all turned to the sound of the car horn, beeping from the small parking area by the gates.

"It's Chalky," said dad leading us quickly toward the car. "Come on, Titch he's come back for us?"

"Is he taking us home, Dad?" Lizzie asked, dragging me by the arm.

"It looks like it, come on don't keep him waiting!"

Lizzie shoved me from behind, while lowering the umbrella into the well between the seats. "Jaimie stop hanging about and get in the car?"

"I am, so stop pushing me. Dad Lizzies pushing me!"

"Son, just get in the car like a good boy? Thanks Chalky, you're a life saver!"

"That's okay mate, you would've done the same for me!"

"How did you know what time we were leaving?" dad asked closing the car door.

"I didn't, so just in case you'd already left, I drove the way you would've been walking. I'm the only car on the road so you wouldn't have missed me."

"We can't thank you enough Chalky," said mom. "Especially as its Christmas day and you should be with your family?"

"It was Madge, the wife's mother who told me too, Titch. One thing I've learned being married to Ruth is not to contradict, or argue with her mother. And anyway I probably would have come, even if she hadn't insisted I should! So what's happening with the little man then?"

Mom was going to answer Chalky's question but she couldn't. Dad offered Chalky a park drive, and lit them both from a single match.

"He needs an operation to save his life, Chalky; but there isn't anyone who's skilled enough over here who can do it. The hospital have found a surgeon who can, but he'll have to come from America."

"Someone will have to come from abroad to operate on Patrick?"

"Yes, and to do that, Chalky will cost one thousand-five hundred pounds!"

"One thousand five hundred pounds," repeated Chalky. "Bloody hell mate! You can buy two houses with that! How can you raise that amount of money; I know I couldn't, even if I had three jobs?"

"We couldn't. There's a young girl with the same illness opposite Patrick. We've spoken to her parents, and the specialists in the hospital, and the surgeon has agreed to come and perform the same operation on the girl and Patrick for the same cost."

"So you'll be paying half each then?"

"Yes!"

"Seven hundred and fifty pounds is still a lot of money, Jim. Will you be able to raise that amount?"

"Not without borrowing it, Chalky. If it means having to pay it back for the rest of my life, then that's what it means!"

*

That evening I was sitting cross-legged on the mat, with the gas-lamp burning away, inches from the streamers tied to it across the ceiling. In those days the possibility of them bursting into flames from a naked flame was never considered; and to my knowledge none ever did. The wireless was playing Christmas songs. Dad was preparing a little snack of turkey sandwiches, while mom and Lizzie looked through the photo album, sharing loved moments. If Pat's had been there, I would have been teasing him with Rupert, pretending to give it him then snatching it away; and mom would be threatening to send my Christmas toys back to Father Christmas – again; but with him not being there I couldn't. I thought Patrick had been taken away because I was always being naughty with him. I'd had a feeling of loss since he had gone, and my nightmares had become more frequent. I was wetting the bed more often too, and I believed the stairs leading toward the small landing were hunted. Dad said it was my imagination being over active, and told me to think of good things before going to bed.

Eleven
1952

March had suddenly appeared on the calendar as if from nowhere. After spending several months at Hill croft, Patrick was sent to convalesce at Uffculm open air clinic in Kings Heath. They told mom and dad if he continued in becoming stronger, he could come home before the end of the year.

Money had been really tight because of the loan dad had borrowed from work. Mom and dad had been saving hard for the uniform for when I joined the cubs, and the day came when I could proudly wear my uniform.

"Socks!" said dad, referring to one being higher than the other. I quickly adjusted both knee-high socks, to the level of my knee length shorts.

"Stand upright; put your shoulders back, and let's see if you've remembered the cub motto?"

I was happy to, for at last I was wearing the peaked cap with yellowy golden bands, a neckerchief around my green jumper, grey knee length shorts, and green tabs lapping over grey knee-high socks. "Do your best." I said proudly, for now I was an affiliated cub, with a hat and a badge to prove it. "Can I go and show everyone before I go to cubs, Dad," I said without hiding my excitement.

"You can, but no showing off!"

"And no coming back with dirt on it," warned Mom.

"I won't Mom, you can watch me from the gate if you want?"

Lizzie came in from the toilet before I went outside, rubbing her hands from the cold. "Dad, it's our turn to put the paper in the toilet again, it's almost gone and you need to cut up some more - and the chains not flushing properly! I had to pull it three times. Lizzie gave me an approving look and said, "Hmm, very smart; you better not get bored and say you're not going anymore! Mom and dad have saved a long time for that uniform!"

"I won't!"

"Mom, Jessie's having her birthday party on Saturday. She said she wants me to go because I'm her best friend."

"Saturday!" said mom. "We were taking you and Jaimie to the pictures on Saturday, Lizzie!"

"But Jaimie's going to Saturday matinee with the kids in the grove?"

"Mom, aren't I going to Saturday matinee?"

"Yes you are; were taking you in the evening."

"You mean I'm going to the pictures two times on Saturday, Mom?"

Lizzie hovered between the cupboard and the couch. "Can't you go without me, Mom? Jessie will be really upset if I don't go to her party."

"Well what time is she having the party? If it's in the afternoon, you can still come to the pictures with us; we won't be going till around seven?"

"Jessie said the party won't start until about six o-clock. It should've been in the afternoon, but her dad had to go to work, so they're having it after he comes home."

Mom nodded to dad. "Well we want you back in the house before ten, it gets dark about eight, and a couple of gas lamps aren't working between Mary Street and Hallam Street!"

"The gas-lamps not working by the coal-yard either Mom," I said, behaving more grown up in my uniform. "I think someone's been throwing stones at it because the glass is smashed!"

Mom nodded while gently moving the peak of my hat central. "Now you can see why we didn't mind you joining the cubs. If you're there doing something useful, you're not doing anything you shouldn't be, like throwing stones at gas-lamps!" Mom quickly went to the outhouse, and came back with the disinfected wee bucket, placing it on the second winding tread, ready to be taken up stairs at bedtime.

"What are we going to see, Dad," I asked, not really caring what the picture was.

"Snow White and the Severn Dwarfs, Jaimie; Lizzie you would have loved it."

"If it's anything to do with Cowboys and Indians, Dad, then I'm glad I'm not going!"

I intervened quickly, bringing the conversation to me. "Well I like Cowboys and Indians, Dad. Roy Rogers was on Saturday's Matinee last week!"

"It isn't about Cowboys or Indians," said mom returning to the couch. "It's an animated fairy story about a beautiful princess and a wicked witch!"

Lizzie gave mom a little, "Hmm! Popeye the Sailor man's an animated film – isn't it, Mom?"

"Yes, but this one's different, Lizzie, this one's for grownups too!"

"Have you seen it before then," Lizzie asked out of girly curiosity.

Dad lit his park drive, and exhaled a cloud of white smoke toward the ceiling. "Your mom and I went to see it a few months after you Jaimie was born. It was only on the Imperial for a week, and one of the foremen at work recommended we see it before it came off. Jaimie was a really miserable sod for the first six months; screaming and wailing for your mom every-time she was out of sight. You couldn't even go to the toilet, without him screaming - could you, Titch?"

"No I couldn't, Mo looked after you two and Patrick, and I went with your dad to the pictures for a little break. It's a shame your brother isn't here to see it with us, Jay. It's a film no one should miss seeing."

"That's okay, Mom, he can come with us when he comes home - can't he Dad," I said looking for approval.

"I doubt it Son! It's been nine years since we last saw it; it'll probably be another nine before it comes to the Imperial again!"

*

Snow White and the Severn Dwarfs did come back to the Imperial. It came back in nineteen fifty eight. (The year I left school and started work.)

*

It was around ten o-clock when we got home from the pictures. Even if Lizzie had got home before us, the house would be in darkness. No one was allowed to light the gas lamp only dad, and Lizzie had tried to light it last Christmas. I was at auntie Mo's with mom and dad, and Lizzie was at her friend Jessie's. It was about four o-clock, and already dark when Lizzie got home. Instead of lighting the candle, waiting for us to come home, she pulled the table toward the couch, climbed on it and tried to light the mantle with one of dad's long swan matches. Instead of pulling the chain gently, so the gas was not so fierce, she pulled it down fully. When she put the flame close to the mantle, it exploded, sending bits of hot mantle across the room. Dad said it was a good job Lizzie had pulled the chain opposite, closing off the gas so quickly; and that bits of the hot mantle hadn't settled on the trimmings.

The moment dad lit the mantle, bringing light into the room, the cockroaches were scurrying back behind the wooden panelling. We had lived in their presence since I was born; their sounds were an everyday part of my life and so ignored. When I went to bed that night, it took me ages to get to sleep. My head was a whirl of wonderment from watching an animated film, and the name: Walt Disney becoming something special.

*

There had been several visits from people in suits throughout the first half of the year. Even though I was never there when they came, I knew because mom and dad kept mentioning them in their conversations. When I came home from school one day, the grove was full of workmen, carrying pipes and coils of something on their shoulders, I was quickly led to one side by dad, who I was surprised to see, because he was usually still at work. The garden was strewn with bits of old gas pipe, and reals of wire, next to lengths of wooden sheathing. I had been so eager to get home from school, I hadn't noticed the several vans parked in a line up the street

"Right you're coming with me to your Auntie Mo's," said dad, leading me by the arm back through the gate.

"What for; why can't I go in the house?"

"Because workmen are in there - that's why!"

"What are they doing?" I asked, straining to look behind.

"They're taking the gas pipes out, and replacing them with electricity."

I dragged my feet while continuing to look round in curiosity. "But if they take the gas pipes out, how will we see in the dark?"

"Because we're having light bulbs instead!"

"Light bulbs?"

"Yes, light bulbs!"

*

The coldness of wintery air had finally gone, and spring was in full, bringing each day closer to Easter time. I had just come from cubs, stripping and throwing my uniform across the floor. "At cubs today our leader said the Sunday after Easter is, bob a job week - Look," I said, handing mom a letter.

I watched mom reading the letter, impatient for her to finish.

"Hmm, it's a form asking permission for Jaimie to take part in the, bob a job, Hal!"

"We all had one," I said excitedly. "I have to do jobs for people, and they give me a bob for doing it."

Lizzie grasped the letter off mom, humming sarcastically as she read it. "Jaimie, you won't even do anything mom asks you to do around the house; I can't see you doing jobs for other people without whinging about it!"

"It's for a good cause, Mom, that's why I want to do it," I said snatching the letter from Lizzie. "All the cubs will be doing it!"

"Well if you're doing jobs, and being paid to do it, you've got to do them properly. Not like you do here, throwing your clothes across the floor when you're told to fold them properly!"

"So I can do it then, Dad?"

"Yes - and perhaps some of it will rub off, and you'll start doing what your mom asks, without making a sing and dance of it?"

"I will Dad."

Lizzie was meandering from the cupboard under the stairs, to the scullery, with her pigtails flapping either side of her ears. "Dad, can you help me lift the bath off the hook, I want to get it ready for mom," she shouted. "It's Easter Sunday this Sunday, and I'm singing with the Sunday school again!"

"Go and help her, Hal, one of these days she's going to end up inside it when it falls on top of her. There's no room in the scullery for it, it's cramped in there as it is."

"Yes I know it is Titch, but she won't have it resting on the cobbles outside since seeing spider inside it!"

"But if you built the lean to, like you said you would, none of us would have to!"

"There's a stack of old pallets at work, I'll ask if I can have them tomorrow!"

Mom heaved a long sigh. "Thank you, at last!"

"So you're singing with the Sunday school again," said dad, helping to lift the bath off the hook. "That's good, Lizzie, you'll need to start exercising that voice of yours more then?"

"I was on the second row last year, I'm up on the back row this time because of my height."

"You'll have to make sure you're the one who's singing the loudest then, Lizzie."

"It's at two o-clock in the Methodist hall, Dad; will you and mom come and see me?"

"Did we come and see you when you sang last year?"

"Yes."

"And we'll be coming to watch you this year too."

Lizzie gave a contented smile, lighting up her eyes. "Thanks Dad, all the other parents will be there too!"

*

Before 1952 came to an end, another change in my early childhood was to take place while at school. My beautiful cast iron fireplace, with the shelf of mystery above it, edged in dark red ribbon was gone, and replaced with a tiled covered fireplace. The world I knew was slowly changing around me, and although it was for the better, for me it never felt like it.

Twelve
1953

It was the 29th of May, Pat's birthday, and Mom and dad had gone to see Patrick at Ufculm clinic, contented to leave Lizzie and me together at home. I was ten, and my attitude toward my sister had changed. The sticky outie pigtails above her ears had gone, and her hair was now long enough to be put into a neatly brushed ponytail. I was listening to, and obeying Lizzie more so now than I did mom.

"Mom and dad said they might be bringing Patrick home with them, Jay," Lizzie said hopefully. "We could have a party for him, I could help mom make the cake I'm good at helping mom make cakes. You can help dad make a streamer, and we could put, 'Happy birthday Patrick' on it!"

I just hummed. I'd only seen Patrick twice since he was taking to hospital. The first time was a few months after his operation at Hilltop hospital. One of the nurses had walked him to the ward door, and I waved at him through the doors glass panel. The second time was when he was moved to Ufculm - and then it was from a distance.

"It's going to be really nice having Patrick back home with us!"

Again I just hummed! Almost two years was a long time, and although it was my brother Pat's, it felt like a stranger was coming to live with us.

Lizzie opened the stairs door, beckoning me to follow. "Come on, you can help me get the bed ready, just in case he does come home!"

The bed was another thing displacing my life of normality. Two weekends ago, only Lizzie and my bed was in the bedroom; now I was helping Lizzie to prepare the bed next to me, and I wasn't sure how I felt about that!

*

"Now you see Willy behaves himself today Jamie," said William's mom with a pointing finger. "I don't want him getting in trouble again?"

Willy's mom always walked Willy to school in the mornings because he was always late. One time he followed his mom home, and she had to bring him back. Willy never liked school, and when two lads in the juniors were caned by the head, in front of everyone in assembly, he decided school wasn't for him. I heard they had been caned for breaking the nibs off their pens, leaving the two barbs protruding on the ends. While the teacher was absent from the classroom for a few minutes, they threw them across the classroom, seeing who could stick one into the teacher's desk. Willy had tried to break the nib off his pen, but couldn't do it, so he made a plane out of his blotting paper, and threw it toward Jemma Watts - I bet he never told his mom that?"

"Right off you go; and William," called his mother with an accusing stare. "You're going to school to learn, not to mess about?"

Willy half turned answering with sigh of boredom. "Okay Mom."

The bell sounded with Mr Jeffery's voice rising above the chatter. "Okay everyone, stand still and be silent please. That means you too Jennifer Riley," he said, waving a finger at the female chatterbox with a swaying blond pigtail. "Form your lines quickly please, girls on the left, boys on the right! JAIMIE COLBROOK! Walk sensibly please, and stop pushing the one in front of you?"

"I'm not sir," I voiced innocently. "Archie Stevenson behind pushed me."

Mr Jeffery immediately looked at the boy behind me. "Archie Stevenson, you have been told before about pushing in a line. If someone falls on the concrete they can be hurt. I won't be telling you again, because I'll be telling the headmaster; do you understand?"

"Yes sir," came the voice from behind me. I felt Archie's breath brushing against the nape of my neck, and my heart thumped as he whispered, "You little snitch, Colbrook, I'm going beat you up after school!"

As we settled into the seats of our new classroom, Mrs Watson welcomed us back from our Christmas break.

"Welcome back children, I hope you had a good Christmas. You all had a few months to settle in before the Christmas break, and during this first year in the juniors, I will be expanding your knowledge of the twelve times table, and your spelling. Both are an integral part of your education, and both will be part of you daily lessons." Mrs Watson turned to the chalkboard behind her. "On the chalkboard I have chalked a graph of the first six tables. Hands up anyone who is already familiar with any of them?"

Thankfully no one did, and before anyone could it was morning break.

I was still fretting over Archie's threat when the school prefect placed the one third bottle of pasteurised milk on my desk.

"What have you got?" I said lifting the lid of my desk.

Willi opened his two slices of bread. "Spam," he said unenthusiastically "What have you got?"

"Luncheon meat. I hate luncheon meat, we have it all the time at home."

"I hate spam - want to swop sandwiches?"

"Are you scared of beating up by Archie," said Willy, slurping his milk through the straw. "I know I would be!"

"No!" I responded adamantly," slurping the milk through my straw.

"I've never seen you fight! Are you a good fighter then?"

"No, but my sister is!"

William took a huge bite out of his luncheon meat sandwich, followed by another slurp of milk. "Yeah I know, you told me she was in the brownies!"

"Yeah, and when these boys threw snowballs at me when I was five. Lizzies chased them away."

"I haven't got a sister; I've just got a dog," said Willie.

"I know! His name is Toby!"

*

Minutes after the bell rang for home time, Willy and I were running out of school.

"Mom won't like it if I get into a fight, Jamie," said Willy, constantly looking behind in case Archie was behind us. "She'll start meeting me from school again!"

"Archie said he's going to fight me, not you Willy!"

"I know, but you're my best friend, and he might want to fight me as well!"

We ran along the Mosely road, stopping only to go our different ways at the corner of the New Inns. I turned left down Edward Road, and Willie ran on to Vincent Street calling, "See you tomorrow then, Jay!"

"Yeah, see you tomorrow, Willy," I called back.

Elizabeth was going to Upper Highgate Street school for girls, and her first day back was on Tuesday. She was helping mom with the Monday washing when I arrived home.

"Take your coat off and hang it on the door, please," said Lizzie, draping damp clothes over the wooden horse in front of the fire. "Did you come home with Willy?"

"Yes," I answered, as though I was answering mom.

"Mom hummed. "And how was William today?"

"Fine, Mom – why?"

"Because she's been having trouble with him coming straight home!"

"But Willy comes home with me, mom!"

"Only as far as the top of the road! I think she's going to start picking him up from school again. Anyway, how was your first day back?" asked mom talking as she placed the dry clothes into folded piles on the table. "Doing everything Mrs Watson tells you I hope?"

"Yes, we've really started learning our two times table."

"Good, did you tell the class what you did over Christmas?"

"No, Mrs Watson said we wouldn't have time to do it today; she said were going to do it tomorrow!"

"What can I do now Mom?" asked Lizzie, giving me a cautious look.

"You can carry on hand wringing the clothes from the bath, Lizzie, and put them in the copper for me."

Lizzie always helped mom with the washing on Mondays after school. Either she was pounding the clothes in the copper with the wooden dolly, or wringing them in the mangle. Lizzie being home on a

Monday was a big help for mom, it was like her having an extra pair of hands.

"Mom, can I go and see Lizzie? I want to ask her something."

"If it's anything to do with school, Jaimie yes, but quickly; if not you can do it later?"

"It is, Mom," I responded truthfully.

"Go on then, but don't go distracting her too much. It's dangerous when the fires burning under the copper."

"Okay Mom, I won't!"

I was doing what mom asked as I stood outside the brew house, waiting for Lizzie to look at me without calling her. The smell of dirty washing, mixing with steam from the copper hung like a mist, trickling down the walls like little rivers. Lizzie glared at me when she saw me in the doorway.

"You're not supposed to come in here when the washing is being done! Does mom know?"

"Yes, I told her I wanted to ask you something. She said if it was something to do with school, and I didn't distract you I could."

Elizabeth instantly nudged me aside as I walked in. "Jay, ask me about school tonight, you're in the way – move," she said carrying the hand wrung clothes from the tin bath to the copper of boiling water. "There isn't enough room in here when the baths full! It's too dangerous for little squirts to hang around in!"

"Well can you come outside then?" I asked side stepping around Lizzie.

"No I can't," retorted Elizabeth. "Unless you want to take these damp clothes to mom, leave me alone."

"But Lizzie!"

Elizabeth turned toward me, clearly agitated; and instead of nudging me toward the door, she accidently nudged me toward the bath. I did backflip and instantly disappeared under the grey water of soaking clothes.

Elizabeth reached quickly for my hand as I floundered amongst the clothes, gasping for breath in the freezing cold water. "It's your own fault, Jamie," she said dragging me out. "You shouldn't have been in here."

I stood before Lizzie crying my eyes out. Not because I could have drown; but because my spare clothes were behind me, floating in the bath.

"I'm telling mom you pushed me in the bath on purpose," I said walking tearful to the back door, with my clothes hanging wet, and water squelching inside my shoes.

"Good, and I'll tell mom you wouldn't move out of the way when I asked you to."

"Mom," I called sobbing pathetically.

Mom turned from the clothes horse, looking at me dripping water all over the rug.

"For goodness sake, Jamie," mom said, stripping me down to my underpants. "You've been in the outhouse less than five minutes, and you come back looking like that; what on earth happened in there?"

"Lizzie pushed me in the bath!"

"Well I won't be able to dry them for tomorrow! And I don't know what are you going to wear for school?"

*

"Hi Jamie, you're late, I thought you wasn't coming!" Willy's eyes suddenly widened behind his glasses. "What's happened to your school clothes?"

"I had an accident!"

"What accident?"

"Lizzie was helping mom with the washing, and she pushed me in the bath."

"William walked on quickly, flitting his eyes between the footpath ahead, and my play clothes, stitched together with patches of different fabric.

"What're you going to say to the kids at school?"

"The truth; why, don't you think I should?"

"No I don't! If I had a sister and she pushed me in the bath, I wouldn't tell anyone."

"Why?"

"Because they'd call me a cissy,"

"Oh!"

We ran through the gates just as Mr Jeffery came out ringing the bell. "Okay children, into two lines please?"

I followed closely behind Willy to the boy's line, with my cheeks glowing red from embarrassment. Some of the girls were looking at me, while concealing their amusement behind their hands.

"Hey look at Colbrook," called Archie, seizing the opportunity to ridicule me. "He's wearing old clothes covered with patches to school! Did you tell your mom I was gonna fight you after school, and she made you wear those in case I ripped your school one's?"

"Archie Stevenson stop talking please," voiced Mr Jeffery's. "Right everyone in line to your classroom." Mr Jeffery's eyes settled momentarily on me as I walked past him; and my cheeks were flushing even more as l walked into the classroom.

Mrs Watson closed the door and walked to her desk, turning her eyes toward me every so often. "Settle down; settle down now please – I said everyone settle down now!" Mrs Watson waited for silence, then began again. "Our lessons today will begin with each of you, telling the class what you remember most about Christmas - And we will begin with!" Mrs Watson's finger swung from the left to the right of the classroom, settling on John Simmons. "John, come to the front of the class please?"

John walked to the front and faced the class grinning shyly. His hands were behind him as he spoke, looking at the teacher and swaying in embarrassment. After a few words he said, "I can't remember anything else!"

Mrs Watson praised him for the short interesting account; and after her finger had settled on another four children, it settled on me. "Jaimie, come to the front please?"

I walked to the front and faced the class with cheeks flushing; not from having to talk about Christmas, but from the class whispering and tittering behind me, with Archie's voice being the loudest.

"Oi, Jamie, where does your mom by your clothes, from the rag and bone man?"

"Archie, no more of that please," voiced Mrs Watson sternly. "Everyone sit quietly, and stop being so unkind!"

I just stood quietly looking at everyone, staunching the urge to walk out and go home.

Mrs Watson lent toward me, asking quietly. "Jaimie, do you want to sit back down?"

Reluctantly I whispered in her ear, telling her some of the unfortunate events I'd incurred at home.

Mrs Watson, raised herself fully and faced the class. Her eyes were singling out the ones who had jeered the loudest; and in a calm voice she said. "Jamie, please tell the class why you came to school in the clothes you are wearing. Tell the children what you have just told me?"

"Yes, Mrs Watson." I was more afraid of them finding out my sister had pushed me in the bath, than to talk in front of them, so that's what I did. "When I got home from school yesterday, my sister Lizzie was in the scullery helping mom with the washing. Mom was upset because Patrick - my brother's in hospital, and he couldn't come home for Christmas. He's only three and he's really poorly. He's got a favourite teddy called Rupert, and my sister Lizzie was going to wash him so he was nice and clean for when he came home. Lizzie brought some washing for mom to dry, and I went to the toilet for a wee. When I came from the toilet, I saw a cat in the scullery with Rupert in its mouth! I thought it was going to run off and claw it into little pieces. I ran in shut the door so it couldn't get out. The cat was snarling at me when I tried to pull Rupert from its mouth." I quickly displayed the graze on my hand, inflicted from hitting the shelf when I fell in the bath. I took a gulp of air, convincing myself the whole contrived story was the truth. "That's what the cat did when I tried to get Rupert from him - but I didn't care because it was my brother's favourite teddy." The whole class was in silence as the lie unfolded, and my clothes were becoming less important. "I grabbed Rupert when the cat tried to run off with him, so the cat let go, and I fell back into the bath. My mom didn't have any dry clothes for me to wear, so I came to school in these. I don't care if I look scruffy, because I saved my brother's favourite teddy for when he comes home from hospital."

Mrs Watson stepped from behind her desk, and stood behind me with her hands on my shoulders. "Now you've heard why Jaimie is wearing the clothes he has, does anyone have anything to say?"

Lucy held up her arm before anyone. "Yes Mrs, I don't care how scruffy Jamie is, he saved his brother's teddy from a nasty cat. I think he's the bravest boy in the class." Lucy offered me a smile, and subconsciously I smiled back.

"Yes, and I believe we all feel the same – don't we children?"

I was surprised to see everyone responding. Even Archie's mouth moved slightly.

"Jamie," said Mrs Watson – "You could have stayed at home, hiding your shame by having nothing but old clothes to wear - But you did not; you came to school facing everyone's unkind remarks, and ignoring them because you knew why."

As I resumed my place next to Willy, his hand nudged me under the desk, while whispering. "I thought you said your sister pushed you in the bath?"

"She did, but Archie doesn't know that!"

"But what if your mom finds out you told a lie to the teacher?"

"Then I'll tell her Archie doesn't like me, and he was going to fight me after school. I'll tell her I pretended to fall in the bath so he couldn't rip my new clothes."

"And what if your mom comes to school, and tells the teacher Archie was going to fight you?"

"I thought you was supposed to be my friend, Willy?"

"I am," he said.

"Well shut up then!"

While everyone praised my heroic deed, Archie sat quietly, mulling over the fact I had ousted aside his status of leadership; not from bullying or fear, but from true bravery. I was happy to conceal my lie for as long as I could. If Lizzie had listened to me I would have told her about Archie wanting to fight me after school, and she would have been there, waiting by the gates ready to fight him for me. As it was, she wasn't, and instead of the class watching my sister standing up to Archie, belittling me even further; I was being surrounded by the class praising me like a hero for telling a good story. It was after concocting my story about the bath when I wrote my first simple story. 'A voice in the night' on lined paper.

Thirteen

June the 25th and Lizzie's thirteenth birthday had been celebrated as always. Lots of hugs and kisses showered upon her. The a cake with thirteen candles on it, was carried in from the outhouse, with my rendition of happy birthday to you, sung by us all – 'Happy Birthday to you-squashed tomatoes and stew-Bread an' Butta' in the Gutta' an' a bag of horse poo!' I of course was singing the loudest.

Mom and dad had bought Lizzie a new coat, announcing her transfer from child to teenager was now official. On Friday I left Willy at the top of the road, and walked down Edward road to the entry. A van was parked just before the entry, with the words on the side saying: Uffculm open air clinic' and a rainbow arching over the lettering. It was a name I was familiar with, and apprehension slowed my steps up the entry to my house. I knew dad was home from work, because I saw him looking through the window when I walked through the gate. Mom opened the door to me, and her eyes were creating a smile as I hadn't seen for a long time.

"You'll never guess who's inside waiting for you, Jaimie," mom said, eagerly leading me into the house. Two people from the clinic were sitting on the couch, drinking cups of tea from mom's posh cups. Lizzie was already home from school, standing by the coal cupboard, and dad was sitting on the chair I always sat on with my brother snuggling next to him. For a moment he looked like a stranger sitting next to dad.

"Come on then, come and say hello to your brother," said mom, leading me round the couch to the chair.

I felt awkward standing in front of my brother; I knew I should be saying something, but I wasn't sure what to say. "Are you better now?" was the first thing I thought of.

"Yes!"

"Do you want to come and play with my toys upstairs," was the second thing I thought of saying. Patrick's eyes turned to the two people sitting on the couch, almost as if he was asking their permission to do so.

"Right we'll be going then," said one rising from the couch. "Any worries or concerns you have, just let us know, but I think he's going to be just fine, aren't you Patrick?"

Patrick nodded, then followed me up stairs to the bedroom.

Mom went with the two people as far as the gate, with her smile showing her appreciation. "Thank you for everything you've all done, we really are grateful."

"It's a pleasure to see someone going home to their family, well and healthy. He's been a good patient, and he's got the rest of his life to look forward to now."

Mom walked back into the house, wandering round grinning like a Cheshire cat. "I'm glad we didn't tell you both Patrick was coming home, Lizzie, it might have interfered with your day, and we wanted to surprise you!"

"I'm glad you didn't tell us too, Mom; I think I would've been running home from school before the bell went!"

Mom kicked the snake knitted draught excluder against the back door, mainly to make her point clear. "You really have to have to finish that lean-to, Hal, the draught through the door's sucking out all the heat from the fire. Patrick might be well enough to come home, but that doesn't mean him sitting in a draught from the back door. It's enough going to the toilet outside in pyjamas; at least the lean- to will keep out some of the draught!"

"Okay, Titch I'll sort it!" Dad inhaled a lungful of park drive - ejecting it instantly from both corners of his mouth. Two of dad's favourite comedians were, Jimmy Jewel, and Ben Warris. Known as Jewel and Warris; ejecting cigarette smoke in this way was Jewels trade mark.

"Mom, do you think Patrick looks different?"

"As in what way, Lizzie?"

"As in he's lost his baby looks, and his hair's darker!"

Dad reached for the ashtray stubbing out the cigarette. "Lizzie, Patrick probably thinks the same about you; he's been away for nearly two years, he's not going to look the same is he?"

*

"This one's my bed now," I said jumping onto to the bed closest to the window. "Dad said you can't sleep too close the window, because the cold comes in through the gaps!" The springs twanged as I bounced up and down on mine, encouraging Patrick to do the same on his.

"Patrick was laughing as he did. "In hospital I wasn't allowed to do anything like this. I had to lie still, and the beds didn't make any sounds!"

"Why did you have to lie still? Was it because you could've fell out?"

"No, it was because I had lots of tubes in my arms and legs. Sometimes I had to have a mask over my mouth because I couldn't breathe properly."

"What? Like if you went underwater, and if you didn't wear a mask you'd drown?"

"I think so!"

"I had a train set from Father Christmas," I said changing the conversation. "If you want you can play with it with me?"

"Okay! I had a race track with a big key. I haven't played with it yet, because Father Christmas took it back to fairyland until I was better."

"Mom and dad said you're better now! Do you think they've told Father Christmas so he can give you the race track back?"

"I don't know!"

"Hmm, you probably have to wait until Christmas because he's too busy."

"Probably!"

Mom's voice escalated toward the bedroom, ending our first conversation as brothers. "Down now you two, it's warmer down here than it is upstairs!"

The stairs were not that wide, and the curve at the bottom was not meant for more than one to negotiate, especially with the wee bucket shoved in the corner,

"What are we having for tea," I asked throwing myself on the chair, urging Patrick to sit next to me.

"Same as we always have on Friday," said Lizzie, helping mom flit back and forth from the outhouse. "Grilled sausage and tomatoes, mash, cabbage and peas!"

"Hal, we never got the treacle again!"

"That's okay, the breads stale, I'll make a bread and butter pudding!"

"Then there won't be enough to butter the toast in the morning, Hal!"

Lizzie seemed to be floating from one part of the room to the other, adding to the chatter in casual comments. "I told you there wasn't much left in the butter dish yesterday, Mom. Dad can't you make some pancakes, there's a half a tin of dried egg in the cupboard!"

"I love pancakes, I had them for tea at Uffculm," Pat's said quietly.

"Dad, Patrick said he loves pancakes 'cause he had them for tea at the clinic."

"I love rhubarb as well!"

"Dad, Patrick said he likes Rhubarb as well."

Lizzie gave a little chuckle, while giving Patrick one of her looks. "I bet you won't like Rhubarb when you know what dad puts on them?"

"What does dad put on them," Patrick asked innocently.

Mom stopped the conversation going further. "Never mind what your dad puts on them. And change the subject please Lizzie!"

*

It was a though Patrick had never been away, and while I still went to Tindal Street, Patrick began his schooling at Park Hill school before going to Tindal Street.

"Have you got everything Jaimie?"

"Yes, Mom!"

"Good, I don't want you saying you've forgotten something when we're at Tindal Street; there's still a good walk from there to Park Hill, so we won't be going back for it!"

As Patrick and I walked side by side in front of Mom, I nudged his hand while quietly sniggering. "I don't think I put my gym trousers in my bag, Pat's!"

"Ahh you're going to be in trouble!"

"Your cousin Robert's giving you his bike next week, Patrick," said mom.

Patrick turned and walked backward. "He's giving me his bike, wow that's brilliant, Mom?"

"Hmm, apparently he's grown out of it. Your Uncle Teddy's getting him one much bigger, so you're having his."

As we all walked up Edward Road I kept on turning toward mom, excited by the announcement of Patrick having a bike. "We can ask dad if we can all ride to the allotment the next time he goes!"

"What's the allotment?"

"It's where dad grows things, Patrick. There's an old shed there with an old fire you burn wood on. I asked dad if we could go camping there, but he said no. If we've all got bikes he might say yes!"

Mom squashed that idea instantly. "I wouldn't agree to either of you staying there overnight; but riding a bike and filling your lungs with fresh air on the allotment is exactly what Dr Cronian ordered!"

"I caught a frog there once," I said proudly.

"A frog?"

"Yeah, it was massive!"

"What did you do with it?"

"I put it in my pocket and brought it home without dad knowing!"

"Did you keep it in your pocket?"

"No, it jumped out of my hand when I took it out. It hopped under next doors privet and I couldn't find it."

"It could still be there then?"

"It could be; we'll have a look when we come home from school."

"Okay!"

Mom suddenly yanked Patrick by the arm from behind. "Can both of you concentrate more on walking, and not talking please; Patrick you almost walked into some dog poo then!"

*

Bonfire night this year was on a Wednesday, and everyone in the grove agreed to celebrate the occasion on Saturday. Edward's garden was nominated to have the bonfire, being the biggest due to him having the entry on the left, and a fence not privet between his and Jean Oliver's on the right. Everyone had agreed to contribute something. Jean Oliver had agreed to stage the firework display in her garden. Dad's contribution was two boxes of standard fireworks, and a van load of old pallets from work – Plus helping to clean up the garden the day after.

"What time are we going to the bonfire, Lizzie?" Patrick asked, staring through the window.

Lizzie squeezed between us, carrying her wellingtons. "Dad said seven o-clock; if it's not raining again!"

Patrick quickly pressed his face against the window again. "It's not raining Lizzie!"

"Err, I thought you said you were ready, Patrick?" Lizzie asked, eying Patrick's socks.

"I am ready, Lizzie!"

"No you're not! Where's your wellingtons?"

"Over the coal cupboard."

"Well they should on your feet, Pat's? It's been raining all day, and the grounds probably muddy. You better get them on your feet before mom comes in from the outhouse!"

While Lizzie was reprimanding Pat's I'd wandered to the cupboard for mine and put them on.

"It's not just me, Lizzie, Jay hasn't got his on either," Patrick moaned.

I saw Lizzie glancing at my feet, then push Patrick toward the cupboard. "Patrick stop whinging and put your wellingtons on, or you can watch the fireworks from the window!"

As Patrick reached for his wellingtons in the cupboard, he turned and pulled his tongue out at me.

The window suddenly lit from an explosion, as the bonfire ignited from half a can of petrol.

"MOM, the bonfires on fire!!" Patrick yelled.

Mom came in, happy to see us all ready and prepared. "Okay, we'll all wait here a bit for the fire to take hold, and the smoke to clear."

"But the bonfires burning now mom, I can see it from the window," I said, in throes of impatience.

Again Patrick pressed his nose against the window, wondering if there would be any bonfire left before he got there.

"Did you hear the bang, Mom, I thought it was a firework," Lizzie said, making sure Pat's and me were ready.

"No, it was just your dad and Erick trying to light damp wood. He did the same last year if you remember, only our bonfire was a few bits of wood compared to the one over there!"

Lizzie hummed at the memory. "He put too much petrol on it then didn't he, Mom?"

*

The bonfire was burning well, and most of the grove was there when we left our house. Strapped to the topmost pallet was the effigy of Guy Fawkes, with his eyes nose and mouth, painted on a stocking filled ball, looking down as worried as dad.

"Hal, your eyebrows," said mom, scrutinising dad's singed hairs.

"Have you noticed how it always rains on bonfire night, Titch? It took three attempts just to light it. We both thought Guy Fawkes was going to topple when the petrol ignited!"

Edward's muddy garden was now drying out nicely; and the dark choking smoke was now plumes of light grey rising toward the heavens.

"Anyone like roasted chestnuts, because I'm taking them out now!" called Erick.

"I'll have one!"

"Me too!"

"How long before the baked potatoes are done?"

A moment passed while Erick probed the blackened potatoes, smouldering in the hot glowing ash. "About five minutes I'd say, Jean!"

"Get one ready for me then will you Erick? The butter and salt's in the living room."

Patrick, Lizzie, me, and four friends in the grove were half leaning over the fence, watching Edward lighting the fireworks with a box of matches.

Sounds like gunshots were followed with clusters of glistening stars, lighting up the sky beyond the grove. I was holding Pat's hand, mingling with, Tommy, Arthur, Philip, and Jack, under the watchful eyes of mom. Lizzie was mingling with Alice.

With the bonfire's warmth behind us ousting aside the cold air, the first of our fireworks was ignited. We had 'Air Bombs, Pom-pom cannons, and star shells, filling the air to the cries of, OOOH,and AAAR; while, Long Fountains, Short Fountains, Roman Candles, spinning Pin Wheels, and, Flying Imps occupied the ground – all from the boxes of Standard Fireworks.

The sky was now glowing, like the aftermath of the sun setting; and the air was dense with the smell of burning wood.

A volley of penny bangers ignited under the dustbin lids at the rear of the houses, throwing them across the cobbled blocks and creating rolling clatters.

Erick walked briskly toward the entry between the houses, commenting. "I'll go and see who it is, before they blow their hands off!"

*

The weather was turning cold now, and rain was on the verge of becoming droplets of ice. Christmas was only a few weeks away, and the festivities were already in place.

"Your dad and I are taking you to see Father Christmas at Lewis's on Saturday; that's if you want to go and see him?"

I almost dropped my cup of tea when mom said it. "Yeah, 'course we do; don't we, Pat's?"

Patrick responded with enthusiasm, but not as enthusiastic as I was. "Will the Father Christmas at Lewis's be the real one, Mom?" Patrick asked.

"I would think so –Why?"

"Because the one who came to the clinic wasn't!"

Now there was a reason why I was a little bit concerned by Patrick's question. Some boys at school had been telling everyone it was their moms and dads who brought them their presents - not Father Christmas because he didn't exist. And our presents didn't come from Santa's work shop at the north-pole, but from the shops in carrier bags. "How do you know he wasn't the real Father Christmas then," I asked Patrick. "It might've been him who came here as well - couldn't it, Mom?"

"Because the real father Christmas would've had a real beard. The one at the clinic wasn't because his beard fell off when Richard Smith grabbed it?"

I turned to mom, waiting with Patrick for the most important answer of the year to be answered.

Mom settled herself between me and Patrick; determined to keep the legend of Father Christmas alive for another year at least. "Father Christmas has too many children to see now; he could never see them all on his own! The Father Christmas who came to you in the clinic, Patrick was one of his helpers from the North Pole. They couldn't all have a big beard and moustache like the real one, they would have got in the way when they were making the toys!"

"So Father Christmas is real then, Mom?" I asked adding to the illusion.

Mom thought for a little before answering. "When I was your age, I asked my mom and dad the very same question. They said if Father Christmas and Rudolph didn't exist, then the glass of milk, the biscuit, and the carrot for Rudolph would've still been in front of the fireplace in the morning!"

"And they wasn't?"

"No, because Father Christmas and Rudolph must have been while we were asleep!"

"I'm going to ask Father Christmas for the big spinning top that hums when you spin it, Jaimie!"

"And I'm going to ask him for a mouthorgan, like the one dad plays!"

*

We were at the bus stop on Mosely Road, waiting for another number fifty bus to town. It was a cold and wintery day, with hints of ice mingling with the random flutters of rain. Lizzie had come well prepared wearing her pink woolly hat, with a white pom-pom; and her woolly coat and scarf, with knee high thick woollen socks. Patrick and I wore peaked hats, thick coats, and short trousers with our long socks rolled up over our knees.

Two buses had already gone past without stopping; and the third only slowed down for someone to jump off. The conductor was hanging from the pole, saying. "Sorry the bus is full, there'll be another one along in five minutes!"

"We've been here for half an hour now, Hal; the kids are cold, and so am I. It's Saturday and everyone's going to Town; perhaps we should leave it for one day in the week?"

"I'm at work all week, Titch; and the kids haven't broken up from school yet - if we don't go today, we won't be going at all!"

"Dad! Aren't we going to see Father Christmas then?"

"Your mom thinks it's too cold waiting for an empty bus to come, Jay, you'd better ask her!"

"Mom, it's not too cold; look we're all wearing scarfs and everything!"

"And I want to ask Father Christmas for a spinning top," said Patrick.

Lizzie came to our rescue by saying. "I don't mind waiting Mom, we're first in the queue now, and there'll be loads of room on the next one!"

"Okay then, Lizzie, but don't you go complaining when we've all got colds for Christmas!"

*

"No room on top; inside standing only," said the conductor, half hanging from the platform pole.

Dad quickly ushered us onto the bus, mumbling. "Great - now I can't even have fag till we get to town!"

The cold wintery air felt even colder as we travelled close to the platform; and not until several passengers from the lower deck jumped off, taking their bags from under the stairs, did dad managed to squeeze Patrick and me under them; halving the wintry air by also standing in front of us.

Mom, dad, and Lizzie had been standing for the whole bus ride to Dale End; and the first thing dad did when he got off the bus was to reach for his cigarette packet.

Lewis's was the largest and most prominent department store in Birmingham's Town centre; dominating the corners of Corporation Street and Bull Street. In a young boy's vivid imagination, it resembled the stern end of a huge galleon; with hundreds of windows shedding their lights onto the streets, coated in films of icy rainwater. With the Salvation Army brass band playing: Deck the Halls, under the Christmas decorations, we were two boys, walking with our family through a kingdom of magic and wonder. The first to greet us was the length of the queue outside Lewis's, waiting to go through the doors.

Lizzie's chest instantly deflated from a long sigh. "Mom, we're going to be waiting for hours!"

Patrick and I didn't mind, because each street window was displaying different themes of a Christmas wonderland. The first was a Christmas fairy, floating above elves and pixies waving her magical wand. I think if mom and dad had said to us, 'let's just spend the day, walking backward and forward from window to window, Pat's and I would have both agreed - and gone home happy.

The queue was moving toward the doors one step at the time, with a gap of two or three minutes between. Thankfully the window displays were amazing enough to forget the boredom of waiting.

"Do any of you want to use the toilets? If so say so, and one of us will go with you?" said watching Lizzie, standing the way she always does when wanting a wee.

I didn't, and neither did Patrick, but Lizzie certainly did.

"Can you look after my bag while I go with Lizzie, Hal," said mom. "I don't want to forget it and leave it in the toilets? You two keep by your dad; Hal make sure they stay by your side!"

"Titch, I think Lizzie would appreciate it if you went with her now?"

"Thanks, Dad," Lizzie said, hurrying mom along.

Patrick grasped the sleeve on dad's coat, ruffling it for his attention. "Dad, what if we all wanted to go to the toilet at the same time; who would keep our place in the queue?"

Like dad, I was more concerned about the random drops of rain, becoming more persistent, than going to the toilet.

*

We were already through the doors when mom and Lizzie came back, thankful to be squeezing themselves into the building with us, and not still outside standing in the rain.

"It's bucketing down out there now, Hal!"

"And my feet are soaking wet, Dad," Lizzie moaned, flicking the water from her coat.

"Lizzie, you're flicking water in my face!" Patrick nudged mom's arm when Lizzie ignored him. "Mom, Lizzies flicking water in my face, tell her to stop!"

"Lizzie, stop flicking water into your brother's face, please!"

The woman in front turned to mom, and in a harsh un-motherly tone said. "My two are just the same, always finding something to bickering about – kids eh?"

"Yes, kids," responded mom.

"We aren't always bickering, Mom," said the boy, revealing his discontented face.

The hard faced woman's fingers flicked against her son's hat, almost knocking it from his head. "Just face the front and shut up?"

I gave a silent snigger to mom, thankful that the woman wasn't my mom.

The landing on the first flight of stairs had a fire extinguisher, and a bucket of sand in the corner. The second landing had been transformed into a scene from, Charles Dickens: A Christmas Carol, with all the characters moving mechanically.

Each of the six landings had been transformed into magical scenes and moving figures, absorbing the drudgery of climbing the concrete stairs between them.

My excitement spilled over when we walked from the sixth floor landing, and into a grotto with elves, and pixies greeting us.

"Patrick, Look - there's Father Christmas," I said with my voice spilling in awe and wonder.

Patrick's neck extended above my arm, with his eyes widening larger than mom's saucer's. "It's him isn't it, Jaimie – the real Father Christmas?"

I nodded slowly, while affirming Patrick's question in a meaningful. "Yes, Pat's it is – It's the real Father Christmas!"

We were suddenly approached by the overzealous elf, leading me and Patrick to Uncle Holly's tent in the guise of a grotto.

When I was Pat's age, mom told me, Uncle Holly was Santa's helper, and only Santa wore red; that's why he wore a short jacket twinkling from a million sequins, a bright yellow dickey-bow, green tights, and twigs of holly bound around a hat, resembling the one the mad hatter wore in: Alice in Wonderland.

We were in Uncle Holly's grotto for about three minutes, and an elf from Santa came in and held Patrick's hand. "Come with me, Santa's ready to see you now," she said.

Pat's face turned instantly white as he was led from the tent, with mom, dad, and Lizzie watching as he sat on Santa's lap, hoping his hands remained by his side - and not trying to remove his beard.

I was next, and my heart was thumping as I entered the magical domain of Father Christmas.

"And what is your name?" Santa asked me.

"Jaimie!" I replied timidly.

"And have you been a good boy for your Mother and Father?" he asked me in a deep voice.

"Yes," I said, savouring the magical person that was not real – but was!"

"Good - so what would you like me to bring you for Christmas, Jaimie?"

"A mouthorgan," I answered truthfully.

"A mouthorgan - is that all?"

"Yes - you've already given me my best present ever!"

"I have, and what is that?"

"Making my brother, Patrick better so he could come home!"

*

Patrick's first Christmas following his recovery from TB would be special. Nothing was going to be too much, and mom and dad had made sure Father Christmas came to all of us this year.

"Mom, have we got anymore wall paper; I've nearly used it up, and I still need to make more streamers?"

"You haven't cut up the whole roll of wallpaper already, Lizzie?"

"Well you said you wanted the posh room decorated as well this year!"

"There's half a roll tucked under the stairs; your dad was keeping it to patch up where the old cast iron fire was! You can use that and, and if he ever gets around to do it, I'll tell him he must have put it somewhere else!"

"I've already seen it, Mom; it's all ripped and covered in beetroot juice?"

"Oh, so that's what happened to the jar of beetroot?"

"So what am I going to use for streamers then?"

"Lizzie, stop worrying, there's still three weeks left before Christmas; we'll pick one up in, Archers down the lane. There's always the odd roll going on the top shelf!"

A layer of fine snow had fell overnight, creating a beautiful wintery scene on the privets and roofs. Unfortunately it wasn't enough to build the snowman dad had promised, but it was enough for a few snowball fights amongst us kids in the grove.

Patrick and I were never naughty kids, a little boisterous when it came to playing games maybe, but never intentionally naughty. We had already played - what's the time Mr Wolf – Moonlight Starlight, and the Farmers in his den; then as we marched around the grove, with me in front, I thought of singing something I'd heard at school in the playground. It made everyone laugh, and I decided marching around the grove, with the kids marching behind me, singing the song would be more fun than our games, or scooping up snow to make snowballs. In full voice I yelled. "I can laugh – I can swear – shitta bugga aresole – I don't care!" I was halfway through singing it for the third time, when mom came storming out of the house, grabbing my arm and marching me back into the house. I couldn't understand why mom was so mad, because all the kids in the grove were laughing - just like the ones in the playground.

*

"Hal, I'm thinking we should go to Town again - before it gets too busy!"

"It's already too busy, Titch, the buses into town are always packed now! What is it you want from Town, you can't get from the lane?"

"I won't know till I see it, and I want to walk round the market anyway! We haven't walked round the market for ages, and we used to go once a month!"

"That was when Patrick was in hospital, Titch, it's a bit cold dragging everyone around the market this time of year!"

"We won't be dragging them around in the cold all the time, for goodness sake. We'll be in the shops, all nice and warm. I know you don't like shopping, Hal, so stop making excuses!"

"I'm not making excuses, I'm just saying – that's all!"

"You'd like to go to town and see the lights again, wouldn't you," said mom, drawing mine and Patrick's eyes away from our comics.

"Can we go and see Father Christmas again," I asked.

"No - once is enough; and anyway he'll be coming to see you in a few weeks - if you still behave!"

"Naa, Ide rather go to the lane then, Mom, the buses always smell!"

Dad was meandering between the living room and the posh room, quietly counting how much he saved by not walking around Town.

Fourteen
1954

I had exchange my precious Cubs hat, for the four dents flat brim hat of the boy scouts; and dad had begun to build the lean-to covering the back door, and the outhouse. My monthly visits to the baths on Mosley road now included Pat's, and well worth the six pence for both of us to lie in the white glass enamelled bath, filled with hot steaming water - and the bar of carbolic soap traveling to and fro between us.

Lizzie had not long come home from school, and was scrutinising dad's handy-work on the lean-to.

"Mom, is dad leaving the door on the scullery?"

"I don't know, Lizzie, why?"

"Well if he does, it's going to hit the lean-to and not open properly!"

"I'm sure your dads already thought of that, Lizzie."

"Well I'm going to ask dad if he's leaving it on when he comes home!"

"Why - does it matter if he leaves it on or not so long we're dry Lizzie?"

"Well yes, Mom it does; we could put the clotheshorse there, and we wouldn't have to move it when the baths down."

"Well you'd better ask him then Lizzie?"

"I will!"

Lizzie came back into the living room with her pigtails flapping, kicking mine and Pat's feet to one side so she could sit down.

"I'm going swimming with Jessie on Saturday again, Mom! I can swim the length of the baths twice now; I want to be able to swim four lengths, so I can join the GLB swimming team with Jessie!"

"Mom, can we go swimming with Lizzie," I asked knowing Lizzie wouldn't want us to.

Lizzie's eyes turned toward me, and I knew from the look she was going to say. "No Mom! Remember when I took, Jaimie three years ago, and he ran back home saying I'd tried to drown him. I'm practising for the swimming team, and I'm not taking Jaimie so I have to bring him back when he sees water!"

"I went with dad in the sea at Rhyl, didn't I?"

"Yes, but you was piggyback on dad's shoulders Jaimie."

"Yes – well, only because I saw a jellyfish!"

"It was seaweed, Jaimie and you know it!"

Mom intervened, preventing the discussion from becoming an argument. "Just let Jaimie go with you this time, Lizzie, Jaimie you're nine, and your dad should have learnt you how to swim by now; Patrick you stay here with me, your dad can to take you both swimming later where he can keep an eye on you."

"Well, go on then," snapped Lizzie. "Get your trunks?"

*

I was eight when I went to the baths with Lizzie and Maisie - another of Lizzie's friends. It could have been yesterday when I approached the steps into the pool, hanging onto the side rail of the shallow end hiding my fear.

"I'm going for a swim with Maisie now," said Lizzie. "So no showing off. Stay close to the edge until we come back, okay?"

"Okay," I answered, as Lizzie gave me a visual warning too. While Lizzie and Maisie went off bobbing up and down like fish toward the deep end, I began jumping up and down, splashing the water either side, just like a family of children were doing a little way along. Things were going great, and I was enjoying the children pointing at me, thinking I could swim. On about the fifteenth jump, my feet slipped and I went under. All I could remember was panic as the water went over my head. I was splashing about trying to regain my footing, and to the family of children frolicking in the water, it must have looked as though I was enjoying myself - but I wasn't because I was drowning. My feet suddenly touched the steps and I crawled out, coughing and crying. I ran from the baths and down Edward Road soaking wet in just my trunks, crying to mom that Lizzie had tried to drown me. It must have been half an hour before Lizzie came running to the house, talking loud and tearfully.

"MOM, is Jay here?"

"Yes he is, Lizzie, he's in the bedroom changing into dry clothes. What on earth happened? He came running in, screaming and telling me you tried to drown him!"

"He just disappeared, Mom; me and Maisie were looking everywhere for him. The lifeguard was searching the pool, and we searched the changing cubicles.

"You shouldn't have left him on his own, Lizzie, You know he's petrified of being under water!"

"I didn't leave him Mom, I told him to stay close to the side while I swam with Maisie."

I came through the stairs door at that moment, still tearful at my near death experience. "Yes you did leave me; I was under the water, and I couldn't get out!"

"Well I'm never taking you again! MOM, I'm never taking him again!"

But Lizzie did, and I was quietly grateful for her doing it. Most of my friends at school could swim, and on several occasions I was too embarrassed to admit it. Pat's and I would go swimming with Lizzie again, and it would become something we did regular.

*

Sunday morning, and Pat's and I were going to the allotment on our bikes with dad. We were at the bike shed, waiting for dad to drag the bikes out, and the coarse rasping voice of the rag and bone man cut through the Sunday air. "Any old rags – any old rags?"

I instantly raced into the house calling, "Dad, the rag and bone man's here!"

Dad walked swiftly to the coal cupboard, and came out with the empty coal bucket and shovel. "Go up the road and see if the horse has done a whatsit? If you're lucky this time, you might get a shovel full before someone beats you to it?"

"Okay, Dad." Quickly I grabbed Patricks arm. "Come on, someone's always scooped it up before I get there!"

"Get where - scoop what?"

"The horse muck; dad puts it on the rhubarb!"

"What for?"

"To it make the rhubarb grow bigger."

"They didn't put horse muck on the rhubarb in the clinic," Patrick said running with me down the entry.

Along the pavement, kids were already playing hopscotch between lines drawn in chalk. One young girl with a ponytail saw me, and ran to me with a piece of brick in her hand - probably from one of the bombsites! In a squeaky voice she asked. "Can you throw this onto the roof please; we've run out of chalk."

I waited first for the adult at the top of the road to disappear, then I lobbed the chunk onto the nearest roof. A chunk of broken slate fell, and shattered into smaller pieces on the pavement.

"Thank you," said the girl, grabbing the pieces of slate and running back her friends. Most of the slabs along Edward Road were covered in hopscotch markings, made from broken roof slate.

Between the horse's rear, and the cart, a pile of muck had been freshly delivered, steaming nicely.

"Aww, Pat's, look at that, there's loads of it? You hold the bucket and I'll scoop the muck!"

Patrick grimaced as I reached between the horse and cart, easing the gardener's golden manure onto my shovel.

"Urgg, it stinks," said Pat's, as a half shovel full dropped into the bucket under his nose.

The second shovel weighed the bucket down, and the third filled the bucket just below the rim.

With the shovel in one hand, I grabbed the buckets handle with the other. "Come on, we'll carry the bucket between us!"

The journey back up the entry took a lot longer than coming down, and every now and then we stopped for a little rest.

"Did you have to do this on your own, Jay?" Patrick asked me.

"No! Lizzie came with me. She carried the bucket, and I carried the shovel."

"She carried the bucket on her own?"

"Yes! Lizzies really strong. She chased after some boys who threw snowballs at me, Lizzies not afraid of anything – except wasps!"

"I don't like wasps either, they can sting you death!"

"I know, I like dragon flies."

"I've never seen a dragon fly!"

"You haven't!"

"No, I don't think I was allowed to at the clinic."

"Well I'm big now, and I can go down the entry on my own. I'll ask mom if you can come with me, and you can say hello to them – just like I did with Lizzie, when I was your age!!"

Fifteen

The bike shed dad had built in the garden was just high enough to stand in, and wide enough for the three bikes. Dad's bike hadn't left the shed for ages, because the tires needed new inner-tubs – which he replaced before Patrick came home. Mine was the result of bartering with the rag and bone man for bits and pieces, and a coat of paint to make it look new. Lizzie had outgrown hers and had given away ages ago. She was preferring to push a pram now, than the pedals of a bike.

Although Russell road wasn't tremendously long, it was a road with a steady incline to the allotment gates at the top. Aligned with chestnut trees on both sides the road felt and seemed longer than it was. The houses either side were large, with bay windows made of stone; and steeply pitched roofs with a fancy brickwork chimney's, soaring above the ornate ridge tiles. Some houses had trees growing in the front garden, and it was a million miles from Edward road in status - even though it was only a twenty minute cycle ride away.

The moment Patrick entered the allotment shed, his hands and eyes were everywhere. The shed had been put together bits of wood, and old windows nailed together; and a rusty corrugated iron roof, overhung either side flapping up and down in the wind. The shed was something that resembled an abandoned log cabin, lost in the wilderness, and long way from civilisation.

"I saw a fire place like this in a picture book I had in the clinic," said Patrick, picking up things with rusty nails, and tools with sharp edges. Patrick suddenly made a beeline toward a spider web, occupying the corner of the shed. The huge spider never moved as Patrick poked it with a finger. "Cor! Jaimie - look how big it is; it's nearly as big as my finger," he said, poking the eight legged thing.

"Patrick, don't do that?" Dad warned easing Patrick away from the web. "Spiders are best left alone!"

"Spiders are okay, Dad; when I was in the clinic someone came with a spider, and he asked if someone wanted to hold it!"

"And did you hold it," I asked in curiosity.

"Yeah, it was massive; its legs were dangling over my hand. The man said it was a tarantula and he told me to keep still. He said I mustn't be afraid because it wouldn't bite me. A lot of us held it!"

Dad gently led Patrick away from the web, and ushered us both from the shed. "That's because the spider you held was familiar with being held, Patrick. Spiders like that one in there won't appreciate being messed about with - and best left alone!" Dad sighed, worrying if bringing us both to the allotment was tempting fate. "I want you both going home in the same condition you came in. The last thing I want is one of you going home with so much as a splinter; your mom wouldn't let me hear the last of it!"

Walking to the far end of the allotment, away from anything dad considered harmful, I was quietly in awe of Patrick. Not only had my brother survived a life threatening operation – he had also held a spider the size of a hand in his hand, *AND* was three years younger than I was.

On the left side of Dad's allotment was as a small wood or dell; at the far end were the gooseberry bushes covering almost two thirds of the plot; the remaining third was the place dad threw everything to burn. Dad was growing potatoes, carrots, suede, runner beans, cucumber, and cabbage - in fact most of our vegetables came from the allotment. I was walking around with Pat's, introducing him to this wonderful garden a hundred times bigger than the one at home.

"What's in there?" Patrick asked pointing the wood like dell.

"I don't know! Dad said it was haunted, and he told me not to go in there, so I haven't!"

Patrick took a step closer, peering between the trees, then took another two steps closer.

"Pat's, dad said I'm not to go in there!"

"I only want to have a look, that's all!"

I turned slyly toward dad, just to see if he was looking, then cautiously followed Patrick past the first of the trees. The birds were in the trees singing, and the sun was filtering in through the trees canopy. It was an idyllic place to be in, until Patrick suddenly stopped, straining his left ear toward the sound of something moving.

"What is it," I said, peering at the same spot Patrick was.

A sudden noise just behind turned us both at the same time.

I tugged Patrick's arm, with my eyes focused on the area of sound. "Come on," I said stepping cautiously backward, "Dad's not going to like us being in here!"

Our heads suddenly turned to the sound on the right. And the moment something heavy dropped with the roar of a dragon, I was running from the dell crying, and Patrick was overtaking me with snot running from his nose, and a face whiter than our table cloth.

"DAD," cried Patrick the moment he saw him. "There's a monster in the wood!"

My voice followed Patrick's cry of terror. "It's massive, Dad, and I think I saw his teeth!"

It took me less than a second to realise dad was laughing, and a clump of earth in either hand. "It was you; we thought it was a monster, Dad," I said sniffing back the tears.

"I think I've wet myself," said Patrick, with his eyes still turning back toward the dell.

"Good, now perhaps you'll both listen when I tell you not to do something. This is an allotment, not the garden, and if you're going to come with me, you have to do what I say - or you don't come at all – is that okay?"

"Yes, Dad," I said nodding first.

"Yes, Dad," said Patrick, looking at me as though it was all my fault.

"If you want something to do, you can take all those twigs to the bottom and put them with the others!" Dad pointed the small branches and twigs he'd cut from the trees, overlapping the edge the plot.

"Can me and Pat make a den with them, Dad, we won't be in the way - will we, Pat's!"

Patrick nodded, while still glancing toward the dell.

"Go on then; but don't go making too much mess down there – and don't either of you go telling your mom about the dragon in the dell; especially you, Patrick, your still in that bubble she's wrapped you in!"

It took us an hour to build it, but it was a great den, just enough room for the two of us. Inside this den was our little world, with the smell of compost, wheel barrows with squeaky wheels rumbling from two plots away, and the bells of 'All Saints church' coming toward us on a light and westerly wind.

"When you was in hospital for a long time, mom said it was because you was really poorly?"

"Yeah I was," Patrick answered as though it was nothing important to talk about. "I had lots of tubes in my arms and legs, and I had to lie still so they didn't come out"

"How long did you have the tubes for?"

"I'm not sure! But I think it was a long time!" Patrick half leaned out of the den to see what dad was doing. "A man with big glasses who talked funny came to see me. He said he'd come from a long way, and he was going to make me better!"

I looked out of the den too, to see what dad was doing. "You know the big scar you have there," I said pointing to where the scar half circled around Patrick body under his clothes, "Is that where the man cut you with the knife?"

"Yes," Pat's answered.

"Why did he have to cut you with a knife?"

"He said I had something on my lung that was making me poorly, and he was going to take it out."

I eased back into our den, pursing answers for my ignorance. "When he took it out, did you cry? I did when I had a splinter in my thumb, and dad tried to get it out!"

"No I didn't cry because I was asleep when he did it!"

"But what if you woke up? I had nightmares and they woke me up when you wasn't at home - and I wet the bed. Dad had to change my blankets in the middle of the night." I added.

"They put a mask over my mouth so I couldn't wake up. I think I only woke up because the man in the white gown said I could!"

"But you said you was asleep! How did you hear the man say you could wake up if you was asleep? Lizzie tried to wake me up for school once, and I couldn't hear her because I was asleep. I only woke up because she hit me!"

"Because I wasn't in the hospital, I was in the clouds, looking down at a man in a white gown. It wasn't like the gowns they have in hospital, this one was really long, and it had long sleeves. The man had long white hair, and a long white beard; he was shouting really loud."

"Why was he shouting - was he angry?"

"I think so! Every time he shouted a big flash of light made me close my eyes."

"Was he shouting at you?"

"No - he was shouting at someone else in the sky because he was looking up. He kept pointing at me, and holding out his arms when he shouted."

"Well if you was asleep you could've been dreaming, everybody dreams, Patrick - even Lizzie!"

Pat's head swayed when he said, "No - it wasn't a dream, Jay. I was in the clouds looking down at the man. He kept shouting – not yet - not yet. When I opened my eyes I was in the ward, with the nurses walking round my bed."

Patrick had genuinely envisaged - and felt something that for him was very real in the operating theatre. There was one thing however that would have made his vision more than just that. It was me overhearing mom's conversation with dad, saying Patrick had died for five minutes in the operating theatre.

Sixteen

July 1954 was the first time we saw a television. Erick next door had bought a Bush with a twenty inch screen for the staggering price of - one hundred and fifty pounds. Like all good neighbours, Erick and Hilda invited the kids in the grove to theirs for a viewing after school.

It was like Pat's and I were in a tiny version of the Imperial picture house, with everyone sitting cross legged on the floor, staring at a mini black and white screen displaying a flower with, 'Watch with Mother' on the petals. Then came the title: Bill and Ben the Flowerpot Men, and we all sat watching the puppets on string, delighting and enthralling us on the small magical screen.

I was first to reach our door, with Patrick trying to outdo me between the doorframe.

"Mom, their television's brilliant, they can watch something on a screen, like we can at the pictures, only they don't have to go to the pictures now - do they, Pat's?"

"No, they can stay at home and watch the television instead!"

Mom only half heard us, focusing her attention more on her chores than her overexcited sons. "Go and take your school uniforms off please? I asked you to do it before you went next door!"

"Yes, okay, Mom we will in a minute, but you have to listen, a television's got a screen; like the one at the pictures."

"And you can hear it as well, just like a wireless."

"Only the wireless doesn't have a screen like a television. Can we have one - Mom pleeese?"

"Don't talk to me about wanting television; talk about it with your dad. The knob fell off the wireless over a week ago, and it's still not fixed. Now go upstairs and take off those uniforms before I have to ask you for a third time!"

"Okay," we both said.

"And stop racing up those stairs," mom shouted, as the clumping sound of feet reached the ceiling.

Pat's was struggling to remove the jumper over his head, giving me the advantage pulling my draw open first. I was looking for anything that was already ripped, or soiled by something that wouldn't wash out. "Lizzie's going to be annoyed when she knows we've watched a television you know, Pat's!"

"Well she should've been home on time like we was." Patrick finally removed the jumper, throwing it to one side to get to his draw. "She could've watched it with us!"

I was hopping on my left foot with my trousers half on, trying to get my right one into the right trouser leg. "Yeah I know, she'll probably be so jealous she'll go next door and ask if she can watch it now."

Both draws were closed almost at the same time, creating a kafuffle on the landing as we both tried descending the stairs together.

"Right, I'm telling your dad!" Mom shouted as we both wedged ourselves in the stairs doorway. "Jaimie let Patrick through first please, if that scar opens up and he's back in hospital I'll blame you!"

Reluctantly I let my brother leave the stairs first, protesting my innocence with a sour face. "It wasn't just me, Mom, Patrick almost pushed me down the stairs."

"Yes I know it wasn't just you. But you're the oldest, Jay, and you should be setting an example for your brother. And you, Patrick, you can stop your smirking. You were told by the clinic be careful for the first year home; and cavorting on the stairs means you're not doing as you were told either."

"Sorry Mom," Patrick murmured.

I also said I was sorry. "You're not telling dad are you?"

"No, not this time, you're dads already stressed with the jobs I'm nagging him to do!"

The front door opened to Lizzie's voice calling, "Hi Mom."

"Lizzie you'll never guess what Patrick and I saw," I said, brushing aside my apology to mom. This was far more important knowing something Lizzie didn't, than being wedged in between the stairs doorframe with Pat's.

"No, I don't want to guess!"

"Well we saw a television, and people and things were on a screen, just like at the pictures."

"Only smaller," said Patrick just as excited as I was telling her.

"Yeah, only smaller."

Lizzie placed her satchel on the floor and took off her coat, seemingly uninterested in our amazing news. "Mom, the G L B are putting on a show in my school hall. It's all about fitness; I'm doing a hoola hoop dance routine with three girls. The tickets are nine pence a family, will you all come and watch? I've got the leaflet in my satchel, I'll show it to you so you and dad can read it later."

"Yes okay, we'll look at it after tea when were all settled, Lizzie."

I took hold of Lizzie's jumper, preparing to do anything to gain her attention. "Aren't you going to ask us where we saw the television?"

"Well - where did you see the television then?" Lizzie asked me in a droll response.

"Next door! All the kids in the grove watched it. We saw two funny people who lived in flower pots, Lizzie."

"And there was a flower with eyes and a mouth, smiling at us," added Patrick.

"Yes, they're Bill and Ben the flowerpot men; and the flower's called, Little Weed; they always show that on a Wednesday," said Lizzie with a hint of boredom.

Mom seemed as surprised as Patrick and I was. "You seem to know a lot about television, Lizzie! Is there a television at your school?"

Lizzie shrugged, preferring not to talk about it.

I grasped mom's arm, while looking at Lizzie suspiciously "Mom, Lizzie's hiding something; Lizzie always looks like that when she's hiding something!"

"Why don't you both go upstairs and play with your toys brats?" Lizzie voiced at being interrogated.

"Lizzie doesn't want to tell you mom; I bet she doesn't go to school and watches the television in someone's house instead!"

Mom turned to Lizzie, asking her. "Lizzie, have you been doing the after school activities like you said you were!"

Lizzie released a heavy sigh. "Yes I was, Mom – but only for a few weeks. Mrs Raybon, our gym teacher became ill, and they said they were postponing the activities until she got better!"

"But you've still been coming home at this time, where have you been going after school?"

"I've been going to Jessie's, watching her television, Mom." Lizzie confessed. "Mrs Raybon cancelled the session half way through, and Jessie invited me to hers till it was time to come home."

At this point, Pat's and I were becoming a little upset! Jessie had been watching the magical box for ages, and we'd only seen if for the first time today.

"Jessie's mom always put the television on for, Fred her brother when he comes home from school;

and we began to watch it with him. Television's really good, Mom! On Monday it's 'Picture Book,' on Tuesday it's 'Andy Pandy,' on Wednesday it's, 'Bill and Ben the Flower pot men,' on Thursday it's 'Rag Tag and Bobtail,' and on Friday the 'Wooden Tops! You don't just have to listen to the wireless any more, Mom, there's lots of programs on the television – not just 'Watch with Mother!"

"Yes there probably is love, and televisions are a lot of money to buy too!"

"So we couldn't have one then?"

"Not at the moment, Lizzie, perhaps when the price has come down."

Patrick seemed on the verge of crying when he said to mom. "Lizzie's watching Jessie's television after school, Mom? Jay and me can't, we have to listen to the wireless. We can't watch Bill and Ben the flower pot men, on the wireless!"

I suddenly made a thoughtful gesture with my index finger "I've got a good idea, Mom; we can go with Lizzie and watch Jessie's!"

"OH NO YOU CAN'T," Lizzie voiced aloud. "That's the reason why I never said anything, Mom. Jessie's got two brothers, and her mom won't like my two brothers watching her television after school as well!"

"But, Mom?"

"No butts, Jaimie please! Jessie's Lizzie's friend, not yours. Have you decided yet what you want to do when you leave school, Lizzie?"

"Well, I wasn't going to say anything yet, but I have an interview at Rayland's on the eighteenth of June!"

"That's a week before your birthday, Lizzie!"

"Yes, I know, Mom! Mrs Atkins my head teacher said I could have the day off from school. She said because I had excelled in typing, she would type me a reference to give them too!"

"I'm so pleased for you Lizzie, I know your dad will be. Right, we have three weeks to get you ready for your interview! Saturday were all going down the lane for new clothes, there's a sale on at Jenkins!"

"Saturday," I voiced in concern. "But that's when we go to the Imperial for the Saturday matinee, Mom!"

"Well you'll both have to miss the matinee this week won't you, Jaimie?"

"But that's not fair, Mom! Everyone in the road will be going to Saturday matinee! We watched Roy Rogers, and Lassie last week!"

"Well they'll probably be on the week after that, you can both watch them then! When your sister goes for her first interview, she will be the best dressed person they have interviewed. Anyway Jaimie, aren't you supposed to be going to scouts?"

1954 ended with us also having a television, standing in pride of place on the corner shelf next to the window.

Seventeen
1955

Nineteen Fifty five was to be an important year for memories. Dad had bought a second hand bike with a small engine, powerful enough to propel dad along at thirty five miles an hour on flat roads, but having to pedal as well on roads that wasn't. An old helmet came with the bike, and Dad probably knew people were sniggering when he rode past them. But apart from getting him to work and back, it was half the cost of going by bus, which meant saving for our holiday to Rhyl in August was less stressful. It was also the means to acquiring a motorbike licence.

Larry Adler was the Harmonicist I listened to on the wireless; and then several times on television. Dad could play the mouth organ brilliantly, and I wanted him to teach me too. Dad bought me a cheap one, just in case my love for the instrument was a fad.

Sometimes I practiced in the bedroom, sometimes I practised on the way to school, but most of the time I practised in the outside toilet - which was a lot better than shouting 'I'M ON THE TOILET,' whenever next door wanted to use it. Secretly I'd learned how to play: Cherry Pink, Larry Adler's hit song and was just about to announce my first gig to mom, dad, Pat's, and Lizzie.

"When we go to Rhyl, I'm going on Discovery Time, playing, Cherry Pink on the mouth organ!"

"That's good, Jaimie," said mom without even digesting the enormity of my intention.

Lizzie released a controlled laugh, sounding more like a raspberry than a laugh. "Yeah of course you are, Jaimie! And I'm going to sing on the stage too!"

"Are you, Lizzie," I responded with a hint of surprise -and joy.

"No-of course I'm not, stupid, I'm not making a fool of myself standing on a stage in front of lots of people."

Mom intervened at last, actually sounding like she was happy for me to go on the stage. "That's not a very nice thing to say to your brother - is it, Lizzie?"

"No it isn't, Lizzie," agreed dad, "You've been singing in front of people most of the year!"

"Yes I know I have, Dad, but that's in church!"

"Singing at Golden Sands is no different than singing in church, Lizzie; you're still singing in front of people!"

"I'm going on the stage with, Jaimie as well, Dad," announced Pat's, to my surprise!"

"Are you, Patrick?"

"Yes, Dad!"

Mom came to the rescue yet again. "And what will you be doing then, Son?"

"I'm going to tell a joke!"

The raspberry laugh came from Lizzie's mouth again – only this time full blown. "Pat's is going on the stage as - A COMEDIAN? Come on, Dad say it; Patrick telling jokes on stage is stupid isn't it; he doesn't even know any jokes?"

"Yes I do, Dad! A man with a funny hat and a red nose made us laugh at the clinic; I can tell one of his jokes!"

"Go on then, Pat's, tell us one now?" Lizzie asked making herself comfortable on the chair.

Patrick began to sway from nervousness, intertwining the fingers on each hand in front of him. "A man was holding a candle, and he was trying to blow it out, but he could only blow from the side of his mouth. Every time he tried to blow out the candle he missed, so he asked a friend to blow out the candle for him. Instead of his friend blowing out the candle, he licked his fingers and squashed out the flame between them - That's it; that's the joke I'm going to tell!"

Mom quickly reached for Patrick's hands, displaying her motherly proudness. "That was brilliant, Patrick, well done Son!"

"Yes, well done, Patrick," dad said too.

Lizzie never clapped, she just nodded her head with a, "Hmm."

Patrick was being showered with, well-done for his joke; now I wanted to show them how good I was on my mouthorgan. "I can play, Cherry Pink on my mouthorgan if you want?"

Lizzie's hmm for Patrick became long huff for me, "Not that thing again, Jaimie, Mom it sounds like a church organ out of tune?"

Mom turned her eyes to Lizzie, while nudging me. "Jaimie, go and get your mouthorgan. Lizzie, what did you say you're singing on the stage?"

"I told you I wasn't going to, Mom!"

Patrick returned Lizzie's huff, commenting for me. "I think Lizzie's too scared, Mom! She probably thinks she's not good enough, and everyone will laugh at her!"

"I've got the best voice at Sunday school, and you know, squirt?" Lizzie retaliated.

"Well, I haven't heard it!" Pat's retaliated back.

"That's because you're never at Sunday school when I'm singing, Twit!"

"Right! That's enough now," Dad stood by the stairs door, shouting. "Jaimie how long before you come down with that mouthorgan?"

"I'm looking for it, Dad!"

"Jaimie, you should know where it is! You've got one minute!"

"Okay!"

"Lizzie, if you can't listen to your brother without making a comment, then go into the scullery and clear up the mess you made this morning!"

"You mean the sink?"

"Yes, I mean the sink! Just because you're a typist at Raylands, doesn't mean you can't tidy up after yourself!"

I almost flew down the stairs with one hand on the handrail, the other clutching my precious harmonica. Mom, Dad, Patrick and Lizzie were waiting for me like an audience, and it felt like, 'Discovery Time' at Rhyl had come early. My rendition of Larry Adler's 'Cherry Pink' was flawless, and well worthy of everyone's praise - even Lizzies.

Eighteen

Unlike our holiday in 1948, we arrived at Rhyl by coach on time, and without a worrying frown on dad's forehead. Our caravan was as close to the sea as could be, without the waves lapping against the caravan door; and it was spacious in comparison to the others we had spent our holidays in.

My heart beat with joy as the voice on the loud speaker announced the first birthday message! And a hundred voices singing, Happy Birthday, travelled around the camp in gusto.

"Dad, can we go and have a look at the pavilion while you unpack the cases?"

"Okay, Patrick, but wait for Lizzie; I don't want you both wandering off camp to the souvenir shop down the ramp."

"Don't worry, they won't Dad," Lizzie called from her own little bedroom.

Patrick and I were strutting impatiently on the grass around the caravan, discussing what to spend our money on.

"I'm going to buy one of those big balls, so we can play football on the beach!"

"And I'm going to by a kite, like the one I saw in the shop window, dad said he'd help me fly it."

We both walked around aimlessly, waiting for Lizzie, calling now and then. "Lizzie are you ready - we're waiting?"

Lizzie appeared in her shorts, a white blouse and mauve cardigan, short white socks and pumps, and her hair redone with a ribbon round her ponytail. "Come on then," she ordered strutting past us.

"Now behave properly, and no shoving each other?"

"We won't," I said, pushing Patrick away from me from behind Lizzie's back. Patrick then pushed me too, and then it became one after the other. We were both seeing how far one could push the other, and a camps four wheeled bike came along the pathway, veering slightly toward us.

"I love your shorts!" called the boy, peddling the bike with a young boy sitting next to him.

"I love your hair," Lizzie called back, unabashed.

The boy half turned calling. "What's the number of your caravan?"

"Seventy eight, on the front - What number's yours," Lizzie called back.

"Hundred and five, just by the washrooms and toilets," was the boy's reply.

After walking for a few minutes, curiosity made me ask, "Lizzie why did you tell the boy what number our caravan was?"

Lizzie shrugged while seemingly unconcerned. "Because he asked me Jaimie!"

"Well why did you want to know his?"

Lizzie's shoulders shrugged again – because I was being polite."

*

The pavilion doors were always open to campers; and when it rained those with children took advantage of the activities laid on by the yellow and green coats. Today it was cloudy only, and only a few were in there, familiarising themselves with the camps central building of entertainment.

While Lizzie meandered around on her own, Patrick and I walked the length of the building to the stage at the far end.

"It's a big stage isn't it, Jay?" came Pat's voice.

"Yeah," I said, visualising the moment when I walked on it on Friday; and every camper at Golden Sands were sitting on chairs waiting for me to play, Cherry Pink on my harmonica. This was the first time ever, when I wished Friday was tomorrow on the first day of my holiday. "I can't wait till Friday, Pat's - it's going to be great, isn't it?"

"Is it," followed the uncertain response.

"Did you tell your joke to your friends at school, like mom asked you too," I asked

"Course I did, I practised on my teacher as well!"

"Did she all laugh?"

"No! She just told me to keep on practising! Jaimie - What if nobody laughs at my joke on Friday?!

I noticed the hesitancy in Patrick's voice, and knew he was giving it second thoughts. "Well Lizzie, me, mom and dad will be, Pat's!"

"I know you will – But!"

I could sense Patrick was a little scared, but the stage didn't frighten me; I wanted everyone to hear me play the harmonica. But had I been three years younger like Patrick, I don't think I would have been too willing to on the stage either. "You don't have to go on the stage if you don't want to, Pat's; mom and dad won't mind!"

"But you're going on, Jaimie?"

"I know I am – but when I was your age I wouldn't; I would've been too scared."

*

"The stage looks a lot bigger close up, than it does from over there," said Lizzie joining us at the stage. "Aren't you both scared?"

As I already knew what my answer would be, I answered for both of us. "We are little bit, Lizzie, but we can't wait can we, Patrick!"

Patrick half nodded, not sure if his answer was the same as mine.

Lizzie turned, and walked us across the pavilion to the doors, talking to us casually. "You know mom and dad are very proud of you, going on the stage with Jaimie, Patrick?"

"Are they, Lizzie?"

"Yes – And I told them I couldn't do it because I'm not confident, or brave enough."

"But you sing in the church - and when you're having a bath in the outhouse; we can hear you sometimes in the living room."

Lizzie tittered a little. "Patrick, singing in the church, and in the bath isn't the same as singing in front of a lot of people. And I think you're both very brave doing it too!"

Lizzie's words of encouragement were the words of mom walking in front of us. The joyous feeling overwhelming me was lightening my footsteps as we left the Pavilion - And from the way Patrick was walking, they were lightening his too.

*

Sunday began with requests being played over the loud speaker. While the songs were being played, Patrick and I were helping mom put away the beds under the seats, and generally tidying up. Dad was making our holiday breakfast of eggs and bacon, and Lizzie was in the bedroom, preening herself in case a certain person came along.

Mom's eyes turned to Lizzie as she sauntered from the bedroom. "You look very nice, Lizzie. I thought you were saving those clothes for the evenings?"

"Lizzies met a boy, Mom, that's why she's dressing up!"

"Jaimie, shut up please and play with your beach ball."

"Oh, and whose the boy then," mom asked in motherly curiosity.

Lizzie shrugged, curling her mouth into a grimace at me. "Mom, I don't know who he is; I only saw him when he rode past on the bike. He waved at me, and I waved at him back."

"That's nice, perhaps you'll see him again in the pavilion - when were all there?"

"Lizzie won't have to wait till tonight, Mom," said Patrick. "Lizzie told the boy our caravan number!"

Mom glanced at Lizzie while fluffing the cushions on the seats. "Did she now?"

"Why don't you two play jumping into the sea from the breakwater?"

Dad always kept clear of any discussions between mom and Lizzie, Mainly because he was the one ending up in trouble. But a little bit of his advice seemed appropriate to prevent the discussion from brewing. "Titch, let's not make an issue of this; we're on holiday at a holiday camp. Lizzie's thirteen and she's bound to bump into a boy her age!"

"Yes, Hal I know. But like you say, we're in a holiday camp, and that's where trouble begins - in a holiday camp!"

Lizzie fired back, venting her lack of trust from mom openly. "Mom, I know how to behave; but if you're going to question everything I do while I'm here, I might as well stay in the caravan till it's time to go home!"

Lizzie walked back into the bedroom, a little tearful and shut the door behind her.

Mom walked to the door, and knocked gently. "Lizzie what are you doing, come out now?"

"I'm taking these clothes off, and put my other's on."

It was obvious to dad, mom was reluctant to let Lizzie grow up! But also obvious if mom couldn't trust Lizzie here, on a campsite; she wouldn't trust her back in Birmingham either.

"No, don't take them off, Lizzie; like your dad say's - you're thirteen now, and bound to bump into a boy your own age. Come on come out, all I'm asking you to do is be careful!"

Lizzie came from the bedroom, sniffing back the tears. "I will be careful, Mom, you just have to trust me that's all?"

I was as bewildered as Patrick as we had our breakfast. Trust, and being careful? Why was mom and dad asking Lizzie that; they never asked me, or Pat's - and we'd fell over loads of times!

The sky had become overcast, but the wind had remained light. We were all preparing to go for a stroll on the beach, so Patrick and I could say hello to the sea, then take a leisurely stroll to the souvenir shop and buy the beach ball for me, and the kite for Patrick.

We were the first outside, running around the caravan and playing tag, while waiting for mom, dad and Lizzie.

"Excuse me!"

I stopped before my second run around the caravan.

"Is this the caravan where the girl with the ponytail is staying?"

I was standing almost to attention, and with a slight nod ran into the caravan. "Lizzie, that boy who waved at you is outside on one of those bikes!"

Lizzie instantly pulled the curtain on the window slightly to one side. "It's him, Mom, it's the boy who asked for our caravan number!"

Mom also took a little peep through the window. "Well you'd better go and see what he wants, Lizzie," said mom without discussion or argument.

I had run back outside next to Pat's, both of us watching in naive curiosity as Lizzie talked to the boy on the camp bike.

Lizzie's cheeks were red when she went back into the caravan, talking loud enough for me and Patrick to hear.

"He's asked me if I wanted to go for a ride around the camp with him, Mom!"

Mom again peeped through the caravan window "Ask the boy his name, and the number caravan he's staying at?"

Lizzie raced down the steps, talked for a moment to the boy, then raced back up them into the caravan.

"He said his name is, Bryn, and his caravan is one hundred and five, by the washrooms!"

"Ask this, Bryn how long he's hired the bike for," dad asked.

Again Lizzie raced down the steps, then back up them just as quickly.

Lizzie was puffing as she said, "He said he's got the bike for two hours, Dad."

"Right, well if we're not back by then, you come back and wait outside the caravan. Bryn can wait with you if he wants, but you wait here – okay?"

"Okay, thanks Dad, thanks Mom!" Lizzie almost fell down the steps in excitement, smiling like a Cheshire cat as she climbed onto the bike.

*

The afternoon seemed to have passed quickly; it was eight o-clock and we were making our way across the camp to the Pavilion, smartly dressed.

"Patrick, Jaimie slow down, the pavilions not going to close before we get there?"

"I know, Dad, but what if we don't get a seat!"

"Patrick, half the campers aren't even there yet, there's plenty of time to find a seat!"

Lizzie was purposely doing the opposite to us, slowing our walk to disguise her excitement at seeing Bryn again.

"Dad are you still going to buy us some chips on our way back to the caravan?"

"Only if you and Patrick are good, Jaimie!"

"Can we have some crisps and pop in the Pavilion?"

"Yes, Patrick, is there anything else you both want - while I still have some money in my pocket?"

I laughed. "Dad you're so funny!"

Mom was walking beside Lizzie, with her conversation low and casual.

"Bryn seems a nice boy, Lizzie?"

"Yes he is, Mom."

"Does he any brothers and sisters?"

"Yes, a younger brother called, Dewi; and an older sister called, Wynne. They come from Wrexham."

"Wrexham? That's quite a distance from Birmingham, Lizzie!"

"Yes it is!"

*

Golden Sands Pavilion was an integral part of my holiday. It's atmosphere was created from music and dancing, with moms and dads sitting around the dance floor tapping their feet to the music; while children ran around, not yet old enough to appreciate its importance like me.

"Mom, there's Bryn," said Lizzie, pointing discreetly to the boy with blondish hair, waving to them.

"Well hurry and save the table next to them before it's taken then!"

As Lizzie walked quickly to the family, dad said to mom. "You're happy for Lizzie to see the boy while we're here then, Titch?"

"No not really, Hal, but I won't spoil the holiday for her. If his mom and dad are anything like us, they've probably warned him as well. At least when she's not with us we'll know where she is - and who she's with!"

Once our greetings were over, and we'd settled into our seats the evening began. 'The Tennessee Waltz, was the first to be played, and mom was quickly on her feet, dragging dad from the chair.

"Come on Hal, we haven't danced for ages?"

While mom and dad danced to the tunes of - The Blue Tango, Till I Waltz with You Again, Earth Angel, and more, Lizzie was gushing with holiday love, flitting between our two tables.

Patrick and I were bonding our friendship with Bryn's family, all laughing and discussing our different accents; and the Pavilion continued to wrap itself around me like an old close friend.

The evening ended with Patrick and me, strolling toward our caravan with mom and dad, eating our chips from a cone of newspaper. Lizzie had asked mom if she could walk alone with Bryn to our caravan; to which mom said yes so long as Bryn behaved like a gentleman.

The further we walked from the pavilion, the darker it became. Only the moon, and the caravans shedding light through curtains were casting any light across the camp toward our caravan.

Dad suddenly stopped us at the caravan door, shushing us with a finger to his mouth, "Listen, can you hear it?"

"Hear what, Dad?" I asked listening for anything resembling a sound.

"What about you, Patrick, can you hear it?"

Patrick stood quietly, looking warily around him. "I can hear the sea, Dad, that's all!"

Dad lent toward us, displaying the excitement two young boys should have been. "Yes, Patrick we can hear the sea; we can't hear the sea from our door back home! But we can hear it from our caravan door here!" Dad handed the caravan key to mom. "You go inside, Titch, and I'll take them down to the beach."

"I'm beginning to wonder who the biggest child is in the family, Hal! It's cold and it's dark, and too late to be going on the beach?"

"No it's not, Mom," I voiced instantly. "It's not too cold or dark - is it Patrick!"

Patrick agreed with me, undoing his coat and throwing it open. "No - look I don't even want my coat buttoned up, Mom!"

"Well, if you're so intent of standing in the dark looking at the sea, do your coats up! I don't know why you can't wait until the morning, Hal, but don't be down there too long please?"

Patrick and I held dad's hand as we walked the narrow path between the dunes, and onto the beach. The sea was still quite a way out, coming and the moonlight was glinting against the waves rolling toward the shingles. From where we stood, we could see the dim lights from caravans following the coastline.

Strangely it was more windy and cold where the caravans were above us, than down here on the beach. Dad was rummaging amongst the pebbles, looking for the flattest to skim across the water. I was doing the same as Patrick, seeing who could throw the pebbles furthest.

"Can we play on the beach with the ball tomorrow, Dad," I said, lobbing a pebble into the waves.

"And go in the sea?" Patrick said, lobbing a pebble as far as he could.

"You bet we can," said dad, enjoying this moment with his son's lobbing pebbles into the sea. "It's what we came to the seaside for!"

During the night the weather had turned for the worst. Light raindrops had become heavy, beating against the caravan roof like a thousand small drums. The waves were now crashing against the shingles, sounding as though they were trying to reach us; and every now and then a gush of wind rocked the caravan, almost lifting it from the concrete blocks underneath it. I lay on the couch bed next to Patrick, both wide awake, and both relishing every moment of Natures strop in boyish wonder.

*

I must have fell asleep, because the next thing I could here was the voice on the speaker, announcing requests for music to be played. Dad was pondering around in the small space called the kitchen, and the bacon slices in the pan had just begun to sizzle.

"Wakey - Wakey everyone - breakfast won't be long," dad called, shoving the bacon already done into the space below the cooker. "That was real storm last night! Did you two sleep okay?"

I yawned, and Patrick answered. "Yes, Dad!"

"Well it's gone now, so up you get you've both slept in long enough." Dad pulled back the curtains, announcing in a thankful tone. "Sunshine!" Dad knocked on Lizzie's door, calling. "Up now, stop dreaming about lover boy, Lizzie, breakfast is almost ready!"

Dad didn't have to call me and Patrick twice, we were up, grateful and ready to devour another fried breakfast, instead of the bread and milk we would be having back home.

"So are we going in the sea today, Dad?" Patrick asked, nudging me.

"And playing with the ball?" I said, nudging Patrick back.

"If it'll stop you two from tormenting each other - then yes."

Mom slowly emerged from the bedroom, with her eyes showing lack of sleep. "Tormenting who," mom asked slumping onto the couch. "I don't know about you, Hal, but I never had a wink of sleep last night! What about you two - did you manage to sleep through it?"

"Yes, Mom, But I tried to stay awake so I could listen to it."

"And me," said Patrick, nudging my arm.

"You must be mad, all of you, I think me and Lizzie are the only sane one's in this family."

"Lizzie, up please," called dad, tapping on Lizzie's door again. "If you're not up by the time I dish out the breakfast, yours is going in the bin!"

"Now we are playing a request for, Jimmy Williams. He will be nine years old next week, and his request is for, 'The Runaway Train, by Burl Hives. Now every time the whistle blows, we want all the children on the camp going, whoo-whoo, so we can all hear?"

"Pat's, they're playing our favourite song!" I said running down the caravan steps before the song began. Patrick followed and we both stood facing in the direction of the speaker.

The song began with. *'Oh the runaway train went over the hill and she blew,'*

Almost every child on the camp yelled out, *Whoo!'* with Patrick and me shouting the loudest. Then came the songs chorus, played on the Jaws harp, and I was rocking my head while mimicking the sound.

"Hey, Pat's, we could pretend it was your birthday tomorrow, and ask them to play the Runaway Train again!"

"But mom and dad will hear them saying my name!"

"Not if you use another name they won't!"

*

Eleven o-clock and we were finally on our way to the beach. Dad was in his white shirt and grey trousers with trunks underneath, carrying the two fold up chairs, blankets, and the bag with the beach ball shoved inside. Lizzie was in her pink bathing costume, carrying her magazines in a shoulder bag, and the towels and blankets under her arms. Mom had the bag with the drinks, soggy sandwiches of cheese and tomato's, and everything else she could think of - and I led the way with Patrick, annoying dad by playing tag on the narrow sandy path to the beach.

With the sea retreating far enough to expose the sand, we set up our little area of towels, blankets and folding chairs, as others on the beach had already done.

No sooner had dad put the bag on the sand, Patrick grabbed ball and ran across the sand calling. "I'V GOT THE BAAAL, YOU CAN'T HAVE IT - I'V GOT THE BAAAL YOU CAN'T HAVE IT!"

I immediately chased after him, calling playfully. "YES I CAAAN - YES I CAAAN!"

"Here, Lizzie put some sun lotion on your arms and legs love," said dad; digging into mom's bag of whatnots. "You're like you're mom; you can both burn quicker than frying an egg?

Dad was down to his trunks, also plastering on the sun lotion when mom voiced her concern.

"Hal, go to those two please, they're being too boisterous. The balls bounced twice now over that couple!"

"No rest for the wicked then!" Dad strode toward us, conceding the fact he was on the beach to play with us, not to sunbathe.

"Dad, are you playing football with us," Patrick asked kicking the ball hard into the air. The light wind turned the large bouncing ball quickly toward the sea, and dad was after it before the waves could capture it.

*

For the umpteenth time, dad returned with the ball from the retreating waves, and walked directly to the bag on the blanket. "This ball's going back in the bag; and you can paddle in the sea! You might as well make the most of it, there's no sea to paddle in back home!"

"Okay, Dad,"

"But up to your ankles only, no further than that."

"Okay, Dad," we both said again.

The moment dad turned away with the ball I shoved Patrick aside, "I'm going to be first to the sea!"

Patrick overtook me like a greyhound and was in the sea, kicking and jumping over the waves before I was.

"I just beat you – I just beat you!"

"I don't caaare, I don't caaare!"

"Right you two, I'm off to the toilet," dad called. "Do you need to come with me?"

"No, Dad," we both answered, knowing we had already peed in the sea.

"What about you, Lizzie, do you want to go to the toilet?"

"No, Dad, I'm fine."

"You can go after me if you want, Titch."

Dad had only been gone for five minutes, and we were both getting bored just splashing about in the waves.

Patrick kicked the water in boredom, splashing the salty brine into my eyes. "Let's play with the ball again?"

"But dad told us not to," I said rubbing my eyes.

"No - dad told us not to kick it near any people, or in the sea; he didn't say we couldn't kick it!"

"I'll go and get the ball!"

Mom was in conversation with Lizzie when I slyly eased the ball from the bag. I think the conversation was about Lizzie's reluctance to do anything regarding us, and blamed it on her flirtation with a certain boy from Wrexham.

We were only minutes into playing, and a hefty kick from me sent it bouncing across the sand toward the sea. "Quick, Pat's get the ball, dad's gonna be mad if he knows we kicked it into the sea."

"You kicked it into the sea, Jaimie, I didn't!"

"Well you was playing football with me when we shouldn't!" Without realising how far we were in the water, it was lapping around Patrick's waist.

Dad raced past Mom and Lizzie when he saw us - shouting as he ran. "Titch you haven't been watching them, they're both in the sea!"

Mom and Lizzie ran behind dad, shouting at us too.

The sea was past Patrick's chest, rocking us back and forth when dad waded toward us.

"I TOLD YOU TO LEAVE THE BLOODY BALL ALONE." While dad was cursing and dragging us from the danger we were in, I was pointing to the ball, bobbing up and down beyond our reach.

"Dad, the ball?"

"Go to your mom both of you while I get it, and this is the last time!" Dad then waded into the sea as far as he could, then began swimming away from the beach.

Long after mom had reprimanded us from doing what we should've, dad was still in the sea swimming toward the beach with no sign of the ball.

Dad had been swimming for ages and he wasn't getting any closer to the beach. I knew there was something wrong when mom said to Lizzie. "Your dad's in trouble, Lizzie, he's been swimming like that for too long!"

Lizzie panicked instantly, cupping her hands around her mouth calling as loudly as she could. "DAD – DAD!"

Patrick and I began shouting to dad, waving our arms like Lizzie and mom.

Several people on the beach became alerted by our frantic calls, and came walking to us.

"Is dad's going to be alright, Jaimie," Patrick asked me.

I couldn't answer my brother's tearful question, I was crying as mom paced back and forth, calling to dad with distress in her voice.

A man we thought was a camper approached mom, talking loudly enough for us to hear. "Is that your husband?"

"Yes," mom responded.

"And how long has he been out there swimming like that?" He asked again.

"About twenty minuet's now, it could be longer - he went in after a beach ball and he just can't seem to get back to the beach!"

The man sighed while looking toward dad. "Another one after a beach ball! The currents on the turn and he's struggling to swim against it!"

"What happens if dad can't swim against it," Lizzie asked shedding tears.

"Let's not think about that now, I'll go for the people who will try and help your dad, while he's still close enough to help!"

Several people had surrounded mom now, attempting to console her and failing. The gentleman seemed to have gone for hours, then came back with Jayne, one of the Team members, and three men with coils of rope around their shoulders! One was wearing a life jacket.

Jayne approached mom, while the one in the life jacket quickly tied the rope around his waist. Instantly he ran into the sea with the rope trailing behind him.

The two men followed him until they were waist deep, feeding the rope through their hands as he swam towards dad.

Patrick had been quietly standing beside me, staring at the sea. I think he wanted to cry like me, but was trying not to.

"Do you think they can help dad?" Lizzie asked the Team member.

Jayne shrugged slightly. "I hope so; this is the second time it's happened this season. I know them all and they'll do what they can!"

"Jaimie kicked the beach ball into the sea, and we couldn't get it," said Patrick owning up between sobs. "We tried to get it, but we couldn't, and dad went in after it - That's what happened!"

"Look," said Jayne, stooping to hold Pat's hands. "You mustn't blame yourself, neither of you. You didn't know what was going to happen!"

"But it's my fault, I kicked the ball into the sea," I sobbed. "And dad told us not to play with it!"

Jayne then held my hand too, consoling me with her kind voice. "I don't understand the tides and currents fully myself; and I live and work here. When your dad's safe again, and you want to go in the water, tell him to take you to the Marina in Rhyl, it'll be a lot safer!"

A waving arm appeared above the waves, and the two men stood one behind the other up to their waists, hauling the rope through their hands while slowly walking backward. The one in the life jacket was cradling dad, until he could feel the sand beneath his feet.

Mom was crying while the three men half dragged dad from the water onto the beach, and Lizzie wanted to go with mom to him.

"No, it's best if you wait here with your brother's," Jayne said holding Lizzie back. "Let them look after your dad first; they'll call you when it's okay to go to him."

Lizzie was thirteen, and almost a grownup; she didn't think the kindly words were meant for her, but for me Patrick. In a grownup voice she said to Jayne. "I'm going to see if mom and dad are okay! Would you mind staying here with Jaimie and Patrick while I find out?"

Patrick and I never argued on Lizzie's decision to keep us there, and neither did Jayne. It was because of me and Patrick doing what dad said we couldn't, he went into the sea after the ball. When we saw dad, coming toward us wrapped in a blanket; mom and Lizzie on one side, and the one who saved him on the other, relief became guilt and we both burst into tears.

As far as we were concerned the gentleman who saved dad was a hero, and his leaving came with words of advice to all of us.

"Your dad's been a very lucky man; not many men could have swum against the current for as long as he did. When I got to him he hadn't the strength to keep afloat. Another minute or two, and the outcome would have been very different to what it is. Now enjoy the rest of your holiday, and be thankful what could have been tragic - wasn't!"

*

We spent the rest of the day at the caravan, content to be in each other's company. Dad wasn't allowed to do anything, and Patrick and me were happy doing everything mom and Lizzie asked us to do.

Lizzie was doing something for mom in the kitchen, when Bryn showed up, jingling the bikes bell to tell her he was there, and would she like to go for a ride with him. Another time she would have said yes, but she came back into the caravan, leaving Bryn to cycle on without her.

Come seven o-clock we would have been heading to the pavilion for the evening's entertainment. Instead we were staying in the caravan eating fish and chips from the chip shop.

Although we must have talked about everything that evening, no one brought up the moment we thought we'd lost dad, and how it came to happen in the first place. The only thing dad did say was struggling to keep his head above the waves; and seeing us in the distance on the beach, thinking it was going to be the last time he saw us.

Nineteen

The weather over the past few days had been great. We'd spent the most of our time sunbathing on the beach; and whenever there was a slight wind, Patrick's kite came out of its bag, hoping this time we could keep it flying for more than two minutes, before flipping and bouncing along the pebbles again.

On the days when the sun was shining, and the sea was calm, dad would have normally paddled up to his waist. Now he never went further than his ankles, and we never saw him swim again.

Dad had taken us along the breakwater several times, watching the waves curling over the concrete structure, while hoping to see the train travelling toward Rhyl station thundering past. On Thursday the clouds begun to gather, and it rained about midday. I was lounging on one side of the caravan seat, reading comics dad had bought from the shops to keep us occupied; and Patrick was lounging on the other side, swopping comics by throwing them to each other.

Although the rain meant we were being limited to the things we could do outside; inside the caravan there was an unexplainable feeling of contentment.

The rain was tapping against the roof, the waves were rolling over the pebbles; and the cries of the seagulls were coming from all around.

Mom, Dad, and Lizzie were doing things together too, with their chit-chat and laughter adding to the contented mood inside the caravan. Like Pat's I was reading my comic, happy and grateful to be listening, and sharing the moment of it all!

"As it's our last day tomorrow, Hal; if the weather brightens up we could have a walk into Rhyl!" Mom said out of the blue.

"Yes, I'd like that, Titch! What about you three, are you up for a walk into Rhyl tomorrow?"

I looked up from my comic, with the expression of a cod fish on a fishmongers slab, ending my contentment. "Walk there?"

"Yes, Jaimie - walk there!"

"But it's a long way to walk, Mom – If we go on the bus we can sit on the top, and see the sea?"

"We can do that when were on the bus coming back, Jaimie," mom said with her mothering sigh of disappointment. "I just thought it would be nice with us walking together - that's all! And I think I've had enough of the sea for this holiday!"

Lizzie tutted at my thoughtlessness, silently reminding me my actions a few days ago! "Jaimie, you walked from our house to the Bristol Road to go to the Lickey's; and if it meant you walking for two miles then you would've and not moaned. We're at the seaside with seagulls flying over us, Jaimie – not pigeons and magpies. You only go on the bus at the seaside if it's raining! Mom, I don't mind walking with you and dad!"

"And I don't mind walking with you and dad either," Patrick confirmed, smiling at Lizzie.

I saw Lizzie smiling back at Patrick, and suddenly I was the odd one out. "Okay, we'll walk there then!" I thought agreeing to it would bring a smile from Lizzie too; but it didn't!

*

It was Friday morning, and our last day at Golden Sands. The weather was good, and we were walking past the souvenir shop before the speaker announced, *Good morning campers.* Tonight was Discovery Time in the pavilion, and we were on our way to the fair at Rhyl.

Mom's arm was around dad's walking behind us, and we were maybe half way to Rhyl when Lizzie asked Patrick to stop humming because it was annoying her.

"Patrick can you stop it please, you've been making that noise for ages now?"

"It's not a noise, it's a song, Lizzie!"

"No it's not, it's a noise, Patrick!"

"Well my teacher at school didn't say it was a noise, she said it was a song!"

Lizzie released a short laugh, sounding more like a grunt. "Patrick, I know all the songs at school, and that's nothing like any of them!"

Mom's voice came from behind as the discussion became louder. "I hope you three aren't bickering again; we all agreed on no arguing today?"

"It's Patrick, Mom, he said he's humming a song from school, but he's just making an irritating noise. I know all the songs from school, and that's nothing like any of them."

"Yes it is, Mom," I said, siding with Patrick. It's 'The Rag' something song!"

Lizzie's lips instantly exploded outward. "I think you mean - The Rag Taggle Gypsies, don't you Jaimie?"

"That's what I was going to say, Lizzie," I said truthfully.

"Go on then, Jaimie, you sing it if you know what it is?"

I did in a fashion, but to really be truthful it sounded no better than Patrick's version.

Lizzie then gave us her rendition of, The Rag Taggle Gypsies, the way our teacher did at school; only Lizzies version sounded better.

"Go on Lizzie do another," mom called. "And you two can try and join in; hopefully it'll stop the three of you bickering for five minutes!"

Lizzie did; and with Patrick and me singing along in sporadic bursts we sang, 'Oh Soldier- Soldier! Michael Finnegan! A Roving! Oh No John No! We're off to see the Wizard - three times! The Grand Old Duke of York - twice! The Runaway Train – twice! The Teddy Bears Picnic! They're changing the Guards at Buckingham Palace! In fact almost every conceivable song Lizzie could think of.

Without realising it we had walked the distance from Golden Sands to Rhyl. Patrick and I were still singing with our arms swaying and legs striding, and we only stopped when we saw the top of! The Mad Mouse, and other rides appearing.

"Look, Dad there's the fair," I called. "Are we going on something – Are we?"

"If you can be good a bit longer?"

I was nudging, Patrick, and Patrick was nudging me.

"Dad said we can go on some rides!"

"Yeah, I know!"

"I'm going on that big wheel first!"

"And I'm going on that ride," I said, pointing toward the screams and excitement, from the people on the Mad Mouse.

"What about if were not big enough?"

"Dad will let us if we be good! Dad lets us do anything if we be good!"

"Yeah, I know!"

*

Our first port of call was the toilets, then some rest and nourishment at cafeteria beside the Mad Mouse. The building seemed to vibrate from the rides, with the sounds of screaming and music overlapping each other.

"As this is our last day, you three can go on whatever rides you want." said dad, casting a sly look toward mom.

"Yes - so long as they aren't faster than I can walk, or higher than I can jump," added mom, deflating the whole purpose of being at the fair. "I'm joking she said, wiping the sulks of spoilt children from their faces.

I wasn't too happy with mom and dad doing that - but I could see why they did – and that made it alright.

*

Patrick and I were quite tall for our ages, and in features looked nothing like each other. My hair was fair and straight hair, Patricks was dark and curly. Dad once said jokingly that Patrick came from the milkman. But Lizzie said Patrick looked more like Rogers in the coal yard. Being quite tall was the reason Patrick was with me, waiting for the next empty mouse to come. The mouse was a cart, with a seat just wide enough for two people side by side; and with a sigh of trepidation, I climbed into the mouse first. Patrick followed and squeezed in beside me.

"No waving arms or trying to stand- sit back and enjoy the ride!" said the man with the weather-beaten face, lowering the guard across our legs.

Patrick touched my arm, uttering quietly. "Are you scared, Jaimie – I am?"

If dad had been sitting with us, he would have been the one saying, 'Don't be scared I'm with you!' But dad wasn't, so me being the eldest, and bravest it was left to me. "It's alright, Patrick don't be scared - I'm with you!"

Mom, dad, and Lizzie gave us a scanty wave, then our mouse rolled gently forward. We were giggling as the inclines moving chain grasped the mouse, rattling beneath us and taking us steadily toward the top.

"Look, Patrick," I said, turning my eyes to the big wheel. "I'm going on that next!"

"And I'm going on that!" Patrick, pointed to the Bow Slide. I think Patrick wanted to go on the carousel too, but the mouse suddenly lurched to one side when he was pointing, then dropped almost vertical for a whole two seconds. The G force of racing back up was stomach churning, and mine was halfway in my mouth. Patrick though wasn't so lucky, and screamed out a mouthful of sick.

The mouse was now travelling wildly on the narrow track, throwing us from side to side like rag dolls. For one underpants wetting moment, we both thought the mouse was taking us out to sea. Our heads almost left our necks as we rounded the tight bend, and upward to the next gut wrenching drop

The cake Patrick had eaten in the cafe, was splattered across the front of his jumper; and the snot from my nose had formed the silky lines you see behind a snail.

When we finally came to the end, no one was more relieved than I was. I wasn't sure what Patrick was thinking, but I felt as though I'd just come from a fight, and been battered black and blue.

Lizzie was laughing as we walked toward her deathly white. She had warned us not to go on the ride, after seeing someone being sick afterwards; and I thought she was jealous because she was scared - and we wasn't.

"Now they know why it's called, The Mad Mouse - don't they, Dad!" Lizzie said, pretending not to laugh.

For the rest of the time we spent at the fair, Lizzie couldn't even look at me and Patrick without laughing. And she only stopped when we were back in the caravan, displaying the bruises on our arms and legs to her.

*

The moment had come - it was seven o-clock on Friday evening, and we were in our best clothes, heading for the pavilion. The Mad Mouse, had been one experience we wouldn't forget in a hurry; now Patrick and I was about to experience another, on the stage in the Pavilion.

"Have you got your mouthorgan, Jay," dad asked me.

"Yep!" I said retrieving it from my pocket.

"How about you, Pat's? Are you okay with your joke?"

"Yep, Dad," came Patrick's Jovial reply.

Mom touched Lizzie's hand, half whispering to her. "Lizzie, no more laughing please! The Mad Mouse was hours ago, and you're the only one still laughing!"

"I know, sorry, Mom! It's just that!!"

"Jaimie's, been looking forward to playing his mouthorgan on stage all week. Let's not spoil it for him - or Patrick?"

"I won't, Mom!"

Tonight the chairs in the pavilion were laid out in rows facing the stage. Most of the front seven rows were already full, and the campers were filing through the doors one after the other. Some must have been coming from other camps, because there were more people coming through, than there were campers on Golden Sands.

The record playing incidental music was suddenly replaced by! 'There's No business like Show Business,' and the camps compare walked onto the stage. In a smart red suit, a large yellow tie, and a bowler had sitting on a mass of curly hair, he stood in front of the microphone announcing. "Welcome to the Golden Sands Pavilion – and, DISCOVERY TIME! Time – If everyone's happy shout –HELLO BERNIE!"

The roof raising – 'HELLO BERNIE' followed, and the show had begun.

I was number fourteen in the line of children waiting off stage to be called, Patrick was three children behind me. I could just see Bernie on the stage, warming up the audience with witty jokes and comical movements, and each time bringing the audience into fits of laughter.

"What are you doing?" asked the girl in front, half turning toward me.

"I'm playing the mouthorgan - what are you doing?"

"I'm singing - Somewhere over the Rainbow - and I'm going to win!"

I ignored her, and turned to Pat's giving him the thumbs up. Pat's gave me one back, and the line moved forward again.

The rapturous applause and shouts of hurrah's followed the girl singing, 'Somewhere over the Rainbow,' and before I could swallow again, I was being nudged from behind by a camp team member.

"Go on your next!"

Everything was a haze when I walked on. I could hear mom, dad and Lizzie shouting, but I don't remember seeing them, even though they were only eight rows from the stage.

"And a big applause for our next contestant everyone," called Bernie, beckoning me to join him. "And what is your name?"

"Jaimie."

"Jaimie everyone - And where do you come from, Jaimie?"

"Birmingham," I answered, being coached by dad an hour before.

"Buuurmingum! Oi thort oi recognoised thu acceent!"

Everyone was laughing but I didn't know why; No one talked like that in Birmingham.

"So, how old are you, Jaimie from Buuurmingum?"

"Twelve."

"Twelve ladies and gentlemen!"

Bernie's hands revolved in mid-air, encouraging the audience to clap again.

"Okay then, Jaimie, what are you going to do for us tonight?"

"I'm going to play the mouthorgan."

"You're going to play the mouthorgan – He's going to play the mouthorgan everyone!"

Another round of applause followed.

"And what are you going to play?"

"I'm going to play, Cherrie Pink!"

"Okay then, Jaimie from Buuurmingum, the stage is yours."

Bernie walked off to the side, and I was standing alone, in front of a mike, and in the middle of the stage. I drew my mouthorgan from my pocket, faced the audience, and played Cherrie Pink, without a single mistake.

Bernie walked back on, encouraging the applause and shouting to hit the roof of the Pavilion. "Wasn't that great ladies and gentlemen. A musical hit from Larry Adler, and not a wrong note played. Well done young man!"

As I walked to the side opposite from the side I walked on, I could see, mom, dad, and Lizzie clapping and shouting the loudest. Another team member was waiting to usher me from the stage, and I walked to my seat, the happiest boy on the planet.

"Well done, Jaimie," said mom and dad. Even Lizzie said well done, you were brilliant.

The next three acts came and went in the same frenzied manner of claps and cheers, and now we were waiting for Patrick to walk on.

I felt Lizzie touching my arm. "I bet he's really nervous now, Jaimie!"

There was no need for me to bet if Patrick was nervous or not; I knew he was because I was.

"Come on everyone, raise your hands for our next contestant!"

Patrick walked on with a huge smile, looking more confident than I must have looked.

"Now then young man, and what is your name?"

"Patrick!" he answered in a loud voice.

"And Mr Patrick – where do you come from?"

Patrick began to swaying from side to side; and in a loud voice called - "England!"

Everyone in the Pavilion were laughing, even mom Lizzie and dad. Above the laughter, I heard dad saying in light-heartedness, "The Codshead!"

"England," responded, Bernie, extending his smile. "And what part of England is that, Mr Patrick?"

Patrick's swaying became more, and his cheeks were flushing with a crimson glow. "Edward Road in - Birmingham!"

"Another contestant from Buuurmingum, ladies and gentlemen; you're not related to the gentleman playing the mouthorgan are you?" Bernie said jokingly.

"Yes, he's my brother!"

"Two brothers from England everyone - and both from Buuurimigum, I think that deserves a round of applause, don't you everyone?"

Everyone agreed because without even doing anything, Patrick had brought the house down with laughter.

"So then, Mr Patrick, are you going to play the mouthorgan like your brother?"

"No - I'm going to tell a joke!"

"You're a comedian? - Our first comedian is on stage everyone! I have a sneaky suspicion he's been playing with us since he walked on the stage. Right then - Patrick from England, for the next few moments, the stage is yours!" Bernie walk to the edge of the stage, waving an arm for everyone to clap.

In a matter of seconds the clapping had stopped, and apart from the odd cough, or child talking the Pavilion went quiet.

Patrick stood smiling and swaying with his arms behind him. The whole pavilion waited for Patrick to say something, but all he did was sway in front of the microphone, looking wide eyed.

"He's forgotten what to say," I said quietly to mom.

"No hasn't, Jaimie, he's just shy and embarrassed!"

I heard Lizzie sighing before saying to mom. "Shall I go and get him, Mom?"

Dad suddenly called to Patrick. "Come on, Son, were all waiting to hear your joke!"

Lizzie also called "Come on Patrick."

Mom and me were about to call too, and Bernie came onto the stage.

"I think this young man has already made us laugh, don't you everyone?"

Voices of agreement rippled across the pavilion, for everyone thought it was part of his act.

"He's certainly made me laugh! Let's give him a round of applause for that, Ladies and Gentlemen?" Bernie ushered Patrick from the stage as the people applauded. "Well done young man, you were certainly different!"

While we sat through the remaining acts, laughing and cheering along with everyone else, Patrick and I were giving each other suspicious glances. I wasn't totally sure if Patrick's silence was part of his act, and he'd left out the joke on purpose. He never did tell me if it was or not!

*

"I would like to take this opportunity by thanking all you children who have entertained us tonight. As far as I am concerned you are all winners, but it is up to you, the audience to decide who is the winner of, Discovery Time - Nineteen Fifty Five at Golden Sands. In front of the stage you will see three of the team members are spaced equally, and each one is holding a pad and paper. They will write down the names of the acts who are clapped the loudest, and that will decide who comes first, second, or third. Now – can we have all the children back on stage please?"

Patrick and me made our way to the stage, and stood with the other contestants filling the stage behind Bernie.

"Is everyone ready?" Bernie called.

The unanimous cry of, 'YES' followed.

While Bernie called out each act in turn, the team members wrote down the strength of their applause.

"Who do you think is going to win," Patrick asked me.

"The girl singing, somewhere over the Rainbow," I answered without hesitation.

With the acts all clapped, Bernie filled in the time with comical banter.

"You forgot the joke didn't you," I asked. "Go on, Patrick tell me, I won't say anything – promise!!!"

After five anxious minutes, the head team member reached up to the stage, and handed the results to Bernie.

"Okay everyone, I now have the results of the competition."

Music came from the record player, adding suspense. "Coming third in the competition is – Wendy for her dancing!"

Wendy was brought to the front next to Bernie by a team member.

Bernie calmed the clapping and shouting. "Coming second in the competition is – Jaimie for his rendition of, Cherry Pink on the mouthorgan."

My knees were shaking when the team member led me beside Wendy.

Again, Bernie calmed the audience, then proceeded in announcing the winner. "And the winner of, Discovery Time, Nineteen Fifty Five, is ----- Racheal, with her rendition of: Somewhere over the Rainbow."

*

This holiday could have been the one with tragic memories; instead it was the holiday I enjoyed the most. It was also the last time Lizzie came with us on holiday.

Twenty
1956

"I've got gym today, Mom!"

"Yes I know, Jaimie; and because a certain man knocked your shorts off the clothes horse last night, they might still be a bit damp!"

"Mr Bennett said if we don't bring shorts and towel on gym day, it'll be the headmaster, or the slipper!"

"Anyone hitting you with a slipper, or anything else, Jay will have me to reckon with, no mistake! That goes for you as well, Pat's!"

"Patrick goes to Park Hill, Mom; they don't cane you or give you the slipper there - But he will when he comes to Queensbridge road! I had three strokes of the slipper three weeks ago from the assistant head.

"The slipper - What for? You never said anything about that? You must have been playing up then, and you're dad won't like that!"

"I wasn't playing up, Mom. We were waiting for the art teacher to come, and a couple of kids began running around playing tag between the desks."

"So they must have had the slipper too then?"

"No they didn't!"

"What do you mean – no they didn't! You just said they were the ones playing around, not you!"

"Because, Robert knocked my pen onto the floor when he ran past. I was underneath trying to get it, and the teacher came in and saw me!"

"The teacher saw you? What about the two who were playing around, did she see them too?"

"No, they saw her through the glass in the door, and they were sitting down before she came in."

"I think it's best if we don't tell your dad, I don't want you getting another slap across your backside! It's about time punishment like that was stopped anyway; it may have been acceptable in my day - but not now. If it happens again, you wait until the teacher comes – and you put your hand up – that way you can't get in anymore trouble! Come on, hurry up; I don't want you being in trouble for being late too!"

*

My class teacher, Mr Bennett, was a no nonsense man. With a greyish handlebar moustache, and a hardened expression, he looked like an ex- sergeant who'd come straight from the army. The first thing Bennett he did was change our seating positions. I imagined this was done to end any familiarisation with the one sitting next to me.

"Have you all handed in your homework?" Bennett asked in his abrupt manner.

"Yes, Mr Bennett," we all answered together.

Mr Bennett walked around his desk, with the twelve inch wooden ruler he always carried in his hand, tapping against his leg "I am constantly telling you ink blobs are unacceptable on your work, yet some of you are still struggling with the simple task of preventing them. You are the ones with wandering minds, and the simple task of holding and dipping a pen into the inkwell correctly is unimportant to you – Well it may be unimportant to you, but not to me. Those handing in unacceptable work from today will be told to do it again - after school in detention. Just to remind you boys it is gym today; any boy who has not brought a towel, or shorts can give their excuses to the headmaster in the morning. Books on your desk top and open please!"

I raised the top of my desk and withdrew my book, closing the top quietly.

"On the chalkboard you will see I have written some words. I want you to incorporate one of those words into different sentences, giving the words different meanings; for example! The man on the roof was repairing the lead flashing; and the lady took her dog for a walk on the lead! No talking, just writing please!"

I was pretty good with words, because Lizzie was pretty good too, and helped me when needed. Our next lesson after morning break was Maths, and though I was okay with my twelve times table, the game Bennett always played with the ruler made it the most daunting.

"Right everyone, settle down and concentrate? I'll begin with you." he said touching, Smithers shoulder with the ruler. "Seven sevens are?"

"Forty nine, Sir!"

Bennett walked a few steps between the desks. "Six eights are?" he said touching, Larry's shoulder.

"Forty eight, Sir!"

This continued throughout the next fifteen minutes, until every shoulder had been touched. Only Jones failed to answer a sum correctly, and the rule came across his knuckles harshly.

Bennett walked to front his desk and faced the class, tapping the ruler against the side of his leg gently; watching for anyone who looked up. My eyes were glued to the book on my desk, but, Richard's eyes behind me weren't.

Bennett walked to him and rapped Richard's knuckles with the ruler.

*

The bell for dinnertime couldn't have come quick enough. Jones and Ryland had been rapped with the ruler across their knuckles, and I always dreaded it rapping across mine. Before I knew it, the bell was ringing for dinner break over, and I was walking in single file back into the building. I was allowed into the classroom for my gym shorts and towel, joining the others in an orderly walk to the gym.

Bennett closed the gym doors, and walked to the centre. "Right, everyone form an orderly circle around me please?"

We all did so, in the orderly command.

"AND THAT INCLUDES YOU THREE!" Bennett called to the three boys lagging behind. "For the next three minutes, I want you all to run around me shouting and yelling as loud as you can! When I tell you to stop, you will stop and stand quietly while I tell you what to do next! - BEGIN NOW?"

I ran with the others around Bennett, screaming aloud and enjoying the brief moment without discipline.

"ALL STAND STILL NOW?" Bennett strode around our circle, eyeing each of us in turn. When he stopped he was facing away from me, and the two boys either side of me. I could barely hear what Bennett was saying; and when he shouted, "BEGIN AGAIN," I assumed, as did the two either side it was to continue shouting; and so we did, shouting as loud as we could.

"STOP, ALL OF YOU!" Bennett swung around pointing directly to me. "YOU - GET HERE NOW?"

Straight away I knew I was heading for punishment, and the moment I was close enough, Bennett grasped the front of my top and lifted me from the floor.

"HOW DARE YOU DISOBEY ME, YOU WRETCHED BOY?"

Bennett released my top, then punched me in the stomach. As I arched forward he rabbit punched me to the floor. I could barely breathe when he hoisted me to my feet. He threw me around and his fist thumped me from behind.

"Get back in line, and if you do anything wrong again, it's straight to the headmaster for caning."

I was struggling with the rest of the gym lesson, and Bennett was walking around discussing our next movements us as though nothing had happened.

Several boys in my class, with reputations for being hard said to me afterwards; 'we were on the verge of coming to help you!' But of course they never did.

*

I had been home for fifteen minutes, crying on the couch when mom came in with Patrick. Her first words were always, 'Have you had a good day at school today, Jaimie; and I would say, 'Yeah, it was okay, Mom!" But today mom was greeted with tears, and a son in total distress.

"Jay, what on earths the matter?" Mom whispered something to Patrick, then came and sat beside me. "What's happened, why are you crying?"

I couldn't answer mom, my grief wouldn't let me.

"Has someone been fighting with you - is that it?"

All I did was sway my head.

"Then if it isn't fighting, what is it?"

I was still sitting on the couch crying when Lizzie came home.

"Mom, what's the matter with Jaimie?"

"I don't know, Lizzie! I've asked him what's wrong, and he just cries when he tries to answer!"

Lizzie removed her coat, then sat beside me. "It's alright, Mom, you leave him to me, Jaimie's going to tell me what's happened, aren't you Jaimie?"

I managed to nod while releasing an emotional, "Okay!"

"Go on then I'm listening," said Lizzie, holding my hand between hers.

From the moment I could talk, it was always Lizzie I was more comfortable talking to; and the moment I began to talk, it all came out in short none stop breaths.

Lizzie stood to her feet, with her face looking more thunderous than mom's

"I'm not having that, Mom! A teacher beating up my brother! I'm not having that, no one beats up my brother, not even a teacher - wait till dad comes home!"

*

We were only half way through our first morning lesson, and Mr Bennett's attention was drawn to the glass pane in the door. He left the classroom, then walked back in and sat at his desk. For a few minutes Bennett's fingers locked and interlocked with his eyes staring directly at me.

I had my head down and eyes on my work, pretending I couldn't see him looking at me. It was good five minutes before Bennett left his chair, and walked to the front of his desk.

"Colbrook, out here - NOW?"

Everyone's eyes were on me as I walked to the front, and stood before Bennett. Then just as he did in the gym the day before, Bennett grabbed my jumper and half lifted me from the floor again. His face was so close I could smell his breath, and his spittle went into my left eye.

"If you send your father to me again, I'll drag you down to the heads office and I'll cane you myself!"

Bennett threw me backward, sprawling me across the classroom floor. "Now get back to your desk," he said with the wild angered look he had in the gym.

I never did tell dad what happened, it would only have made matters worse for me; and nothing would have come from it anyway. Teachers were always throwing wooden blackboard rubbers across the classroom, and cursing aloud when it missed a pupils head.

Punishment then was delivered in several ways. A ruler across the knuckles; three strokes of a hard soled slipper across your arse; and three strokes of the cane, leaving your buttocks sore for a week. Unfortunately for me I had a teacher who gave out punishment far beyond those; and shouldn't have been a teacher in the first place.

Twenty one
1957

I was in my last full year at, Queensbridge Road, and Pat's was just starting there. Instead of Patrick being taken to Park hill by mom now, he was going to school with me.

"Now listen, Pat's, mom told me to look after you - so no playing up. When you was naughty at Park hill, you only got told off; when you're naughty at Queensbridge, you can be punished with the slipper or the cane!

"Will you be able to play with me in the playground?" Pat's asked, less nervous than I was when I started there.

"Yeah, I can for a bit, but you'll soon make friends with kids your own age!"

When we walked through the gates, and along the path toward the school steps, I remembered my stomach being filled with nervous waves of apprehension, just as Pat's must have been now. The white stone pillars flanking the steps were unlike anything I had seen, and as a new comer to the school in nineteen fifty five, climbing those steps between the pillars was a daunting experience for me. My most favourite lesson of all was in the handicraft shop, with Mr Ferguson, the handicraft shop teacher. I may have lagged behind in every other lesson, but in the shop I excelled. I was making replicas of the tools used for making things, which meant using the lathe, case hardening and brazing. Mr Ferguson was a brilliant teacher, and I adhered to his every word as if he was my dad.

Unbeknown to me, Mr Ferguson had approached the head master, Mr Rollason, requesting my last full year at school would benefit me more by working in the handicraft shop. Mr Rollason agreed on the condition I attended each maths lessons in the classroom. Dad was happy when I told him that, because working with steel in the handicraft shop was following his profession as a welder fabricator.

"And how did my little man do at school?" said mom, fussing over Patrick the moment we walked through the door.

"Alright, Mom, I played with two of the kids in my class. Some of the bigger kids weren't very nice to us, but we took no notice and they left us alone!"

"Good lad, you make sure you tell Jaimie if anyone's bullying you. Jaimie if you see anyone bullying your brother, you tell me or your dad!"

I answered, "Yes, Mom," because that's what mom wanted to hear." When I told mom and dad about Mr Bennett, it just made matters worse. "I won't be able to watch him all the time, Mom! I'm leaving next year!"

"Well hopefully by then, you won't have to watch him, Jaimie! Now come and sit down both of you, and I'll bring you a drink."

"It's not the cabbage water again is it, Mom?"

"Yes it is, Jaimie, so stop moaning it's good for you!"

"Can we have the TV on?"

"Yes, Jay; but no banging the sides again! If the picture starts rolling, leave it for when your dad comes home. If he breaks it I'll be his fault, not yours – or Patrick's!"

It was about half past five when Lizzie came in from work. Before even saying, "Mom, I'm home!" she thumped the side of the television, bringing the rolling picture static in an instant.

"There! That's better isn't it." Lizzie said as though we were incapable of doing it ourselves.

"MOM! Lizzie's just banged the television!"

"LIZZIE, don't bang the television!"

"Snitch! Next time I'll let it roll, and you won't see anything!"

"Mom, Lizzie just called us a snitch!"

"Jaimie, if you can't stop squabbling with your sister I'll turn the television off.

As mom turned her back on us, Lizzie gave me and Patrick a smug look of satisfaction.

*

Without any further harsh words we had our tea, and were settling down for a quiet evening. Mom and dad were laughing and talking between watching the television, Patrick and I were cross legged on the rug, playing snakes and ladders from my compendium box of games; and Lizzie was at the table, swatting up on her shorthand. After about twenty minutes, Lizzie left the table and handed mom an envelope, stamp-marked, 'Mosely Road Methodist Church.'

"Miss Aldridge asked me to give you this letter, Mom," Lizzie said, handing mom the envelope.

"Oh yes, and what's it about?"

"It's about something I've been asked to do at Church on Sunday's!

"It must be something important then?"

"Yes, Mom, it is for me!"

Mom looked up from the envelope in her worrying face mode. "Miss Aldridge must have given you this letter yesterday, when you were at Sunday school?"

"Not this Sunday, Mom, she gave it to me the Sunday before!"

Now dad was finding the envelope more interesting than the television. "If it's important, why didn't you give your mom the envelope then?"

"Because I can't decide whether to do what, Miss Aldridge asked me - or not, Dad!"

We all went quiet while mom opened the envelope, then read the letter slowly to herself. Mom then placed the letter on her lap, and turned to dad. "Hal, the committee's asking Lizzie if she would consider being their infants Sunday School Teacher!"

"Are they?" dad said with a mouthful of cigarette smoke. "Well I know one thing, Lizzie, they wouldn't be asking you if they thought you weren't the right person for it. I would see that as a blooming great compliment!"

"It is a compliment, Dad! Lizzie answered, wafting aside the smoke from her face. "I've been going to Sunday school since I was out of nappies; but I don't know why they've asked me, and not someone else!"

"Have you read what's in the letter Lizzie?"

"No, Mom, it was sealed and I was asked to give it to you!"

"Well let me just read it out to you then, love, then you'll know why they are asking you!"

"On the first Sunday of April last year, Mr, Brown, the infant's teacher was taken suddenly ill while at church. Unfortunately at the time no other person was available to step in for him. Elizabeth was asked if she would occupy the children until he was well again - which she did without question. Instead of Elizabeth finding something other than the scriptures to occupy them, Elizabeth took the class in the form of their teacher, talking about the scriptures in the confidence of an adult. The response we had from the children, and their parents afterwards was good. Now the position of Sunday School Teacher for the infants has become permanently available; and we the committee find Elizabeth the perfect candidate to fulfil this most important position.

Because of Elizabeth's age and maturity, we have to notify the children's parents, and of course your permission as Elizabeth's parents.

Miss Aldridge.

Now I remember when Lizzie was asked to take the class particularly well! It was the month I had my exam at Sunday school. I was given a certificate saying: Scripture Examination. 1956. Third in class. Signed, Bryan-H-Reed.

"Did you hear that, Patrick? Lizzie's going to be a teacher?"

"Yeah, a girl in my class called Ellie keeps on bragging about her mom being an art teacher. When I tell her my sisters a Sunday School Teacher, she'll be really jealous because my sister's better than her mom!"

Wanting more information on the subject, I asked, dad. "Dad, is being a Sunday school teacher better than being an art teacher?"

"Well I wouldn't say one was better than the other, Son," said dad trying to be objective. "Being a Sunday school teacher is a big responsibility. It means teaching children the true meanings of the bible - without making it sound boring and losing their attention – I would think! Am I nearly right, Lizzie?"

"Yes you're right, Dad! That's why I enjoyed going to Sunday school, because our teacher made it sound interesting."

"See," said Patrick with a nudge. "I told you!"

"If I say yes, then it means going to the church in the week as well! I know a lot about the scriptures, Dad, but if I said yes, they'd want me to know more?"

"And is that such a hardship, Lizzie," said dad. "When your mom was your age she was working in the factory, riveting together sections of steel plate six days a week; and doing it while helping her mom!"

"Hal you're right - but you mustn't compare Lizzie to the things I did! Lizzies goes to work five days a week! In between she's helping me around the house – and learning shorthand, which is an important part of her job! She goes to church on Sunday's, and if you think about what she already does, Hal, Lizzie's doing a lot more than I ever did! Lizzie, whatever you decide to do, your dad and I will support you – but it has to be your decision, and no one else's!"

Lizzie nodded to mom, while releasing a short of relief. "Thanks Mom," she said, and returned to the table to continue learning her short hand.

I saw mom giving me a wry look while talking to dad. "At least whatever Lizzie decides to do, Hal, she'll stick to it, and not lose interest!"

I know what mom was referring to when she gave me that look; and it wasn't my fault when I didn't want to be a scout anymore. I think I only became one because I wanted a hat, like the Mounties wore in the films on Saturday Matinee. Camping for me was swatting the flies, congregating around the poles inside the tent; and learning how to make a toilet in a field, then leaving the field as we found it, without sign nor trace of us being there. On the two occasions when the scouts marched around the streets of Ballsall Heath, I was at home, suffering from a snotty nose and a sore throat. My enthusiasm waned even more when I saw Patrick, playing cowboys and Indians with kids in the road, wearing my boy scouts hat.

*

Christmas dinner again was a family affair, only this time the fire was lit in the posh room too, and we were eating our Christmas dinner sitting around our new table, and not cross legged in front of the living room fire. The television was on, bringing the dulcet voices of choir singers into the posh room, mingling with our laughter when dad blew off accidently while reaching across the table for another Yorkshire pudding.

While I sat next to Patrick, easing clumps of gravy coated cabbage into my mouth with my fingers, Patrick was hiding his sprouts by dropping then into the empty gravy jug. Lizzie of course was eating her dinner like mom and dad - with a knife and fork.

"Okay, listen now, I want to say something!" said dad, tapping the side of his beer glass with the fork. Dad's eyes rolled to me and Patrick, shoving a sprout back and forth between the plates. "You two, leave that sprout alone and listen, it might be one of you two I'll be talking about next time!" Dad turned his eyes to Lizzie. "Your mom and I want to take this opportunity, by thanking you for everything you've done this year, Lizzie?"

Lizzie lowered her knife and fork gently onto her plate, flushing a little from embarrassment. "You don't have to, honestly!"

"Yes we do, Lizzie," said mom. "I don't think you know just how proud of you we are!"

While dad was taking something from his pocket, I was licking the gravy off my fingers in curiosity.

Dad handed Lizzie a small rectangular box, delicately wrapped in pink Christmas paper. "This one isn't from Father Christmas! This one is from me and your mom!"

"Mom and dad's giving Lizzie a mouthorgan like mine, Patrick," I said whispering behind my hand.

Lizzie pretended not to hear my whispering, and nervously continued unwrapping the present in front of mom and dad.

The moment Lizzie opened the box, her eyes filled gently with tears.

"We bought it from the jewellers down the lane, Lizzie; it's a parker one of the best! As your always writing something for work - or the church, we thought you should have a good pen to write with! If you look closely, you'll see: Elizabeth, from Mom and Dad, engraved on it?"

Lizzie just sat quietly for a few minutes, staring at a pen unlike any other she had written with before.

We were all looking at each other, with our eyes always returning to Lizzie.

While all our eyes were on Lizzie, I edged my mouth closer to Pat's ear. "I'm glad it wasn't a mouthorgan, she might've played it better than me!"

Lizzie eased herself from her chair, and walked between mom and dad's chairs, spreading her arms so they reached them both. "It's beautiful, thank you, I'll treasure it forever!"

*

The floor joists under the piano were replaced in September, with the workmen remarking, 'You're lucky the piano and the one on the stool hadn't suddenly disappeared under the floor!'

Mom's fingers were warming up on the piano, flicking randomly across the keys, and her eyes on the glass of water balancing on top, testing for any movement on the floorboards.

"I think Jessie's here, Mom," called Lizzie, rushing to open the door.

"Tell her to come in then, Lizzie?"

Lizzie opened the door quickly, greeting her friend with a kiss. "Merry Christmas, Jessie!"

"Merry Christmas, Lizzie!"

"I thought you wasn't going to come," Lizzie asked closing the door quickly.

"Every time I went to leave, mom gave me something else to do?"

Lizzie chuckled while helping Jessie out of her coat. "I know, that's what all mom's do!"

"Merry Christmas everyone," Jessie called.

"Merry Christmas, Jessie," we all responded in one voice.

Lizzie and Jessie walked closely together, discussing the events of today while walking around the table in the posh room.

Mom's fingers were already warming up on the piano, asking Jessie without looking away from the keys. "Has your mom and dad had a nice day, Jessie?"

"Yes thank you!" Jessie answered, half turning her mouth toward Lizzie's ear. "To be honest, Lizzie, I think my mom and dad will be glad when the days over. My brothers have been squabbling since this morning over who had the best presents. I asked dad to ring Father Christmas and ask him to take all their presents back to the North Pole! I said they were ungrateful, and they were spoiling Christmas for us. When I told mom and dad I was coming to yours, I think they were glad I was!"

"And I'm glad I've got someone my own age to spend the evening with, Jessie."

"Right everyone, Titch is ready to start," said dad tapping one of the glasses with a fork handle.

"Start what?" Jessie asked.

"Singing - we all sing at Christmas with mom playing the piano!"

"You know I'm not very good singing, Lizzie?"

"Neither are dad or my brothers, but they sing anyway. That's what makes it fun?"

Mom's fingers ran up and down the keys, then her left hand started vamping. "Right then, what are we singing first?"

"The runaway Train," I shouted.

"No, something more Christmassy than that, Jaimie! What would you like us to sing, Jessie?"

"I love Deck the Halls!"

"That's one of my favourite's Jessie!"

"I know it is, Lizzie!"

No one seemed bothered about the Christmas songs, coming from a church organ on the television. Our songs were being sang in the posh room, accompanied by mom on the upright piano.

With: Silent Night, being sang between gulps of fizzy pop, Jessie asked Lizzie. "Do you think your mom and dad would mind if I had my Christmas here - with your family next year?"

Twenty two
1958

Although at school I worked with metal in the workshop, at home I was always making things from wood. I made mom a box in the shape of a grand piano once, just to put her little things in – and I'd repaired the outhouse door for dad. During the last few months before leaving school, I'd been going on Saturday mornings to Andrew's builder's yard in the road. Saturday mornings was the only time I could go there, because all the machines were switched off, and only Edwards was there, making something for himself.

Andrews was well into his seventies then; he was a big solid man, almost six foot tall, about sixteen stone, with a cigarette or a pipe clamped permanently between his teeth. Every time I saw him he was wearing a trilby and cow-gown; and because he had a deep coarse voice it made him appear intimidating, but I knew he wasn't!

The carpenters work shop was guarded by a blind old terrier dog called Monty, and walking to the workshop meant walking past Monty's kennel.

"So what did you make with the last wood you had then?" Andrews asked me.

"I made a lamp for mom!"

"What sort of lamp?"

"Well, it's like the sign on a pub, it swings if you push it."

Andrews lead me toward the racks where the off cuts were stored, and I paused again before walking past Monty's kennel.

"Why have you stopped?"

I glanced at the dog, straining to sniff me on his lead.

"That leads just long enough to reach the mortising machine. Monty knows who you are; and if he wanted to bite you, he would've already done so!"

"I know – but?"

"But nothing, Lad! He's blind that's all; his bloody ears aren't blocked, and bloody nose hasn't dropped off; now come with me?"

Walking into the carpenters shop meant walking past the circular saw, the mortising machine and the surface plainer. The whole place was oozing with the smells of, Oak, Teak, Deal, Mahogany, and Pine, all being brought together from the distinct smell of button glue, bubbling in the pot, from a gas flame on the window ledge.

Two heavily used wooden benches were almost the length of the shop, each with a vice either end. One was against the wall, with a huge spoke-shave supported on two nails above it; the second was in the middle of the shop. Timber was stacked in a rack the height of the shop, and divided into sections against the opposite wall; and just by that was the rack with the offcuts.

"Right then young man; what's the wood I'm holding?" Andrews asked me, shoving the two foot length of wood under my nose.

"Oak!" I replied instantly.

"And this?" he said doing the same.

"Mahogany!"

"And this?"

"Deal!"

"And what about this?" he said placing his hands on a length of walnut in the rack.

I recognised the smell, but in its rough state, all I could say was - "I'm sorry I don't know!"

Andrews hummed aloud, removed his pipe, and replaced it with a cigarette. "That's okay, half the buggers who've work here for years wouldn't know either. So then, Jaimie, when do you leave school?"

"I leave school on the second of April!"

"And what are you going to do, when you leave school?"

"Well, for nearly a year, I've been working in the metal workshop at school. Dad's a fabricator in a factory, and I know he wants me to work in a factory like he does!"

"But you don't want to – do you?"

"No, I want to be a carpenter, and work in a carpenters shop, like this one," I said almost dizzy from the smells I love.

Andrews was looking at me thoughtfully, while puffing away on his cigarette. "I want to see the lamp you made for your mom!"

"Okay, I'll bring it in the week!"

"No you won't, you'll go home bring it to me right now!"

"What – right now?"

"Yes right now," he growled. "If I'd wanted to see it in the week, I would've said – wouldn't I?"

I left the offcuts of wood, and hurried back toward the workshop door, nudging past Monty's nose with my knee.

*

"Mom where's dad? Andrews at the builders said he wants to see the lamp I've made!"

"Alright, alright calm down, Jaimie, you nearly had the door off the hinges. Now say it slowly so I can understand you?"

I'd run none stop from the builders, so I was talking while inhaling at the same time. "Mr, Andrews said he wants to see the lamp I made for you, Mom!"

"Okay, but what for?"

"I don't know! He was asking me lots of things; like if I knew the names of different wood; and what I wanted to do when I left school! Then he said he wanted to see the lamp - Where's Dad?"

"It's Saturday and he's gone to the butchers; he should be back soon!"

I should've known where dad was without asking, mom! Round about this time, dad always went to the butchers for Hock; then he'd make us all sandwiches from the warm red meat. When Lizzie was home she'd never have one; always commenting on the meat looking disgusting. For me Hock sandwiches were a delicacy, to be eaten on a layer of butter.

"If I wait for dad, Mr, Andrews might be gone, Mom!" I raced up the stairs, grabbed the lamp from mom's bedside table, and raced back down again. "When dad comes back, tell him where I am, Mom?"

An hour later, I was back with the lamp, more excited at seeing dad than going on holiday. "Dad, Mr, Andrews at the builders said can you come with me and see him next Saturday?"

Twenty three

This was the day I had been looking forward to since starting school. Instead of going to school in the green uniform of Queensbridge Road, I was going to school, wearing a bright blue suit with matching tie, and pale blue shirt.

I wanted to be one of those school leavers who stood out more; and after seeing the suit, hanging in the tailors shop window down the lane, I'd been badgering mom and dad for weeks to buy it for me.

"They'll laugh at you for wearing a suit like that," was mom's reactions after our conversations.

"Why won't you let us buy you a suit like everyone else, Jaimie!" was dads.

This leaving day on the, 2nd of April 1958 was my farewell to having a chalkboard rubber bouncing off my head - meant for the boy behind me - a twelve inch wooden ruler across my knuckles – for looking up when the teacher walked past my desk - three strokes of the slipper on my backside – and the very possibility of receiving three strokes of the cane, purely on the word of a teacher, with the tendency of beating up pupils in the gym. The only thing marring the day was the absence of Mr Bennet, denying me the opportunity to tell him what I thought of him – without the threat of being caned hanging over me.

Like the other school leavers, I spent the day strolling from class to class, shaking hands with the teachers, and accepting their words of wisdom with a simple nod and - 'Thank you.'

I spent my final hour with Mr, Ferguson; walking and talking casually around the workshop with him, and being introduced to the boys, attempting to do the things I did. Mr Ferguson was my last teacher to see, and the one I would miss the most.

Before the day ended, and I walked from the school for good, the head handed me my leaving certificate. It read. Scholars leaving certificate; Queensbridge SM School – 'During his last year, has done special work in the handicraft shop. He is quiet and trustworthy.' Mr Rollason – Head teacher. 2nd of April – 1958.

*

The first Monday after leaving school, I was up and getting ready to begin my first day at work.

"Patrick, stop looking at that comic, and get yourself ready for school – Now, please!" came mom's voice a little louder.

"Mom, have you seen my bag?" Lizzie called.

"Yes, Lizzie, it's on the table in the posh room, right where you left it last night!"

"Thanks Mom!"

Mom quickly wrapped the two slices of buttered toast, and shoved them neatly inside my bag. "We've run out of jam, so you'll have to have them without,

Jay! Hal, can you pop in the shop on your way home and get some Jam for me – Oh, and some butter?"

"Yes, now let me go to work before you think of something else! Jaimie, remember what I told you! Listen and do whatever Mr Andrews tells you to do; even if it means sweeping up, or making the tea, you do it. That's how I began; and that's how everyone begins!" Dad grasped my hand with a soft handshake. "You said you wanted to be a carpenter, Son! Well hopefully by the time you're twenty, you will be one. First though you'll have to learn how to make a cup of tea, and use a broom! You do that well, and the rest will come!"

"Okay, Dad! Thanks, Dad!"

"It's ten to eight, Jay, don't forget you start work at eight! And aren't you going to be late, Hal, by now you would have already gone!"

"I told them I would be a little late this morning, Titch; I just wanted to be here to see Jay off on his first day to work!"

"Thanks, Dad," I said.

Lizzie threw her bag quickly over her shoulder, and looked toward me before opening the door. "Good luck for today Jaimie! Just do what dad says and you'll be fine. See you tonight, Mom!" Lizzie called, closing the door smartly behind her.

"Patrick! What did I tell you?"

I gave myself an inward chuckle, then like Lizzie made for the door. "See you dinner time then, Mom!"

*

During my last year at school I was having growth spurts; and when I walked up the drive to my first day at work, I was a five foot ten lanky teenager, buzzing in oodles of enthusiasm and eagerness.

"Ah, here's James, - our new recruit! I'm Roy the plumber," said the man wearing a black beret tilted to one side, and a full moustache covering his top lip. "The one in the bib and brace is Tom! He's the carpenter who'll be teaching you." Roy's moustache brushed against my ear. "A word of warning! Do whatever he tells you, he's not shy giving you a slap if you don't! The rest are all out on jobs, you'll meet those later - So what experience have you got working in wood then?"

"I haven't! In my last year as school, I worked with metal in the school workshop!"

"Well you must've done something for Andrews to give you the job here. The reason I'm asking is, Andrews giving anyone a job here, is like a dustman getting a job as a politician. Andrews has turned down everyone he's interviewed, and they all had some knowledge working in wood. Then along comes you, fresh from school, who only worked with metal and gets the job!"

"I've been coming here for years on a Saturday, buying off cuts of wood. Andrews asked me to show him a lamp I'd made, then he asked to see my dad. After that he offered me the job!"

Tom had been quietly setting up his tools on the bench before acknowledging my presence.

"Well I hope you're better than the last one he employed two years ago! He had more qualifications than me, and he was crap!" Tom then faced me and said. "The name James sounds more like a pen pusher! What's your nick name?"

"Nick name?"

"Yes, son – your nick name!"

"Tom's asking for the name you're family – or your friends call you! If you haven't already got one, Tom will make one up. Everyone who works here have shortened names. It makes us more like a family than workers.

"Oh – that name!" I said with the penny dropping. "Well sometimes I'm called Jaimie, but I'm called Jay the most!"

"And, Jay it is! Right then Jay boy, you can crash the ash now!"

"Crash the ash! I don't know what you mean," I answered in total ignorance.

Tom wriggled a packet of woodbine from his top pocket, brandishing the packet in front of me. "Crash the Ash – Ash as in cigarettes - You smoke don't you?"

"No I don't!"

Tom shrugged off my answer with a swaying head, and an intake of breath. "If you don't smoke, then you don't work here! You want to work with me, then you better go to the shops and buy some now!"

I ran from the shop, down the driveway, and down the road, ignoring the grocers who never opened before nine o-clock. Now I understood why dad had so many names, and smoked like a trooper, because this probably happened to him too when he started work. Dad always said I should have a few shilling in my pocket for emergencies; and my emergency was keeping my job by buying cigarettes.

From then on going to work was making cups of tea on the hour. Sweeping the wood shavings and sawdust from the floor, and sorting out the timber in the racks.

Because I only lived a short distance from the shop, every day at one o-clock I ran home, put on the television and ate my sandwiches watching, Lunch Box, with Noele Gordon, and the Jerry Allen trio.

A whole month had flown bye, and my routine of going to work was honed down to the last minute. It was a Tuesday morning when Andrews came into the shop, strutting around with his pipe clenched between his teeth. Roy was there with Dave, waiting for the instructions on their next job.

"Jay, come here - I've got a little job for you! I want you to go to, Jacks - the hardware shop on Mosely Road. I want you to ask him for a bottle of, Scotch mist – and a Left handed screwdriver! Tell him to put it on my account. Well go on then, Roy needs the scotch mist for his next job!"

"Okay!" I answered, without questioning why I was the one going for the-Scotch mist - and not Dave. I knew, Bill, the shop keeper at Jacks anyway, long before I began working at the builders. I always needed something when making things from the wood

Andrews gave me; and I always learned something from our little conversations.

Bill appeared from the back of the shop as the bell over the door gave a jingle.

"Hello, Jay - mate! You haven't been in here for a while; what are you up too these days?"

"I'm working at Andrews the builders now!"

"Don't tell me – you've got the job as Tom's new mate!"

"Yes!"

"And don't tell me why you're here, I'll tell you! He's sent you for a bottle of Scotch Mist, and a left-handed screwdriver - right!"

"Yes, but how did you know?"

"He does it to all Tom's new mates. I don't want to worry you, but they don't last long at Andrews. You're the forth in two years to ask me for a bottle of Scotch mist, and a left- handed screwdriver!"

"So it's a wind up?"

"Oh yes, they all went back with red cheeks and empty hands." Old Andrews must have had a field day with them!" Bill stared at me in thought for a few seconds, then disappeared to the back of the shop. He came back minutes later with a round clear container, which had a cork as a stopper - and a small screwdriver. "You won't be going back empty handed this time; the old man's had enough laughs at someone else's expense!" Bill placed a white sticker around the tube, and wrote on it, Scotch mist from Dumyat! Then on the handle of the screwdriver, he scratched with a penknife the letters L and H. "Tell the old man I've added, one shilling and sixpence to his account; Sixpence for the screwdriver - and a shilling for the Scotch mist, because it's come all the way from Dumyat. He'll know where that is, because his wife has relatives there. You keep a straight face when you hand it to him, Jaimie; and the joke will be on him - not you!"

Bill placed the two items in a bag, and after signing for them on Andrews account, I legged it back down Edward Road to the shop. Tom, Roy, and Dave were half sniggering behind their hands when I walked in, waiting for Andrews to embarrass me for being so naive.

"Okay there's the left- handed screwdriver," I said placing the tool in Andrews hand; and there's the bottle of Scotch, mist. The screwdriver was sixpence, and the Scotch mist was a shilling, because the mist comes from somewhere called, Dumyat!"

The silence in the shop was unsettling; but I stood in front of Andrews glaring eyes, with the straight face Bill had suggested. The reluctance for anyone to speak first was in their silence, and as I'd already dug my own hole, I asked Andrews. "Do you want me to get you anything else?"

"No thank you – and as this Scotch mist has just cost me a small fortune, no one uses it unless I say so!"

Not until Andrews was halfway across the yard to his office did anyone speak, then they all spoke at once.

"You're the first one who's ever done that to the Gaffa!"

"Did you see the look on his face when Jay gave him the Scotch mist?"

"All the way from Dumyat - bloody brilliant!"

"You'll need to keep your head down for a bit – if you want to keep your job, Jay - All the way from Dumyat!" Tom sniggered again as he walked to the bench. "Bloody brilliant!"

*

Andrews had come to the shop with the plans for constructing four wooden vents, each one almost the length the bench. One of my jobs in the shop was making sure Tom's area of floor was always tidy; run errands for him, and to assist him when necessary.

Because of their size and weight they required the hands of two people to turn them; and this happened least half a dozen times over the next two weeks.

During the first few days of any construction in the shop, I wasn't allowed to talk to Tom, other than ask him if he wanted a cup of tea. And I had to wait until Andrews had taken Tom to the site, for a, look-see, and the first vent was constructed before asking him the question. "Where are the vents for?"

"They're for the Midland Galvanisers, Garrison lane. The roof is pitched with corrugated asbestos sheets, and the top has a wide two foot flat ridge for the vents to sit on. We'll have to lash two pole ladders together to reach them. Andrews specifically wants you to go with us when the vents are ready – I hope you're not too scared of heights, Kid?"

I knew Andrews was somewhere in the shop from the smell of his pipe; and before I could answer Tom, Andrews came striding through carrying a heavy wooden box full of old tools,

"How's Jay doing then Tom?" Andrews asked heading to the middle bench.

"Not too bad – not too bad! He's a grafter if nothing else!"

"Good!"

I watched Andrews rummaging for an offcut of three by two inch deal; then placing it between the jaws of the bench vice. "Jay, get your arse over here?"

I did immediately.

"I know you can cut wood, you've already showed me! But I want to see you cut two inches off that wood with this?" Andrews held the saws handle toward me then stepping back, filling his lungs with tobacco smoke.

The saws teeth jammed the moment I used it, flying off the timber and creating a nasty splintering edge.

"That's what happens when the saw's blunt, and the teeth aren't set properly!" Andrews grasped the saw from my hands, and shoved it back into the box, commenting. "That saw is older than you, and it hasn't cut wood for years. I want that saw cutting through that wood, smoother than a knife cuts through butter; and the same applies to every tool in this box! Until you know how to look after your tools, and use them without cutting your fingers off, you will sweep the floor, make the tea, and help Tom. It's entirely up to you how long it takes, but I want to see improvement taking place. Once you've learned how to use and look after those tools, I'll start deducting half a crown each week from your wages; that'll pay for your new tools - Any questions?"

"No!"

"Good, get on with it then!"

Andrews walked to Tom's bench, discussing the progress of the vents, and with Tom glancing once or twice in my direction, they were discussing mine also!

*

Going to the Midland Galvanizers in the lorry was my first time out of the shop. I was sitting between Tom and Andrews in the cab, and the vents were lashed on the open deck behind us. The others were making their way there in cars.

The two huge pole ladders had been delivered the day before, and when we arrived, almost everyone who worked at the builders were there walking around waiting for us.

Andrews immediately made his way to the doors of the Galvanisers, calling to me and Dave to follow him. "Right then you two, I want you to see something? It might make you appreciate how lucky you are working for me!"

The moment I walked through the doors into the galvanisers, my eyes were watering. Movable racks, with steal parts hung on wire were being lowered into a huge baths of hot zinc. The workers were covering their mouths with scarfs as a powder like substance was thrown in, releasing strange smelling fumes up to the vents we were replacing. We were only in there for a few minutes, but was I glad when we came back out.

"Now when either of you moan about working in all weathers, think about those working in there, and thank your lucky stars you work for me! Jaimie as long as you're not in the way, stand wherever you like! I want you watching and learning! Dave you keep alert in case one of us calls for you!"

"Yes boss!" responded Dave, answering for both of us.

I sidled next to Dave, reassured by being with someone not far from my age. "So how long have you been working here then?" I asked, Dave.

"Over a year now - and you?"

"Since April!"

"So being at Andrews is your first job then!"

"Yes!"

"Well I'm, Dave, Roy's apprentice; I've been here over a year, and it took a long time for Andrews to trust me on a job. You do what he says and you'll be fine – here!" he said offering me a park drive. "I know you smoke or you wouldn't be here!"

Dave's manner was bristling with the worldly confidence I lacked! I reckoned he was not much older than me, but strong in physic and character – Someone not one to be messed around with I thought!

The pole ladders were still soaking wet from the last job, almost doubling their weight. Lashing them together, and raising them against the building took a real team effort.

Roy was the first to climb the ladders, with two coils of rope draping around his shoulders; one short and one long. The ladders were flexing and bending so much under his weight, I thought for a minute they were going to snap in the middle.

Without any fear whatsoever, Roy leaned to the cast iron hook in the bricks, lashing the short length of rope around it to the top rungs, then scrambling with the second rope up the pitched corrugated roof to the flat surface of the vents. Dereck followed, climbing the ladders more agile than squirrels could climb trees - Then up went Tom taking his time steady and cautiously.

I just stood around, watching in utter fascination as the old vents were taken apart, then lowered to the ground in sections on the rope.

Dave had climbed to the roof and down several times during the day, taking materials in a bag slung over his back, needed for flashing in the vents. Even if I was still working here next year, I could never imagine me climbing two rungs on a rope ladder, never mind sprinting up them like Dave.

It was about ten to four when the four vents were finished, and the back of the lorry was full of debris from the old vents. The only thing left to do was lower the ladders to the ground, unlash them and tie them on the wagon. But before that happened, Andrews called me to the ladder.

"Jay, get your arse over here there's something I want you to do?"

There was no hesitation from me when I walked past Dave's rolling eyes. I was the only one who hadn't done anything all day, and all I wanted to do was contribute something, no matter how unimportant it was.

"Right then," he said, clutching his pipe between his teeth. "I want you to put both feet on the bottom rung!"

I wasn't exactly sure why I'd been asked to do that, but by the look on Dave's face I think he knew why.

"Now put both feet on the second rung!"

Again I did without questioning the reason – as I did when he asked me to put them on the third. When he asked me to put them on the forth rung, nerves began to creep in and I hesitated.

"Come on what are you waiting for! Put your feet on the forth rung!" he said with impatience lowering his tone. "It's been a long day, and no one's going home until I say! Now before you piss everyone off, stop messing them about and put your feet on the next rung!"

Outwardly I may have looked unconcerned, but inside my stomach was shaking like a jelly. "I'm sorry I can't!"

Andrews then stood on bottom rung, with his tobacco smoke wafting around me from behind. "You're sorry you can't eh!" he growled. "Well unfortunately you're too high to jump off; and I am not going to step down. The only way you're getting off these ladder now son, is by climbing them with me to the top!"

"Come on, Jaimie, lad, get a move on!" Roy called. "Andrews will stay on that ladder all night, and I'd like to get home before the sun sets!"

"Jay I had to do it!" Dave called to me, "You either climb the ladders with the boss, or you won't be coming to work tomorrow!"

Dave's threat of losing the job I liked was very real; and dad would've found me another job, whether I liked it or not!

I did climb the ladders that day; even when Andrews bounced and swayed them under his weight, I climbed them to the top.

*

I was cycling with Tom to Varna Road. He'd been given the job of replacing the sash cords on several houses; and being his mate, I was carrying the rolls of sash cords around my shoulders, as well as his tool bag.

"Hey, Tom! Is Andrews pinching my work again?" called the gentleman on the bike, with rolls of sash cords around both shoulders.

I followed Tom to the other side of the road, where the gentleman dressed in check coloured clothes, and a hat that looked remarkably like my old boy scouts hat, with cork bottle tops swinging on string around the rim, was waiting to talk to him.

"I see you've got another mate then, Tom!" he said looking me up and down. "I'm Kenneth!" he said shaking my hand briskly. "Or Sash cord Ken, as everyone calls me around here! I hope you last longer than the others! So where you off to now?" he said turning the conversation back to Tom.

"A few houses along Varna Road, Ken!"

Ken turned his wide scrutinising eyes toward me. "You stay close to Tom when you're along there, mate! If they think you're interested, they'll eat you alive for a shilling!"

They both turned their heads toward me, while conversing with bouts of tittering. Then Ken gave me a scanty wave, and cycled off in the opposite direction.

"What was all that about?" I asked Tom.

"Something you'll find out for yourself!" came Tom's reply.

*

The houses along Varna Road were like mansions, compared to the little house I lived in; and I imagined once upon a time people of wealth lived in them. Some of the numbers on the houses were not too clear, so we continued by walking on foot beside our bikes.

We both heard a sash widow being raised fully, then the voice of a woman calling to me.

"Hello darling! My-my, you are young aren't you? I bet your apple hasn't been plucked. Come on I'll do it for a shilling!"

"What's she talking about?" I asked glancing toward her window.

"Stop looking, there's a good lad! You walk nice and slowly with me!"

"Yes, but what did she want?" I asked, pursuing my curiosity.

"She wants you for breakfast; now stop asking questions and look for the house number with me!"

*

The jobs I went on at Edwards varied between going to them on the waggon, on our bikes, or with the handcart if it wasn't too far away. I was often pushing a handcart along the road, laden with a set of ladders, a bag of building sand, half a bag of cement, and our tools. Tom never helped with pushing the cart, he always walked beside me on the pavement. Either he was urging me to slow down when the road had a slight incline, or urging me to push harder when the road was uphill.

One of Edwards contracts was repairing the block herringbone floors in telegraph exchanges. The blocks were laid with hot pitch, and to re-lay them meant chipping off the tar from the blocks and floor.

We had relayed the blocks that required re-laying - except the last one, which Tom shoved across the floor to me.

Tom eased himself from kneeling, saying to me. "That one's yours, Jay! Now I'll see me how well you've been watching, I'm going outside for a fag!"

"No problem!" I said with the sure fired confidence of someone experienced.

"Don't call me unless you've poured the pitch over your hands, instead of the floor!"

After only a few minutes being left on my own, I was painfully reminded how a simple job could have consequences. As I pressed the block down hard into the molten pitch, a streak of hot pitch oozed between the blocks, coating the thumb and forefinger of my right hand.

Tom returned ten minutes later, conscious I was concealing my hand from him. "Okay then, what have you done?"

"Relayed the block like you asked!

"I can see you've relayed the block – block head! I can also see the pitch all over the floor. Show me your hands?"

"There's nothing wrong with my hands, Tom!"

Tom grasped my arm, forcing my hand toward him. The pitch was like a furnace, eating away my skin to the bone, and Tom's moment of sympathy was scant.

"See those," he said, showing me the scars on his fingers. "Hot pitch did that when I was about your age; and it never happened again. Come on, let's get you some first aid before you pass out!"

Twenty four

Nineteen fifty nine had come and gone, and so was my fear of heights, I was now climbing and sliding down ladders quicker than, Dave. My love of working with wood was being fulfilled in the tests Andrews gave me; and my commitment to the yard showed by having my toolbox finished - and filled with new tools. I had mastered the art of replacing sash cords quickly; and on occasions Andrews sent me out to replace them without, Tom.

I was earning three pounds ten shillings a week now! One pound seventeen shillings and sixpence I gave to mom, and the remainder I was saving in a tin in the bedroom. The half a crown I needed to pay for my tools, I earned going to the workshop Saturday mornings, helping Andrews with the bits and bobs we couldn't do in the week.

"Mom I've saved enough to start having driving lessons!"

"Have you, Jay?" mom said, hinting her surprise. "Well if you can afford to have them, then do it; but your dad and I can't help you, your dads saving hard to by a motorbike, just to get around instead of waiting for buses!"

"No, that's fine, Mom," I said instantly. "Next month I won't have the half a crown for my tools stopped from my wages! I can put it towards the fifteen shillings the driving school charge!"

"And which school are you going to?"

"The Premier driving school in Town!" Mom suddenly noticed another dark bruise on my head again.

"Jaimie, are you bumping into something? That's the third time you've come from work with a bruise on your head!"

"Yeah! I bumped it walking under on the beam in the workshop again, Mom!"

"Well, Andrews needs to do something about that beam, Jaimie! One of these days you're going to knock yourself out walking under it - and I'll be going over there with a rolling pin and knocking him out!"

"Right, Mom I'll tell him," I said laughing at the thought of mom confronting Andrews with her rolling pin.

"Well see that you do, Son?"

But of course I wasn't going to tell mom the mark was from Tom's ruler, bouncing off my head again for not concentrating – or doing something for him that wasn't good enough. And yes, sometimes when things were not going right in the shop, it felt like being back at school, doing what I was told, and being hit with the ruler if I didn't! But thankfully I was not at school, and I wasn't of a mind to let the past hold me back. Being chastised, and hit with the ruler in the workshop was essential to my wellbeing; it was honing my need for concentration while working on the bench; and most importantly when working around things that could easily take my hand off.

"Jay, leave your bib and brace in the outhouse, and I'll have it ready for Monday. Have you managed to remove all the sawdust from the bib this time?"

"Most of it, Mom!"

"I wish you'd ask Andrews for another pair? No matter how you clean it out, there's always sawdust in the bottom. I have to wash it separate from the others, and sometimes I haven't the time!"

"I'll ask him on Monday!"

"Jay, are you coming to Saturday Matinee today?" Patrick asked me.

"No – I can't this week, Pat's, I need to repair the puncture on my bike! Anyway you're going with a friend from school today?"

"Yeah, but it's more fun when you come as well!"

"I'll definitely come next week!"

"Okay!"

Mom waited until Patrick had run upstairs before asking. "You could have mended you puncture tomorrow, Jaimie. You haven't gone to Saturday matinee for weeks, and you used to go with him every week!"

"I can't go to the matinee today, Mom! I need to mend the puncture on my bike for tomorrow, I'm cycling with Tom to Chase water!"

"Chase water! – And where is that?"

"Cannock!"

"Cannock," repeated mom again. "And how far is it to there?"

"Tom reckons it's about fifteen miles. He's already ridden to Body More Heath twice! Chase waters a little further on; sometimes they race yachts on the lake! I've never seen a yacht, Mom!"

Pat's had heard me and mom talking from upstairs, and when he came back down, mom was waiting for dad to come back with the hock. He could see from mom's face she wasn't happy.

"Mom's in a mood, I don't think she wants you to go!" Patrick whispered to me.

I glanced toward mom, totally convinced she didn't want me to go. "I'm not going to get lost, Mom, I'll be riding behind Tom there and back!"

Dad had only been back a minute, and mom was airing her concerns about me.

"Jaimie says he's cycling to Chase water with Tom tomorrow!"

"Chase water," confirmed dad. "It's a good ride from here, Jaimie - I hope you're fit; I cycled there with one of my friends before I met your mom, so I know how far it is! - Right then, let's have the bread buttered, and the plates on the table before gets cold - I'll carve!"

"And where are you supposed to be meeting Tom tomorrow?" mom said airing her concerns again.

"I'm meeting him at his house!"

"You said he lives in Alum Rock?"

"He does!"

"Well you won't be following him from here, will you?"

"No, of course I won't!"

Dad butted in quickly, preventing the discussion from becoming heated. "I think your mom is concerned about how far you're riding, Jay! As far as we know, the furthest you've ridden is to the allotment and back, and cycling to Chase water is a hundred times further than that, Son!"

"I bet you don't even remember when I last cycled to the allotment with you, Dad?"

"Yes I do, Son – you brought back the bag of gooseberry's for your mom to make the pie, and that couldn't have been more than a few months ago!"

"Only Patrick went with you - I didn't, Dad," I said, correcting dad's forgetfulness. "I was working that weekend, helping Tom and Andrews to strengthen the timber racks in the shop; and that was over six months ago!"

"Jaimie's right, Dad," said Patrick in my defence. "Only you and I went; and on the way back the bag fell off my handlebars, and the back wheel ran over the bag. The gooseberry's got squashed and the bag fell to pieces. We threw the rest in someone's garden - remember!"

"Yes I do, Son! And we had the apple pie for afters instead!"

"And I bet you don't know how many times I've cycled around Cannon Hill Park, Dad, seeing who can cycle the longest before giving up with my friends. I never came first, but I never came last either! If I thought couldn't ride as far as Chase Water and back with Tom, I would've said no when he asked me!"

Mom gave me a sigh, then reluctantly agreed. "Well! If you think you can do it, then do it, Jay! But you make sure you stay with Tom, and not go riding off on your own!"

"Mom, stop fussing! I'm not going to get tired, and I'm not going to get lost!"

"So where did you say you're meeting Tom?"

"At his house, in Allen Rock, Mom!"

"Allen Rock! I don't remember you telling me you've been to his house before?"

"That's because I haven't – and before you ask me if I know how to get there, Mom, I'll be going along Mosely Road to Highgate Road, then over Stratford Road to Walford Road, Then Golden Hillock Road to!!!"

"Okay," said mom before I'd finished. "You've convinced me to mind my own business, but you can't blame me from worrying!"

"I know, Mom!"

*

During the nineteen fifties, the big bands were dominating the airwaves; and programs were ruled by the stiff upper lips; drawing lines across anything deemed tacky or disrespectful. The nineteen sixties began like a gentle breeze that soon became a hurricane, sucking up the stiff upper lips, and replacing them with a new era of music, clothes and talk.

My driving lessons finally began in August, 1961; the same time Lizzie met Sean, her new boyfriend. They were fifteen shillings for each lesson, and I had saved enough money for twenty lessons. All the cars at the school were Ford Anglia's – some of which had so many faults, they should have been banned from the road.

"I am your new instructor, Mr Broadshaw," said the gentleman, totally opposite in appearance to Maison, who had been my instructor for the last six months. After a brief handshake, I followed the stout gentleman to the closest of the Ford Anglia's, then sat in the passenger seat next to him.

Maison's manner always made me feel easy before a lesson, but there was nothing easy about Broadshaw's.

"Where is Mr Maison?" I asked.

"Maison's left the school, I'm taking over his lessons from now on!"

Broadshaw drove the car from under the arch - to the less congested roads circling Birmingham's Town centre. At a quiet stretch of road he pulled along the curb, stopped and walked around the car. "Right, into the driving seat young man; show me how much you've learned?"

I did everything Maison had taught me, and I thought my first fifteen minutes went well.

"At the next available place, I want you to pull over to the curb, stop and turn off the engine?"

Broadshaw sat quietly writing something on his notepad. "How do you think you did?" he asked me while still writing.

"Not too bad!" I answered airing my confidence.

Broadshaw closed the notepad, and half turned toward me. "Well, if you were taking your driving test with me, I would fail you right here and now!"

I felt my cheeks flushing from embarrassment! I thought I'd driven okay, and his comment was not the one I had expected.

"Apart from the few things you did wrong, your driving was acceptable to pass your test. What do you think you did that was an immediate fail?"

I answered, "I don't know," because I didn't!

"You stopped at the Zebra crossings, junctions, and traffic lights nine times. And each time you snatched up the handbrake on the ratchets. Nine times in half an hour, each time wearing down the ratchets tips. Imagine how many times those ratchets are being dragged across each other in one year - two years, or even ten! All it would need for the break to slip on those worn ratchets is a gust of wind, or the vibration of a vehicle driving past. Parked on the flat, maybe the car would roll gently into the curb, or the car behind it! But what if the car was parked on a hill? Then your car would be rolling down at great speed, and we know what would happen then?"

I raised myself a little in the seat, allowing myself to see Broadshaw's notepad when he opened it again.

"I'm not going to discuss your faults with you now; we'll be addressing those as we go along. Maison has gone, and I am here - So when you are ready, drive on please; and from now on you will raise the handbrake with the button pressed in, and released only when fully raised?"

1962

"Okay everyone, it's here!" Dad called to us from the other side of the gate.

Patrick and I were through the gate, running down the entry, and standing on the pavement, while dad was still walking down the entry with mom.

The black shiny motor bike and sidecar, LUN156 was parked along the curb, more beautiful than dad had described to us. The 650cc Triumph was a powerful looking machine; and the enclosed sidecar attached to it was like a small caravan, big enough for to two people to sit in comfortably.

We were walking around the machine, proudly displaying the bike to the people walking along the pavement.

"Is that yours," asked the gentleman walking past with his wife.

"Yes, our dads just bought it." Patrick answered.

The gentleman paused briefly, showing enthusiasm in his words. "I had one just like that - but without the sidecar. Powerful thing it was. It was like sitting on the back of a bull, racing full speed – powerful thing!" The gentleman stood for a few moment until his wife urged him to walk on.

Both mine and Pat's excitement had been fuelled by the gentleman's interest, and our eagerness to ride on it began the moment dad walked from the entry. "It's brilliant, Dad! Can we go for a ride on it now?"

"I think your dad should have more practice riding it on his own for a bit, Patrick!"

"Dads just ridden it all the way from Saltley, Mom. Remember what you said to me when I was going to Cannock with Tom on my bike!"

"I don't know, Jaimie, it might be a bit too soon. What do you think, Hal?"

"I think we should go for a ride, Titch!"

Mom only agreed because she was outnumbered three to one. "Go on then, but not too fast, Hal - not until were all used to it!"

"Patrick you'll have to go in the sidecar with your mom. Jaimie's lanky legs won't fit inside it!"

Dad removing the two old-fashion helmets from the sidecar first, then helped Patrick and mom into the sidecar.

My heart was pumping as dads leg thrust down the starting pedal, waiting for the engine to erupt in a roar of a snorting bull. Dad must have pumped the pedal half a dozen times before conceding it wasn't going to start.

Dad thought no one saw him kick the front tyre in frustration, but Pat's and I did!

"The plugs must be damp, Titch, you'll have to go back to the house while I clean them!"

To add to mom's frustration, as she scrambled out of the sidecar, she banged her head on the roof.

"Don't tell me you've bought a pig in a poke, Hal!" she said straightening her hat.

"You two go with your mom while she's in a mood!"

We'd only walked halfway up the entry, and the sound of an engine on full throttle over took us.

"Dad's started the motorbike, Jaimie," Patrick called while legging it down the entry.

I grasped mom's arm, encouraging her to come with me back down the entry. "Come on, Mom, Dad's got the motorbike started!"

Dad's revving was creating short bursts of power, belching out in smoke from the exhaust pipe, and foolishly he turned the engine off as mom walked on the pavement.

"Come on, Titch, get in the sidecar!"

"It is going to start again isn't it, Hal?"

"Yes it is, now get a move on before it gets dark!"

I sat behind dad again, tightening the strap on the helmet. "What did you do to make it start again, Dad?"

"Nothing, I Just pressed the start pedal, and away she went."

"Are you ready?" Dad called tapping the cellophane window on the sidecar.

Patrick gave dad the thumbs up. And mom just nodded while miming, 'yes get a move on.'

Dad's leg thrust down the starting pedal – then he did it again – and again, with each downward thrust producing the dull sounds of compression.

"That's it, everybody off!" Dad voice with frustrated annoyance.

"What's wrong with it, Dad?" I asked.

"Nothing – there's nothing wrong with it! It's your mom, she's a bloody jinx!"

"Let me know if – and when you've fixed the bike, Hal," mom called, storming off up the entry.

Pat's and I were happy to stay with dad by the bike, even though it wouldn't work.

"I'll try one more time; and if it doesn't fire then, I'll have to take it back to the garage!"

The moment dad's let thrust down the pedal, the bikes powerful 650cc engine burst to life, throbbing like a dragon breathing in and out. Mom hadn't yet reached the end of the entry, so she must have heard it. But she never came back down.

"Right then, who's first for a ride to the lane and back?"

We both put our hands up, but we only wanted to ride on the pillion, not in the sidecar. It was the toss of a coin who went first behind dad, wearing the helmet and goggles.

*

Once every month, Pat's and I paid a visit to 'Rick's Car Sales' along Mosely Road, just opposite Vincent Street. We had almost talked dad into having one, and looking for cars in our price range was a good way of keeping our conversation ongoing. This monthly visit came on Saturday March the 31st 1962.

Coming back from the car sales, Pat's stopped and looked through the window of the pet shop.

"Hey, Jay, look at this?"

I looked through the window, and like Patrick I fell in love with the small dog, barking and whimpering at us from pen inside.

"Ahh, look Pat's, all he wants is someone to love him!"

Pat's walked instantly into the pet shop, with me following. "How much is the dog in the pen?" Pat's asked the person, feeding the cockatoo on the perch.

"Ten shillings, but if you buy her today, you can have her for eight!"

I looked at Pat's, Pat's looked at me and grasped my arm. "Jay, shall we ask mom and dad?"

"Yeah, let's ask them, all they can say is yes or no!"

*

"And - who do you thinks going to feed her, Patrick – take her for walks, pay the vet bills if something happens to her, because I won't be," mom said adamantly.

Any hope of us having the dog now depended on dad, and how convincing we could be to make him say yes.

"We're going to do all that – aren't we Jay?"

"Yes - you and mom won't have to pay or do anything!"

"And how much did you say the dog was?" Dad asked Pat's.

"Ten shillings, but if we buy her today, we can have her for eight!"

"Right then! Providing we won't be the ones left to look after her - and I back the winner of the Grand National this afternoon, I will say you can have the dog!"

Pat's and I were together on the couch, and dad was in the chair opposite, glued to the television, waiting for race to begin.

Dad had placed a one shilling bet on, Kilmore, ridden by Fred Winter to win at twenty eight to one.

Even though mom said she wasn't in the slightest interested who won or not, as the race began she was hovering around the room, while keeping one eye on the television. During the next few minutes, it was a tossup which house in the grove was shouting the loudest, but as the horses past the winning post, ours was the one still shouting.

We were bouncing up and down on the couch, shouting loudly enough for the whole grove to hear. "Dad, you've won – your horse has just won the Grand National!"

"How much have you won, Dad?" I asked so the whole grove could hear that too.

"I'd say about one pound and eight shilling!"

"A pound and eight shilling? So we can get the dog then?"

"As far as I'm concerned you can Pat's – but you'll have to confirm that with your mom first."

*

We were in the house no more than a minute, and mom was walking round with the dog in her arms.

"You like her then Mom," I asked.

"She's lovely, how old did the shop say she was, Patrick?"

"About six months, Mom!"

"What are we going to call her Mom?" I asked.

"Trixie's a nice name," said Pat's.

"Nah, Pat's, everyone calls their dog Trixie. I like Molly' that's a nice name for a dog. Mom."

"We could have called the dog, Fred, after the jockey Fred Winter if it were a he!"

"Well the dog's not a he, Hal, she's a she."

"Yes I know she's a she; that's why I said we couldn't call her, Fred!"

Mom gave dad one of her looks. "Hal if you're going to be awkward over a name, go and put the kettle on the stove.

"I was going to suggest we called her Sally!"

"Sally! That's a nice name!"

*

Since leaving school, Patrick had worked for, Bradleys the butchers on Mosely Road; and on the odd occasion, he came home with scraps of stomach turning offal. Regardless how it looked, mom would always turn it into something really tasty.

"Pat's your brother's in the backyard fiddling with something oily his bike again - and it's all over one of my tea-towels. Just tell him if he does it again he'll have me to answer to."

"Yes, Mom!"

I had just about finished changing the rear break pad, and Pat's came from the lean-to with mom's message.

"Mom said if you put any more oil on her tea towels, you're in trouble."

"That's okay, I'm nearly finished."

Pat's shoved the wooden crate across the purple bricks with his shoe, and sat on the crate next to me. "I've applied for another job, Jay," he said in a casual way.

"Why - you haven't been at Bradleys that long; I thought you liked working there?"

"I do, that's why I've been there nearly a year and a half!"

"Wow, it doesn't seem that long! So why are you looking for somewhere else then?" I carried on adjusting the rear break cable, aware something was not right with my brother. "Well dad won't be happy he's losing his free Sunday meat, Pat's!"

"He'll still have his Sunday meat, Jay, I've applied for a transfer to the butchers shop in Gooch Street. I know the boss Frank. I went to see him last week, and he said he'll put a good word in for me!"

Now I was looking confused. "Pat's, you can walk to the butchers in Mosely Road; you can't walk to the butchers in Gooch Street. Why leave Mosely Road and go to Gooch Street? Dad will want to know why!"

"Because I'm being bullied there - That's why, Jay!"

Now Pat's had my full attention; if anyone knew about being bullied by and adult, I certainly did. "Who's been bullying you?"

"Rick, the manager and Bob!" Patrick rolled down his shirt top, revealing the bruise marks around his neck. "They did this – and this," he said, showing me the bruise marks around the tops of both arms.

My full attention wasn't just been given out of curiosity now, it was being fuelled by anger. "How long have they been doing that, Pat's?"

"What! Throwing me against the wall, with a fist against my head! Or bending my arms behind my back?"

"I was slowly feeling sick from the anger knotting my stomach, and I said. "Both!"

"About six months after I started, when they changed the management!"

"Why didn't you tell me or dad then – when it started?"

"What happened when you told dad about Bennet, beating you up in the gym? It made things worse didn't it?"

Pat's was right - and that's why I never continued on with that question.

"They were calling me Bonehead for everything I did; and when I said something in 'back slang' they both pushed my head against the wall; threatening to break both arms if I said it again!"

"Back slang? What's back slang?"

"The language they use, so customers in the shop don't know what they're talking about!"

"Like what?"

"Like - if a woman came into the shop with nice legs, Rick the boss would say to Bob, 'Ehtta kool the Namow with ecin gells!'

"Can you teach me the back slang, Pat's," I said genuinely wanting to know.

"Yeah, I can, but why?"

"Because when you get the job in Gooch Street, I'm going to stand outside the shop in Mosely road, and I'm going to tell everyone why you left! Then I'm going into the shop, and tell, Rick the manager he's a cowardly bastard in back slang!"

"No you won't, Jay because then we'll both be in trouble with dad!"

*

For a long time now, Lizzie had been going out with the boy she met at the Locarno in Town. It was Jessie's birthday, and she had gone with Jessie to celebrate. His name was Sean, twenty one – the same age as Lizzie, and although he had Irish blood running through his veins, he never have an Irish accent. According to Lizzie, Jessie had fancied Sean's friend, and persuaded Lizzie to dance with Sean, just to make things even. For Jessie it was a few dances only; for Lizzie her meeting with Sean carried on with a few dates, then became a relationship.

"Sean took me to the Odeon in town last night, Mom!"

"That was nice of him, Lizzie; what did you see?"

"West Side Story! It's been on there for nearly a year now. I would never have gone to see it, but Sean insisted I see it with him before it was taken off!"

"What's West Side Story?" I asked Lizzie.

"It's a film about two gangs in America: the Sharks and the Jets! The Jets had this special whistle, to let each other know it was safe to meet! It made the hairs on my arms tingle each time they did it!"

"You mean a whistle like this!" said Pat's, whistling something like a bird in distress.

"No - a whistle like this," she said slapping Patricks hand from his mouth. Lizzie's whistle was like someone being lost in a mist, and was calling for help.

"It's a musical, Jay, you like musicals so you'll love this - and the songs are brilliant," Lizzie released a gentle sigh. "It's the most amazing film I've ever seen, I was almost crying at the end."

"I love Top Hat, that's because I love Fred Astaire and Ginger Rogers, Lizzie." I shrugged both shoulders, showing my indifference to Lizzie's musical. "I love all their musicals – but Top Hat's my favourite – I think!"

"I don't like musicals, I like war films and cowboy films!" said Pat's, looking less interested than I was.

"Well when you've seen this one, you'll love this one too, I guarantee it," continued Lizzie! "Sean's taking me to see it again in the week, Jaimie, you can come and see it with us if you want?"

It was Lizzie's enthusiasm that convinced me into saying. "Okay."

"So when are we going out on the motorbike again, Dad?" said Pat's, asking purely to change the boring subject of musicals.

"You better ask your mom, Son, she's not very happy with the bike at the moment – Are you, Titch?"

"Why aren't you happy with the bike, Mom?" asked Pat's.

"Ask your dad, Patrick, he's the one who bought it!"

"Dad, why isn't Mom happy with the bike?"

Lizzie opened the door to Sean's knock, and grabbed his arm in the doorway. "Come on, Sean, we'll go to the park before I'm dragged into an argument again."

"Bye, nice to see you both again," Sean called, ushered outside and along the path to the gate by Lizzie.

"Mom, if you won't go on the bike, how are we supposed to get to Blackpool?" Patrick's eyes rolled suspiciously to dad. "We ARE still going to Blackpool aren't we, Dad?"

"Well the hotels booked, the routes worked out, so if your mom won't go on the bike, we'll need to book our seats on the charabanc, like - yesterday. Failing that it'll be the train, and that's going to make a hole in our money – again!"

"MOM!"

"MOM!"

"Right then we'll go to the lane and back. But I'm telling you now, Hal, if that bike doesn't start first time, were going by Charabanc!"

*

Our beautiful 650cc Triumph motorbike had been performing well over the following three weeks. Apart from the nail-biting moment when the sidecars wheel dropped into a deep hole, and moms head hit the roof of the sidecar, everything was fine. Dad had spent hours going over our route on the map, with mom always asking dad if knew the way, and dad always telling her he did, and to stop asking.

Patrick and I were just about to go to bed, and the front door flew open with Lizzie calling frantically to dad.

"Dad Sean's been beaten up."

Dad half flew from the chair to the door, taking Sean from Lizzie's arms. "Okay love, I've got him, you go and sit on the couch!"

Mom was clearing the table giving me and Patrick little orders as she did. "Patrick, fetch one of the clean dish cloths from the lean to, and on the way back, grab the first aid box from the shelf."

"Okay, Mom!"

"Jaimie, make sure there's no more than a cupful of water in the kettle, then put it on the stove; don't wait for the water to boil, finger warm will do; wounds need to be cleaned before treating."

Lizzie's sobbing became louder as she sat next to dad on the couch, snuggling herself into his arms.

"Dad - they were like animals, punching and kicking, Sean; I thought they were going to kill him!"

"Well thankfully they didn't, Lizzie - now what happened, why did they set about him?" mom asked.

"We were walking past the chip shop on Mosely Road, Mom, opposite Clifton Road!"

"I know!"

"Sean said he fancied some chips. I didn't want any, but Sean said we could share them while we walked home. Four lads were in there about our age, messing around and swearing. Sean asked them to mind their language in front of a lady, and they gave Sean a funny look as they walked out. They were hanging around outside, and the chip man said we should stay in the shop for a while, just until they had gone - so we did!"

"But they hadn't gone, had they love," said mom tending Sean's wounds.

"No, Mom! The chip man came out to help, but he was pushed back into the shop. They only stopped hitting and kicking Sean when his coat flew open, and they saw his cross and chain!"

I could see the small silver cross, hanging from the chain, and in curiosity I said to Lizzie. "I wonder why they stopped when they saw Sean's chain!"

"Because they were wearing chains too, and they knew Sean was a Catholic."

"Well it's a good job they saw it when they did love," said mom, "Or you'd both be in the hospital now, waiting to have these cuts stitched! Now I'm just going to clean them with this damp cloth and antiseptic! It's going to sting, so no crying like a baby, Sean in front of the lads!"

"I won't, Mrs!!" Sean's attempt to thank mom, was just as confusing as dad's half dozen names; and Sean hesitated between, Colridge, Nellie, or Titch!

"Titch will do fine," said mom kindly. "It's what everyone else calls me!"

Sean's head recoiled away from the cloth the moment it touched a cut. "Whoa, what's on the cloth, Titch?" he said.

"TCP, son – now stop being a cissy, it's how I treat all our cuts here!"

Patrick must have felt quite good he'd never flinched – or whinged when mom treated his cut with TCP!

"Before you go, Sean, I want to give you a little bit of advice," said mom while clearing the table. "In the chip shop, you put Lizzie in danger by being outspoken, when you should have kept quiet. Looking after our daughter doesn't mean confronting people who mean trouble; it's steering her away from trouble that's more important. You use this little incident as an important lesson, Sean – because if you don't, you'll have me to answer to next time. And I can be more brutal than four louts, believe me!"

I saw dad nodding as Sean returned mom's warning with a painful smile; and I nodded too! Mom may have been four feet nothing, but compared to the lads in the chip shop, in one of her moods mom was a force to be reckoned with.

Twenty five

"Hal!" called mom, craning her neck toward the table as she walked past. "How many times are you going to alter that route? I thought you said you had it worked out with Chalky at work!"

"I have got it worked out, Titch. It's been a few years since Chalky drove to Blackpool; it just needed tweaking a bit here and there!"

"But you've been tweaking it here and there for the last two months. Maybe if you'd spent more time tweaking that bike's engine, it wouldn't keep cutting out!"

"How long will it take us to get to Blackpool, Dad?" Pat's asked.

"As the crow flies, about two and a half to three hours, Son!"

"And what if the crow was traveling on the motorbike with us! How long would it be then, Dad?"

Dad shoved the pen scribbled map away from him, pretending to be working out Patrick's question.

"Well – how long, Hal," asked mom.

Dad ignored her, urging mom to say. "Your dad doesn't know, Jaimie; but it's probably double the time your dad will say!"

I heaved a tremendous sigh, because it took me two hours to ride to Chase Water with Tom. Sitting on the bike saddle for two hours gave me a numb bum.

"It's a long way to go on the bike Dad," I said without thinking. "What if it breaks down – like it did on the way back from Cannon Hill Park?"

"You know what, Hal, Jaimie might be right! I'm going to be inside that sidecar with Patrick for - Goodness knows how long – and the thought of being stranded on the side of the road, hundreds of miles from home – Well!!"

Dad slumped wearily into the chair, and unfolded the hand written map flat on the table, "Right! If I go over the route with you now, and you say you would still rather go by Charabanc to Blackpool – then we will - satisfied!"

"Hi, Mom, Hi, Dad, Sean's just dropped me off in his new car. He's got some work to do, so he's coming back later to take me for a pub lunch!"

Lizzie had grown into a great sister. She was the second mom to me and Patrick, and it was hard to imagine that it was only a few years ago, when I was holding her hand, waving at the dragonfly in the ivy along the entry.

"Everyone's looking serious, what are we doing then?" Lizzie asked

"Dad's just about to tell us our route to Blackpool!" said Patrick, "Mom said if we don't like it, were going by Charabanc!"

Lizzie settled herself onto the couch, then emptied the contents of her makeup bag into her lap. "Oh, that's nice!"

"Lizzie, what's Sean's new car like?" I asked craning my neck to look at her.

"A blue one!"

"Sean's new car is a blue one, Patrick" I said tittering quietly behind my hand.

Patrick nudged me while also tittering discreetly.

"Right then, when you two are ready to pay attention I'll start," voiced dad like a school teacher.

"I'm ready now, Dad," I answered, kicking Pat's foot.

"And me," said Patrick, kicking me back.

Dad began by talking us through our journey, while moving his finger along the map. "First we head for the A34 to Perry Bar, then we continue on to Walsall, Cannock, Hednesford Village, and on toward Stafford!"

"Dad, what if it starts raining?" Lizzie suddenly asked – not really caring if it did – or didn't.

Dad's eyes rolled up from the map toward Lizzie. "Now why did you have to mention that?"

"Because if it's raining, you're going to get wet!"

"Lizzie has a point, Hal! No one's mentioned anything about the weather; and what we do if it's raining?"

Patrick's shoulders were lifting on a snigger when he said. "Well we won't care if it's raining, Mom, we'll be in the sidecar nice and dry!"

"Not if we take turns sitting in the sidecar you won't!" I said, trying to remove the smug look on Patrick's face.

"Well you can't, dad said your legs are too lanky!"

"Can we please discuss the route before I put it on the fire," came dad's voice with a hint of exasperation. "The sun could be shining for all we know! And, Lizzie, if you've got any more concerns, keep them to yourself please! Now are we ready to continue?"

The silence was good enough for dad, and again his finger moved along the map.

"So - still on the A34, we go through Stone, then Stoke on Trent towards Newcastle-Under- Lyne, then through a small village called, Kids grove. From there we take the A50 towards, Holmes Chapel, Knutsford, and Warrington. We can stop there for the toilets and something to eat if you want," said dad looking to us all in turn. "Then we take the A49 to Ashton-in-Makerfield, Wigan, and the A6 to Preston. From Preston we take the B6241 toward Cotton Village, then B5411, and, B5269 to Poulton-le-fylde. And the last road we take is the A586, into Blackpool." Dad flopped his hands onto the map, commenting – "There, now you all know how we're getting there!"

I looked at Pat's, and Pat's looked at me, and together we said, "Wow!"

"That sounds like a long way to go by motorbike, Dad," said Lizzie, pursing her lips to apply the lipstick. "I'd prefer going by Charabanc, it would be warmer, and quicker!"

Dad's eyes were not so scathing when he looked at Lizzie this time. "Yes it would, Lizzie, but going by motorbike means we can stop at any one of those Villages and Towns. We can stop and have cups of tea and cake at any one of those if we wanted to! We can make stopping at them a part of our holiday - and we can't do that going by Charabanc!"

"Well, as long as you're happy with the route, Hal," said mom. "I'm happy we can stop when we like. The last time we went to Rhyl on the Charabanc, I almost wet myself before we stopped for a break!"

*

About seven o-clock that evening, Lizzie called in with Sean for an impromptu visit.

"Hi, Mom, Hi Dad!"

"Hello love, we never expected to see you at this time, Hal put on the kettle!"

"No it's alright, Mom, were not stopping long. Sean and I have come to discuss something with you and dad?"

While Lizzie fussed over Sally's welcoming tongue, Mom stood, which she always did when announcements like that were made! "It sounds important, Lizzie?"

"Yes it is, Mom! You know Sean has been talking about us getting married for a while now!"

"Yes, Lizzie."

"Well we've just come from a meeting with Sean's mom and dad. They said if you didn't mind, they would like to pay for the wedding – and everything! They said as they are catholic, and Sean is their only son they would like to do all the arranging.

They said they'd be more than happy for you and dad to be involved!"

Dad was clearly surprised – and in a way relieved – mom however sounded disappointed.

"We know your mom and dad live in a nice house, Sean – a lot better than this house Lizzie lives in. I would hate to think that was the reason for you mom and dad's kind request?"

Sean was about to speak, but Lizzie knew how mom and dad thought. "Sean's mom and dad aren't offering because they think we can't afford it! They're offering because they would like to. You and Mom have done more for this family than any family I know!"

Lizzie was referring to dad, loaning the money to save Pat's life, and will be paying for it for a long time to come.

"Let them do it; you've both already done your bit; and no matter what Sean's mom and dad do, Dad. You're the one who will be walking me down the aisle."

*

Patrick and I were now spending lots of time together. Either we were walking to the lane for new clothes, or riding our bikes, looking for bikes waiting for the rag and bone man to collect.

The bike shed was our workshop, with the salvaged parts from stripped down bikes stored in a wooden box. My bike was built from several bikes, and the only parts we both had to buy were the inner-tubes.

"Dad, what do you think of this bike? It's a little bit bigger than the one I've got, and some of the parts aren't that old?"

Dad's eyes scanned the bikes frame carefully. There was always a reason why bikes were left for the rag and bone man. "There's a hairline crack on both joints," dad said, pointing out the almost invisible lines. "Whoever had this bike must have hit a tree – or a wall!"

"So it's no good then! That's probably why it was on the side of the road."

Patrick was a little peeved by dad's observation. He had helped me carry the wheel less bike from Jakeman Road - in the rain.

"I told you to make sure it was alright, didn't I! People don't throw away bikes if they are any good, Jay!"

"Well it looked good to me; anyway you looked at it as well - and you didn't see the cracks!"

"That's because it was raining! It was you who didn't want to leave it there!"

"Yes, in case the rag and bone man came! And anyway," I said returning the accusations. "Who saw your bike on Russell Road; and who helped you carry it all the way home because the wheels were buckled?"

Dad halted the bickering with some encouraging words. "I'll take it to work and weld the joints on Monday."

"Does that mean you can fix it, Dad?"

"Yes, there's nothing else wrong with it as far as I can see! Apart from the cracked frame and slightly bent forks it'll make a perfectly good bike!"

"You can fix the forks as well?"

"Yes! It'll have to be heated so the paints going to blister!"

"That's okay, Dad, I don't like the colour anyway!"

*

Having good, roadworthy bikes were very important to us. Patrick cycled to work on his, and I could go on little jobs for Andrews; and for that I had one shilling added for each job in my wages. It also meant we could cycle to the park, and meet other kids with their bikes.

My bike was shiny black with silver lines; and chrome cow-horn handlebars that cost a day's wages.

There was a place known to some of the kids, nicknamed Donkeys Hollow in High-burry Park. It was a steep track between trees, and a place where lads went, testing their bikes, and their riding skills.

"Why do you want to go to Donkeys Hollow again, Jay? You rammed your bike into the tree at the bottom last time! You told dad a car ran over your front wheel; what are you going to tell him if you hit the tree again?"

"I'm not going to tell him anything, Pat's, because I won't hit the tree this time!"

"Well I'm not going down it, I've only just finished building my bike!"

"That's okay, you can stay at the top and watch me!"

*

A couple of lad's were already there when we arrived. One was on his bike ready to go down; and the other was hauling his bike to the top with a buckled front wheel.

It was almost a year since I was here last, and the track looked even steeper than I had remembered.

"I hope you've got spares for those posh bikes, because you're gonna' need 'em," said the boy dragging his battered bike toward us. "Hang on," he said staring at me as he got closer. "I've seen you before! You went to Queensbridge!"

"Yeah, about a year ago - and I remember you - your, Barlow!" I said giving him a closer look.

"Yeah, and that's my brother Braiden! You worked in the workshop with Fergusson! You're a lot taller now than you was then - and I bet you got yourself a good job?"

Barlow turned his back on me for good reason; he was one of the lads who bullied lads like me at school.

"Well the tracks got a lot worse since others found out about it! There's a big tree root sticking up halfway down it now! You need to jump your bike over it to miss it!"

"OI YOU, CISSY BOYS, come to see how the big boys do it!" Braiden poised for a moment on the edge

- then he was over, yelling and swerving between the trees. His front wheel reared inches from the root, with the back wheel bouncing him from the saddle. Instantly he dropped into a sideways slide, losing a mudguard scraping the tree. With arms waving, and cries of defiance taunting his brother, he yelled.

"This is how you do it without smashing your bike, Barlow!"

Barlow gave his brother the two fingers sign, then dragged the damaged bike to the trees. "I can't wait for him to smash himself up – then I can laugh at him!"

Now I could see why Barlow was a bully at school; because he was bullied at home. "Patrick I'm not doing it," I said quietly. "The tracks worse than last time, and it's taken me ages to get my bike looking like this!"

"Hang on a minute, Jay, I didn't want to come; you're the one who wanted to. I'm here now and I'm not having those kids thinking I'm a cissy!" Patrick shuffled his bike around me to the edge of the drop. "I'll be waiting for you at the bottom!"

Patrick threw himself over the edge, slewing the bike around the trees with his legs carving lines in the mulch. His front wheel half lifted, and the rear bounced off the root, almost throwing him from the saddle. How he missed the tree at the bottom would forever remain a mystery, but there he was, standing at the bottom, waving both arms. "Come on, it's not that hard,"

Braiden half sauntered past me with the smirk on his face I didn't like. "Go on then posh boy, you're little brothers done it! Now let's see you do it - you don't want him thinking you're afraid – unless you are!" Braiden walked his bike toward his brother, kicking the buckled wheel hard. "I'm not helping you to replace that," he said, hovering to see what I was going to do.

I wasn't fearing for myself when walked my bike to the edge of the drop; it was the fear of having to push my battered bike back home, and facing dad I feared most.

Patrick was still waving at the bottom; and without giving myself time to think myself out of it, I was speeding down the track, slewing my precious bike around the trees either side. As the root came toward me, I jumped from the saddle, allowing my wheels to bounce over the root without any weight. At the last moment, I threw my bike to one side, missing the tree by a hairs width. From being on the top, and standing next to Patrick took seconds, and I was yelling up. "That's the way you do it, Braiden; you hit the tree and I didn't!"

That was the last time Pat's and I went there - And the last time either of us saw Braiden or Barlow.

"I can't believe you actually did that, Pat's," I said cycling beside him up Edward Road. "Kids who've been going there for ages smash their bikes up! I can't believe you did it for the first time - and all your bikes got is a few scratches! My handlebars are loose," I said waggling them back and forth. "And my saddles all skew whiff!"

"I think you've got a puncture as well," said Patrick, pointing out my deflating rear wheel.

"Great - and I only bought it last week!"

*

"So what will you be doing while we're in Blackpool?" Mom asked Lizzie, purely out of interest again.

"Sean's taking me out on day trips in the car! I know were going to Stratford and Evesham; I don't know where we're going after that!"

"Are you sure you don't want to come with us to Blackpool," mom asked Lizzie for the umpteenth time. "Your dad and the boys want to go on the motorbike, but if you wanted to come we'd go by Charabanc – which to be honest, I wouldn't mind!"

"I did ask Sean, Mom, but he wasn't too keen. He said he'd rather save for the wedding, and take me to different places. He said if we went to one I didn't like, he'd take me to another one I did like! I thought that was really nice of him to do that!"

"Yes it was – it was very thoughtful!" Mom continued busying herself, talking as she did. "And how is the wedding going since you haven't spoken about if for a while!"

"It's going okay, Mom, everything's booked and paid for."

"Well it's too late to come with us now even if you wanted to, Lizzie were going on Saturday!"

I came in just as Lizzie was about to go out; making it one of those rare moments when we saw each other now.

"You look taller every time I see you, Jay!"

I gave a slight laugh! "Yeah, it must be the cabbage water mom makes us drink!"

"Mom still gives you that? Mom – you're still giving Jaimie and Patrick cabbage water?"

"Of course, it helps to keep the colds away! And I'd be giving it to you too, Lizzie – if you were here long enough for me to give it you; unfortunately we scarcely see you these days!"

Lizzie gave mom one of her, 'thank you smiles' then slid past me through the door. "Oh, I just remembered; when I passed dad by the bike, he told me to tell you he's fixed the problem."

I watched while Lizzie walked to the gate a fully grown woman. Lizzie had become one without me even noticing, and somehow it felt I'd lost the sister I knew. "Yeah, I meant to tell you dad fixed the problem with the bike this morning, Mom. He said it was the spark plugs, and he's changed them for new ones. He said it will definitely start first time now!"

Mom's melancholy look disappeared at the name, motorbike. "Your dad said that about the battery and the plug leads, Jaimie! You go and tell him if it makes so much as a splutter while I'm wedged in that sidecar, he'll be going to Blackpool on the bike, and I'll be going on the Charabanc! He's had nothing but trouble with it since he had it. The one who sold it to him must have been rubbing his hands when they saw him – don't tell you dad I said that!"

"I paused in the doorway, feeling mom's emotion myself. "You don't have to worry about looking after Lizzie now you know, Mom! She's got Sean to look after her now. Oh - I forgot to mention, Mom, I think Sean and Lizzie are looking for the wedding ring."

Mom turned her eyes quickly toward me, with the look of surprise in them. "They never mentioned anything to me, or your dad about it; what makes you think they are?"

"Because Lizzie went with him to have her finger measured a couple of weeks ago."

"And you never thought to mention that till now!"

"No, because I only overheard it, and I'm not supposed to know. I'm only telling you now to stop you worrying about her!"

Mom was looking at me, but she was lost in a moment of thought. "Okay – thank you Son; go and tell your dad I'll be down in a minute – and tell him woe betide him' if that bike doesn't start! First time!"

"Okay, Mom!"

Twenty six

"Blackpool, here we come! I hope it's going to be a nice day today, Dad," I said looking at the rainclouds! Did you fill the tank up?"

"Yes, Son!"

"The tyre on the sidecar looked a little flat yesterday, Dad; did you use the pump and put some air in?"

"Yes, Son, stop mithering about the bike, you sound like your mom!" Dad walked round the bike, checking the straps around the cases; and I donned my helmet, goggles and waterproofs.

Before I'd seated myself behind dad, one of the policeman from the station stopped and talked to us.

"I see you found the problem with the bike then; what was it - mechanical?" he asked giving the bike the once over.

"No - Just about everything electrical!"

"Yes, mine was the same. So where are you off to?"

"Blackpool!"

The gentleman in uniform stood nodding his head, while rolling his eyes toward the clouds. "It's a fair sized journey to Blackpool in a car, never mind on a bike. Drive carefully and I hope you all have a good holiday!"

Dad thrust down the starting pedal, and the engine fired instantly.

The uniformed gentleman gave me a smile before walking off, which I took for a sign of sympathy.

"Are you okay on the back," dad asked me.

"Yes, Dad, great!" I waved to mom and Pat's in the sidecar, and mom waved back. Patrick laughed at me, pointing at the dark clouds, and mimicking how warm and comfy he was being in the sidecar.

I mouthed something back to Patrick dad would have slapped me for – if he'd heard it!

*

So far the weather had held up, and we were flying nicely along the A34 at fifty miles an hour toward Stoke on Trent. I was now suffering from a numb bum for sitting so long, and every now and then I lifting myself from the saddle.

For the last few miles, Patrick had been goading me with a chocolate bar, waiting for me to look at him before taking another mouthful. It was when the first drops of rain splattered on my goggles I got really angry. I really wanted to thrust my hand through the flimsy screen, and expose him to the elements too; and if mom hadn't been in there with him I would have.

"Dad, when are we stopping to stretch our legs?" I shouted.

Either dad couldn't hear me, or he was ignoring me, so I shouted again. *"DAD. I NEED TO GO TO THE TOILET - AND STRETCH MY LEGS!"*

Dad acknowledged me this time, pointing to the sign, Stoke Town centre.

*

The joy of feeling blood surging through my backside again was indescribable; and for a moment I was walking like a puppet on strings. The ominous clap of thunder overhead came second to the feeling returning to my legs; and strutting back to the bike with dad, carrying a bag of doughnuts, and four cups of tea in cardboard cartons felt good.

"The weather doesn't look promising, does it, Hal?"

Dad heaved a disappointing sigh before answering mom. "No, it doesn't, Titch! Perhaps we should have come by charabanc like you wanted!"

"Well it's no good saying that now, is it, Hal! It's a good job I made you cover the cases in the plastic sheet, you wouldn't have if I hadn't told you to!"

"How many miles to Blackpool now, Dad?" I asked, hoping for a distance that wasn't too far.

"How many miles? We're not even halfway there yet, Son!"

We'd finished drinking our tea and eating our doughnuts half an hour ago, but remained under the shops canopy until the rain eased up a little.

I felt Patrick's elbow gently nudging me - "What!"

"I can't wait till I'm back in the sidecar, all nice and warm, Jay," Pat's said to me in a whispering voice.

"Yeah, well you're not in the sidecar yet, Pats! – Dad!" I called, turning away from Patrick's tormenting smirk. "I'm only a few inches taller than Patrick; I think he should go on the back of the bike now, and I can sit in the sidecar with mom, there's plenty of room for my legs!"

"Yes, but Jaimie's forgotten about the case inside the sidecar, Dad! You know - the one wedged between me and mom on the floor!" Patrick was pretending to be concerned about the case, but I could see him laughing deep inside.

"Okay then I'll put the case on my lap, Dad," I said. "There's no reason why I can't have the case on my lap!"

"Ahh - but then the case would be touching the sidecars roof, Dad. When we were coming from the lane with bags of shopping, you said it was dangerous having bags of shopping on my lap in case we crashed. That's why I had the shopping on the floor between me and mom – right mom," said Patrick, securing his seat in the sidecar.

"Yes, Patrick!" Mom answered, losing the will to look happy.

Patrick's shoulders were rocking from a silent titter; and whether I liked it or not, I would be the one on the back of the motorbike, exposed to the elements like dad.

*

Three thirty, and I had my first glimpse of Blackpool tower. It had taken us six hours to get here, and all I wanted to do was feel the ground beneath my feet again. Thankfully from, Poulton- le-fylde it had been rain free, and the sun was bouncing its light from the waves Blackpool.

Our boarding house was the Lomax along Barton Avenue. It was half way between the south pier, and the pleasure beach, ten minutes from the front. The frontage was immaculately painted in white, with hanging baskets either side of the door. The sign - Lomax, over the hotel doors was the holy grail of our journey; and while dad was doing a few knee-bends next to the bike, I asked him quietly.

"Dad, what's wrong with the bike?"

"What do you mean?"

"Well the bike was making a funny smell like something was burning just before we got here."

"Shush, keep your voice down, Son," dad said, easing me away from the bike! "We've only been here two minutes, and the last thing I want is your mom hearing something bad said the bike! Anyway, what makes you think there's something wrong with it; it got us here didn't it?"

I just nodded in agreement, because dad was already stressed. And he didn't have to say anything, because the smell from the bike said it all.

"Now while I untie the cases, help your mom out of the sidecar, please - if she hurts herself again getting out, she'll blame me for that too!"

We walked in file to the reception, and dad jingled the bell on the counter.

"Hello, and welcome to Lomax, can I have your name please?" said the kindly woman, with an appearance of someone who lived by the sea.

"Colridge," said dad.

"Yes, you are in rooms fifteen and seventeen, on the third floor."

While dad waited for the keys, my eyes were scrutinising the decor surrounding me. Everything from the beautiful lush carpet, to the ornate coving on the ceiling was displaying the elegance of a time gone bye. The banister alone was magnificent, built in a time gone by for the wealthy and class.

"The restaurant is just through those doors, and breakfast is served between eight and ten. The gong will sound when the doors are open. Thank you for choosing, Lomax, and I hope you enjoy your stay here!" On the shelf are leaflets to what's on, and where to go, and I thoroughly recommend an evening at the tower circus!"

*

"Now you two, don't you go treating this room like your bedroom back home; keep it clean and tidy, and no hanging your socks out of the window! That reminds me, how many pairs of socks did you pack?"

"Plenty, Mom, stop fussing!"

"Good, well when you've finished unpacking, we'll go along the prom and have something to eat!" Mom closed the door, and at once I was rummaging amongst my clothes in the suitcase.

"How many socks did you pack," I asked, Patrick.

"I didn't!"

"I didn't either!"

*

335

By the time we'd eaten in the cafe on front, the sun was dipping beyond the horizon. The lamps were coming on along the prom; and every few minutes a tram full of passengers clanged along, with its headlights lighting up the track ahead.

Some holiday makers had chosen the alternative way to travel along the prom; ferried in style on horse drawn carriages

By seven o-clock the front was heaving with holiday makers, heading directly to the pleasure beach. Those with young children were walking in the opposite direction, dragging tired and irate children, clutching half eaten sticks of pink candyfloss back to their lodgings.

The closer we walked to the pleasure beach, the louder came the sounds of enjoyment. Music from the rides were competing with screams and the air was electric with anticipation.

With the smell of fish and chips, and freshly made doughnuts filling my nostrils, Patrick gave me a sideways nudge before asking dad. "Dad, are you and Mom coming on the Grand National with us?"

"No, Son! The first thing your mom and I are doing is finding that cafe, and have a nice cup of tea!"

"But we only had a cup of tea an hour ago, Dad!"

"And we'll be having another at the cafe in the pleasure beach, Son!"

Patrick and I had come to the pleasure beach for the rides, and we didn't want to spend the time in the café, waiting for another cup of tea. "Well while you're looking for the cafe, Dad, Pat's and I will be going to the Grand National?"

"If that's what you want," said mom - without argument. "I just thought we'd have a cup of tea before we all went on it together!"

I turned and continued my walk backwards. "You and dad are going on the ride with us?"

"And why not, Jaimie," said mom, slightly peeved at my lack of enthusiasm. "Do you think your dad and I are too old for rides like that?"

"No – I don't think that!"

Now Patrick was walking backwards, showing more enthusiasm than I had. "Well I think its great mom and dad want to go on it with us, Jay! But I think we should all go on the ride first, and the losers buy the tea and cakes!"

"Well I hope you've both bought enough money then; because you're buying the tickets," said dad, finishing on a false laugh.

On the left, the clown was slowly turning the twin Ferris wheels, while on the right, Noah's Ark was rocking gently back and forth, with animated animals travelling in two's around the huge shaped rock.

"This is a lot bigger than the fair at Rhyl, Pat's!"

"Yeah, I know, great aint it!"

*

Rides such as the Big Dipper, Maxim's flying Rockets, The Mono Rail, and Alice in Wonderland had huge queues. Even the toilets had queues. We'd only been standing in the queue for the Grand National a few minutes, and mom decided she had been there long enough.

"Hal, it's going to be a long wait before it's our turn! My feet are aching, so would you mind if we left the boys here, and looked for the cafe?"

"I told you those shoes you bought were no good for walking; I don't know why you didn't bring the ones you already had, they were perfectly good enough, Titch?"

"Hal, you'd wear shoes with the soles flapping off if I didn't throw them away!"

"Yes, and look where it's got you changing yours – aching feet?"

"Are you coming with me to the cafe, Hal; or do I have to go on my own?"

"Dad relented in favour of the cafe – and mom nagging him for the rest of the evening.

"Right then you two! Keep our tickets safe, your mom and I are going to the cafe – before she accuses me of being inconsiderate again!" Dad glanced quickly at his watch. "The time is now quarter past seven! We'll be at Noah's Ark waiting for you at – Nine! If you're not there by then, your mom will be panicking and giving me grief, which means I'll have to go and look for you, which means leaving her on her own, which she won't be happy about either!"

"Hal, shut up?"

"That's alright, Dad," I said, happy to be left and do whatever we wanted. "We'll just go on a few rides, and have a walk around – won't we Pat's?"

"Yes, just a few rides, and a walk around!"

"Right then – nine o-clock - and no later!" Dad grasped mom's arm, and left us to our own devices.

The Grand National was a three minutes ride, and the trains could hold up to eighteen people. All mom had to do was wait fifteen minutes, and she'd be on the ride with us.

Pat's and I never went anywhere unless our attire was immaculate! We always wore suits, with tapered trousers, and single buttoned jackets. Our white shirts had rounded lapels, and our ties were either bootlace, or the narrow slim-Jim, clasped behind by the gold plated collar pin.

Unbeknown to me, Patrick had been watching two teenage girls keeping pace with us from outside the queue. They were smiling at Pat's when looking our way, and whispering when they weren't. "Hey, Jay! Ehttakool the oat lrig's?"

"Where!" I said, remembering what it meant, and looking in the wrong direction.

"*THERE!*" whispered Pat's louder, while rolling his eyes at two girls looking our way. One was in jeans and short jacket, and the other in loose fitting trousers and a fluffy coat.

"I gave them both one of my cheesy smiles, then looked away, more interested in the ride ahead.

"Well!" said Pat's digging an elbow into my side.

"Well what?"

"They're whispering - and they keep looking at us!"

"Well stop looking at them back! We've only just got here, Pat's, we've got all week to pull the girls"

"I can't, Jay, they're really nice!"

"Yes I know, and they've probably got boyfriends who've gone to the toilets. If you're ogling them when they come back, you'll end up with a fat lip on our first day!"

I was still aching from our long wet journey here; all I wanted to do was go on a couple of rides, go back to our digs and chill out in the bar. "Let's just have a couple of rides before we meet mom and dad!"

"I don't think so, Jay - they walking toward us!"

"Hello! I'm Harriet," said the first girl, talking loudly from the noise around us. "This is my friend, Julia! What's your name?"

"Patrick, but everyone calls me pat's," said my brother, slobbering like a horse on heat.

"And what's yours?" she asked me, bringing her mousy long hair closer to me as she spoke.

"Jaimie," I responded.

"And what does everyone call you?"

"Yay," I responded, lacking in enthusiasm.

"You both look nice - We haven't seen you here before - you must be on holiday?"

"Yes we are," said Patrick still drooling at the mouth. "You both look good too!"

Julia giggled before replying. "We've made a bet you come from the midlands," she said, sideways glancing toward her friend Harriet.

"Yeah we are - from Birmingham!"

Julia giggled again. "I thought you did, I recognised the - Beermingum accent!" she said in the same a poor imitation as Bernie at Golden Sands.

"So where do you come from?" I asked, Harriet, not really caring where the giggling girls came from.

"From Blackpool, silly, don't you recognise our accent?"

"Oh, so you live here – then?" I answered showing no interest whatsoever in how they spoke either. "I suppose you're going to tell us living here, in the fresh sea air, walking on the sands every day is better than where we come from!"

"No I wasn't actually," said Harriet. "Boy your friend's grumpy - is he always like this," she said turning her eyes to Pat's.

"Na, not really! Every holiday we've been on, people have taken the piss when we tell them where we've come from! People think they're better than us because we come from a place with chimneys and smog, and we only see the sea once a year. We don't sound anything like people think we do, do we Jay!"

I just nodded because I couldn't have put my peed off attitude any better.

"Julia! When was the last time we went on the sands, or paddled in the sea?"

"Hmm, Christmas day with our mom and dad I think, Harriet!"

"See, Birmingham boys! We live by the sea – but that's it! We don't go to the beach every day because it's boring! And come the winter almost everywhere on the front is closed. We only come here to watch the visitors having fun – don't we, Julia?"

Patrick nodded toward mom and dad's tickets in my pocket, and before I could say no, Pat's was speaking for me. "We've got two spare tickets; if you want you can come on the Grand National with us!"

"Really?" said Julia in surprise.

"Yes - we don't mind - do we?" said Pat's nudging me again.

"Thank you! But your friend doesn't seem too keen though!"

"He's my brother, he's alright when he gets to know you!"

"He's not like you then?"

Patrick smirked when he looked at me, and I gave him a warning smirk back.

"So how many times have you been on the ride?" Harriet asked, joining us in the queue.

"We haven't, this is our first time in Blackpool!"

Harriet grasped Julia's arm, saying in delight. "Blackpool virgins, Julia! This is going to make the ride even better!"

"OI YOU! STOP PUSHING IN - WAIT YOUR TURN IN THE QUEUE LIKE EVERYONE ELSE!"

Pat's and I turned together, confronting the voice over the heads waiting behind us.

"THEY'RE NOT PUSHING IN, THEY'RE WITH US – OKAY!" Patrick and I waited for the response; then faced ahead when one never came.

Pat's winked at me when Harriet snaked her arm around mine. I was just swaying my head when Julia curled her arm around his.

*

Harriet and Julia had somehow secured the first seats carriage; and the moment the train rolled forward under maze of wooden beams, the girls snuggled up to us.

To think that this morning we were in Birmingham, and this afternoon we were on a train with two girls snuggling up to us was unreal. As our train climbed the steep, 'Lift Hill,' the girls began waving and shouting to the gobby boys on the other train.

"YOU'RE ON THE WRONG TRAIN, THIS ONE'S THE FASTEST, LOSERS!"

Their comments were returned with two fingered gestures.

For few seconds the train rolled along top, curving slightly left toward the sign above saying, 'THEY'RE OFF; then the track suddenly disappeared, and the train dropped almost vertical toward the infamous double dip. While the girls were screaming like everyone else, waving their arms in the air, I was glad to see Patrick doing the same as me, gripping the safety guard, with a wild look distorting his face. The train dipped and climbed along the track, racing at forty-five miles an hour through 'Becher's Brook,' 'Valentines,' 'Canal Turn,' and on toward the,

'Winning Post. I offered a silent prayer when the train rolled under the arch to the finish.

Harriet, and Julia were grasping our arms until we left the ride, then they both stood in front of us, with their arms around each other.

"Thank you that was great!" said Harriet.

"Yes, it really was! So what are you going to do now," Julia asked.

"Well, we were going to walk around the fair for an hour. Come with us if you want!" Patrick asked them, hoping for a yes.

"We can't, we have to go now – Err, you couldn't lend us half a crown for our bus fare home?" Julia asked Patrick, showing no embarrassment from asking.

"Yeah, 'cause we can," said Patrick, who knew he hadn't the loose change to give her.

I only had one shilling and thru-pence in my pocket, and reluctantly I eased out the ten shilling note from my wallet. "You can have this!"

Julia linked arms with Harriet, gave us a smile, and began to walk away. "We sometimes meet at the laughing man by the funhouse." Julia called.

"Or by the Pirate supporting the Mono-rail!" called Harriet. "Maybe you'll see us at one of those again!"

As the girls walked away, I turned to Patrick. "You know they've just taken us for a ride – And I don't mean on the Grand National – and you owe me five shillings!"

"For what?"

"For the ten shilling note I gave them!"

"Well they asked for half a crown! You're the one who gave them ten shillings!"

"No, they asked you for the half a crown, Pat's; they didn't ask me! And next time you fancy a girl with a friend, don't ask me to go with her. You find your own, and I'll find mine!"

"The trouble with you, Jay is you're too fussy!"

"Pat's, you'll go with anything that smiles at you!"

"Well that's better than being too fussy! You're not going to finding anyone; and you'll end up and old man, sitting in a rocking chair all on your own!"

"GOOD!"

"GOOD!"

"And you still owe me five shillings!"

"Okay, we'll come back tomorrow, and I'll bet you the five shillings you don't find anyone you like!"

"And if I do!"

"Then I'll give you ten shillings!"

"Deal!"

"Deal!"

*

"Right, Titch, what do you want to do first," dad asked, soaking up the remains of his breakfast with a slice of toast.

"Pleasure Beach," said Patrick, kicking me under the table.

"Yeah, the Pleasure Beach."

Mom's answer to that was, "We haven't come here to spend every day at the Pleasure Beach, Patrick;

we've been there once, and there's other things to see before we go there again!"

Patrick kicked me hard on the shins, and I kicked him back again. "Okay then, Mom, you and dad do you want; Jaimie and I will go to the Pleasure Beach!"

"But all the rides will be closed until later on in the day, Patrick!"

"That's alright, Mom, we can just walk around till then, can't we, Jay?"

"And is this how you two are going to spend your holiday? Wondering around the Pleasure beach in the mornings, and spending your money there in the evenings?"

I shrugged when Patrick shrugged; drawing dad into the debate by upsetting mom.

"So, if you two want to spend every waking moment at the Pleasure Beach together. That's okay then; but don't either of you come to me or your mom when your money runs out – and it will, trust me it will!"

"But you just like walking around, and going in the shops with mom, Dad!"

"And what's wrong with that, Patrick?"

"Nothing's wrong with that, Dad; but we do that back home, we don't want to spend all week doing it here as well!"

Mom and dad eased back their chairs simultaneously, and walked from the restaurant. "You two do whatever you want; we're going to the Tower – Hal," said mom, pursuing her conversation up the stairs. "We'll go to the ticket office first, and book our seats for the circus! Then we'll go in the Tower, I'd like to look at the famous Tower ballroom while we're here!"

"And if you're not too scared of heights, Titch, we could go in the lift to the top; I would imagine the view of Blackpool is fantastic from up there!"

"It's going to be a nice day today I think, Hal. When we come from the Tower we'll have a stroll along the pier, there might be a cafe on there we can have tea and cake!"

"On the way back, Tick, I'd like to go in the waxworks; I've been told the waxwork figures are so realistic, their eyes follow you as you walk past them! I wouldn't mind going down to the chamber of horrors either!"

Mom's laugh was more of a huff than a laugh. "Well, I'll be waiting for you at the top if you do!"

As mom and dad's conversation continued to their room, my thoughtful silence continued into ours. For as long as I could remember, our holidays by the sea was us doing everything together – as a family. Nothing could prevent us from growing up, and wanting to go our own way! But that didn't mean us doing it right now - here at Blackpool. After fifteen minutes in our room, we made our way toward mom and dad's room.

"Can we come in?" I said knocking the door twice.

Dad turned the lock from the inside, saying. "Come on in, boys, your mom and I are fully clothed now!"

"Hal, do you have to be so course?"

"Mom, Dad, Pat's and I want tell you something!"

"I know - don't tell me," said dad, continuing to get ready to go out. "You both lost your wallets on the rides last night; now your both skint, and you want to know if I can lend you some to go to the fair again!"

"No!" I said adamantly. "We've been having a talk, and while were in Blackpool we'd rather do things with you and mom - instead of on our own!"

Mom never said anything, but her eyes were smiling under her bandana. Dad however didn't look surprised at all, he just looked relieved.

*

"See, I told you we were doing the right thing, Pats," I said emptying the contents of my suitcase on the bed.

"But what about the girls, Jaimie? We could've met them under the mono rail - or by the laughing man like they said!"

"They were never going to be there, Pat's," I said, straitening my slim Jim tie in the mirror. "They were just looking to have fun - with someone like us paying for it!" We both took turns spraying our hair with Cossack hair spray, welding our hair to our heads.

"They live here, and they're probably walking around with some else now. Anyway, Pat's," I said, securing the brass tie stud to my shirt collar. "It sounds like it'll be more fun with mom and dad – and we won't be paying for anything either!"

*

We were in the ticket office, waiting to buy tickets for the circus, and on the wall was the program displaying: George and Alfred Black presents: The big show of 1962 at the Opera House. On the program were, The Derek Taverner Singers, The Malcolm Goddard Dancers, Barbara Law, The Kay Sisters, Ken Dodd, The Three Houcs, The Rain Drops, Eddie Calvert and his C Men, John Padley, Wendy Cameron, Sandra Short, John Harmer, John Frost, and Jimmy Currie's Fabulous Silver Cascade.

With a little more encouragement from Pat's and me - and the offer of paying half for our tickets, we booked that too.

We had done, and seen everything mom and dad wanted through the week. At the Tower circus we were entertained by the slapstick comedy of Charlie Cairoli; and amazed when the lion tamer appeared inside the quickly caged ring, performing tricks with three tigers and a lion with the crack of a whip. We'd been to the top of the Tower, giving us a breath-taking view of Blackpool; walked on the piers, and gone with dad to the chamber of horrors.

During the whole week we'd only peed off mom and dad once; and that was when Patrick bought a whoopi cushion from the joke shop. Each time we walked past a group of girls, Pat's released the sound of someone farting – following with the comment, "Phwar! That was a good one!"

After having dinner in our favourite cafe on Friday, we all walked along the front one more time to the

Pleasure Beach. There were no plans to go any rides from either of us this time! It was just going to be a casual walk around, watching the thrills and spills of the huge entertainment park taking place around us.

We were preparing to take our last walk to Barton Avenue, and amongst the crowd I saw, Julie and Harriet walking arm in arm with two boys toward the ticket office. I just followed behind mom and dad with only one thing on my mind - The long journey home in the morning back to Birmingham.

*

Ten o-clock Saturday morning we were outside Lomax preparing to leave. We had given out our hugs and kisses to the people we had made friends with during our stay; and I was in my waterproofs, waiting for mom and Patrick climb into the sidecar.

"Are you worried about the bike getting us home, Dad?"

"Ask me that when we get to Birmingham!"

Dad fired up the motorbike first time, and straggled the seat while adjusting his goggles. "We'll stop at the first garage and top up the tank," shouted dad.

I tapped dad's shoulder in response.

*

Last Saturday we travelled to Blackpool through cold wind and rain; going back the sky was clear, and the air beating against my face was tinged with warmth. When we stopped at Stoke again, dad and I had discarded our waterproofs for the rest of the journey home.

We were on the A34, traveling through Walsall, and the acrid smell of burning came from beneath us again. The bike was struggling to keep speed and dad steered us toward the curb and turned off the engine.

"That's the smell we had just before we reached Blackpool, Dad!"

"Yes I know!"

"Do you know what it could be?"

"From the smell, I'd say it was the clutch!"

I hadn't a clue what a clutch was, so I just stared at the engine next to dad. "What will we do if it won't get us home?"

Dad's chest inflated while breathing in the air, then deflated on a huge weary sigh. "Your mom's tapping the window! Go and tell her we're just resting the engine for a bit; and for Christ's sake, do not let her leave the sidecar."

"Okay, Dad!"

"Jay, why have we stopped - what's that funny smell? And why is your dad looking like he's carrying the whole world on his shoulders," asked, mom the moment I opened the door.

"Dad said the engines tired, and he's just resting it for a bit, Mom!"

"Well you go and tell him the bikes been resting all week. All I want to do now is get home so I can rest now! Tell him he can rest the engine for as long as he likes then, but not now on the side of the road, miles from home!"

Mom began to leave the sidecar. "No, Jaimie, I'll do it, he won't listen to you!"

"Mom, it's okay, I'll do it!" I said, pushing mom back onto her seat.

Pat's was sniggering while my lie unfolded; and I discreetly showed him my fist.

"Dad, either try and get the bike going again, or tell mom it won't! She just tried to get out of the sidecar!"

"Right, Son it's cooled down enough; get back on the bike before she does!"

*

The rest of the journey was stopping and starting, giving time for the heating clutch to cool in between. What should have taken five hours to get home, took seven. And was dad relieved when we finally pulled up next to our entry, and turned off the engine for the last time.

Mom unfolded from the sidecar without a word to dad, and walked up the entry like someone who had been riding a horse for hours. Pat's and I stayed to help dad unpack, and I was glad our holiday was truly over.

Three days after coming home from Blackpool, our 650cc Triumph motorbike- with sidecar was towed away by the garage dad had sold it to for a pittance, and Lizzie came in with Sean, announcing their wedding date.

Twenty seven
1963

During the sixties, teenagers were drawn to fads and crazes, often following what film was being showing in the pictures. Goodness knows where smoking cigarette tobacco in a clay pipe came from, but Pat's and I did it. Camel Cigarette's-which came in a soft packet were a favoured choice to look cool; offering cigarettes without touching them, flicked up from the pack.

Cigarette's called 'Star' were twice the length of an ordinary cigarette, and could only be bought in singles from a tobacco shop in the Town centre. And offering your mates a cigarette from a silver plated cigarette box, lined in red silk was a must to have.

Around this time, a dance called the: Bossa Nova was making its name at Carnegie Hall-New York; and in 1962 it came to the dance halls in Birmingham. Since then it was a dance everyone wanted to learn, including me!

Since leaving school, Pat's and I had drifted apart a little. He was spending more time with friends, doing the things he liked – which was not doing the things I liked.

After finishing work on Fridays, I always went first to the barbers on Edward road. Having my hair blow dried for the weekend was the weekly event I never missed. After that it was watching Oh Boy on the television, having my tea, then getting ready for the Locarno Ballroom on Hurst Street in Town. Wearing a suit shirt was acceptable, wearing a tie was mandatory; if the bouncer on the door saw someone wasn't wearing one they would not be allowed in.

My Saturday's were all about shopping for clothes – and getting ready for the Ritz, York Road in Kings Heath on the evening. The Ritz was the opposite of going to the Locarno. Tight jeans, tea shirts, winkle pickers - and leather jackets were the requirements for an evening of heavy rock and roll. But this Saturday I had made different plans. I was going to learn the Bossa Nova at Lora Dixons dance school - and I was hoping to take Pat's with me!

"So what are you two doing to today?" asked Mom.

I answered mom first. "Well first I'm going shopping for some new winkle-pickers! Mom, I've seen some shoes in the shoe shop down the lane; they're white leather and look brill!

"And what about you, Patrick, what are you doing?"

I think mom was more concerned about Patrick's movements than mine. A few months ago he came home about ten o-clock, looking as though he'd slid down a muddy bank.

"Well - what are you up to today?" mom asked Pat's again.

Pat's shrugged away mom's question, with a bored, "Don't know yet! Archie's been grounded again – So I don't know yet!"

"Come with me down the lane, Pat's," I said. "There's a sale on in the shoe shop; I'll buy you some new winkle pickers, those have almost had it," I said, looking at shoes that had seen better days. "I've had a ten shilling rise at work, so I've got some money saved!"

"The shoes I've got are okay," said Pat's shrugging off my offer. "Anyway I'd only get new shoes dirty later!"

"Dirty doing what?" I asked mom curiously.

"Things!"

"Things like what?"

"Things like playing football," Pat's answered rattled by my persistence.

"Well couldn't you play football in old shoes," mom asked. "Then it wouldn't matter if they got dirty or not Patrick! You don't' see Jaimie getting his shoes in the state you get yours in!"

"No you don't, Mom," Pat's answered her a little rattled. I'm not like Jay, and Jay's not like me! Jay's been in the cubs, the scouts, and the life boys! Jay paints pictures, writes stories, and makes things, like the big galleon he made and he kept in the posh room. I couldn't paint pictures, write stories, or make things like him, Mom! But I can run faster than you Jamie, I'm better at snooker and darts than you; and I've always beaten you playing chess, haven't I?"

I just shrugged, allowing Pat's to have his opinion of me. "That's okay, Pat's; I was going to ask you if you wanted to come to Laura Dixon's with me this afternoon!"

Pat's gave me look more even more disdainful. "Laura Dixon's - but that's a dance school?!"

"Yeah, I know!"

"I'm going to any dance school with you! My mates would laugh at me doing something like that! Anyway, Jay, why do you want to go there; you tell everyone you can rock and roll?"

"To learn the Bossa Nova, Pat's! It's all the rage now; all the girls are dancing it at the Lacarno!"

Patrick made clear his dislikes this time, by emphasising each work he spoke. "Jay, I've told you – I-don't-like dancing-I'd rather play football; and I wouldn't go to Laura Dixon's even if I did!"

Mom huffed. "Now that's you just saying no to something you haven't tried, Patrick!"

"That's okay I was going on my own anyway, Mom, its Pat's loss, not mine! But - just imagine if we learned to Bossa Nova together, Pat's," I said, giving him one of my meaningful looks. "And dancing it on the dance floor at the Lacarno! The girls will be lining up to dance with us, but it won't happen unless you give it a try!"

"Jaimie's right you know, Patrick," said mom while busying herself around the house. "I've never said I didn't liked something - without first giving it a try. You never know, Patrick, you might like it?"

"Pat's, if you saw the girls who go dancing at the Lacarno, you'd be asking to come with me. Hardly any of the lads who go there can't dance! They just stand around the dance floor wiggling to the music, hoping by the end of the night they'd pulled!"

"Ahh, but have you ever pulled, because I know how fussy you are?"

"Yeah loads, Pat's! You come with me to learn the Bossa Nova, and I guarantee when we go to the Lacarno on Friday, dressed in our besties, the girls will be queuing up to dance with you! Come on, Pat's will you come, we haven't been out together for ages?"

*

After lots ear bending - and a brand new pair of winkle pickers, Patrick was traveling with me to Lora Dixon's, on the corner of Navigation Street, and John Street. We were only going there to learn a dance, but that was no excuse not to look smart.

The dance studio was huge, with a full length mirror on one wall, so people could see themselves dancing. Pat's and I couldn't resist walking past the mirror several times, looking at our reflection. It was the first we'd ever seen ourselves fully; and I looked like Robert Mitchum, with a fag dangling from one side of my mouth! Pat's looked like, Dean Martin with a fag in his mouth. After ten minute's admiring ourselves, Lora, Dixon's voice called us to attention.

"For those who are new here, welcome to Lora Dixon's dance school. We teach all dances here, including the latest dance the: Bossa Nova, which has now become very popular. We will begin our lessons as always by pairing the beginners with our more accomplished dancers. Right everyone, find your partners!"

I lost Pat's in the hunt to find a partner; and I had mine after a few minutes.

"Hello, what's your name?" she asked me.

"Jay!"

"Hello, Jay I'm Celia; this must be your first time, I haven't seen you here before?"

Before I could tell Celia my life story, she was showing me how to dance, along with everyone else to the music from a record player. I eventually saw Pat's dancing with Lora Dixon herself, and he wasn't happy because she was older than mom.

After half an hour we stopped for a break. Celia disappeared to her friends, with the promise of dancing with me in the second half, and Pat's was with me, telling me about the girl who had been giving him the glad eye while dancing.

"Who is it, show me?" I asked, looking across the dance floor.

"There, look!"

I followed his line of vision to the girl sitting on the bench. "She's lovely, Pat's!"

"I know, and I'm going to ask her out!"

Pat's marched off across the dance floor to her, and came back after a few minutes.

"Well – What did she say then?"

"She said she would!"

"See - what did I say? You've been a few minutes, Pat's and already you've got a date. You're glad you came now aren't you?"

Patrick hesitated before saying, "Yeah - the thing is, Jay, she only said she would if you came along too with her friend!"

"Friend? What friend," I said, scanning the whole floor quickly.

"Jackie - That one there." Pat's, pointed to the girl next to the one he fancied. She had hair thicker than a lion's mane, and instantly I was saying. "Oh no – oh no, no, no, no; I'm not doing that again, Pat's, I'm doing great with the girl I'm dancing with thank you!"

"Why not, she looks nice, Jay! And Tina said she fancies you!"

"Tina, who's Tina?" I asked, scanning my eyes around the dance room floor again.

"The girl I've just asked out. I'm talking about her friend, Jackie!"

Lora Dixon called us to the dance floor again, ready for the second half.

"Well, Jay?"

"No, Pat's! We made an agreement remember; you find your girl to go out with, and I find mine!"

"Yeah I know, but that was then!"

"Pat's! – I've come here to learn the dance and that's it. You want to go on a date with someone from here, then go out with her; I'm going to ask Celia if I can take her out!"

"Who's Celia?"

"The one I'm dancing with!"

"But I've told you, Jay, Tina won't come on a date, unless you come too!"

When I saw Celia walking back to me, my future was made very clear. "Pat's I said no! I've told you I'm going to ask Celia to come out with me. You go out with the girl you fancy, and I'll go out with the girl I fancy, remember?"

"Yes I do – but can you do that after you've done this for me! Please, Jay, Tina won't go out with me unless you go out with her friend as well!"

I looked at Celia, then across the dance floor, sensing fear and horror, as the girl with hair like a lions mane waved to me. "I'm telling you now, Pat's, this is the last time I do anything like this for you!"

"You mean you'll do it?"

Reluctantly I said – "Yes!"

Patrick half danced across the floor, swaying his head in jovial conversation with them both. After a few minutes he swaggered back, with his mouth grinning from ear to ear. "They're going to meet us on Monday at the bus stop, just past the Kingsway picture house – six o-clock; Jay, she's beautiful!"

"Who's beautiful," I said, staring at Jackie, staring back at me.

"Tina, the one I'm going out with on Monday!"

All through the rest of Sunday, I avoided any meaningful conversation with my brother. For my sacrifice going with him on his date, he promised he would come with me to the Locarno every Friday.

About seven o-clock that evening, Lizzie called in with Sean for an impromptu visit.

*

"Come on then, Jay, get a move on or we'll be late!"

"Alright, I'm coming."

"What time did you say we were meeting them?"

"Six o-clock, Jay, I've told you that three times now. I know what you're doing; you're taking your time so we'll be late, and they'll think we're not coming."

"Look, we don't want to get there before them do we? They'll think were really interested!"

"I am really interested." Patrick vented his impatience on the bedroom door, then clumped down the stairs, shouting back at the bottom. "I'm waiting for you by the gate!"

I heard dad talking to Patrick at the gate, and hurried to the front door while putting my shoes on. "Dad, did you have a think about what we were talking about?"

"You mean the car, Jay?"

"Yes, you said you was going to have a think about it! Pat's and I said we'd put some money toward it each week. I'm on good money now, and Pat's getting a good wage working in Gooch Street!"

"Hal, shut the gate after you please; Sally only has to see the gate opening and she'll be off again!"

"Don't worry, Titch I will!"

"You said that last time, Hal, and it took all of us half an hour to get her back - Don't blame me if she gets run over!"

Dad waited until mom had shut the door. "Let's see how things are in another six months, Jay, and we'll talk about it then!"

"Okay, I'll have to go Dad, Pat's blowing a gasket." I waited, just to see if dad closed the gate behind him, then walked down the entry.

"You did that on purpose, Jay!"

"Did what on purpose?"

"Stopped and talked to dad about the car, you could've talked to him about it later!"

Patrick was hurrying up the road in front of me, talking in spurts between breaths.

"I bet they'll be early, and they're by the bus stop waiting for us!"

"What!" I said not hearing half of what he said.

"I said I bet the girls are by the bus stop waiting for us! If you walked a bit faster, Jay you'd hear what I was saying?"

"Pat's I'm walking fast enough, stop panicking; they're not going because were a few minutes late!"

"Well that's what you're hoping for isn't it, they'll be gone before we get there!"

"Stop going on, I'm going with you aren't I!"

Our number 50 bus was just leaving the stop before ours; which meant a quick run to the bus stop if we were to catch it. Patrick was instantly on his heels, calling back to me.

"Jay, there's our bus! If we catch it we might just get there before they do!"

Patrick was wearing his normal shoes, but I had decided to wear my new winkle pickers. They were uncomfortable, and a size smaller than normal, but they were white leather, and the only ones in the shop. I soon found out fashion wasn't worth it when I started running, because they were killing me.

Patrick was already on the bus platform, goading me to run faster.

"Jay get a move on, you can run faster than that!"

"I'm trying, Pat's, but my shoes are killing me!"

"Jay if we miss the girls I'll never go anywhere with you again – I mean it!"

"Good, then I won't have to say no to you again," I shouted, running past the bus stop as the bus pulled away. I leapt onto the platform, grasping the pole with both hands, and gasping for breath. "This is the last time, Pat's!"

The upper deck was smoking only, and that's where we headed for.

The moment I sat down, I eased the shoes off my feet. "When we get back home, I'm throwing these shoes in the dustbin,"

Pat' immediately grasp my arm. "No I'll buy them off you! They're really nice shoes, Jay, and my feet are size eight. How much did you pay for them?"

"Seven and six pence."

"Okay if I give you three shillings for them?"

"Done!"

"Done!"

The next stop was ours, and we made our way down the steps to the platform. I was just hanging slightly over the edge of the bus, hanging onto the pole, and I saw the two girls waiting for us at the bus stop. Jackie's both arms were waving feverously the moment she saw me, and in dread I stepped backward to the steps.

"Don't ding the bell, were not getting off!" I said to the conductor.

The bus whizzed past the bus stop, leaving the two girls waving at us.

"Yes were are," said Pat's pulling me away from the stairs to the platform. "Can you ring the bell for the next stop please, were getting off there?"

"Sorry, Pat's I can't do it," I said standing firm against the stairs.

"Your friend doesn't seem too keen to get off," the conductor said pressing the bell once.

"Na, he's alright, he's just a bit shy!"

It took Pat's - and the conductors efforts to remove me from the bus. The man was irate, ringing the bell twice, while voicing it. "If you want to play silly buggers, do it somewhere else and not on my bus?"

Pat's was quick to apologise, blaming me for his inconvenience. "Sorry mate, my brother sometimes acts like this!"

The conductor watched Jackie, running and waving her arms like a child with a new toy; and as the bus pulled away he humorously called. "If I'd been you mate, I'd have definitely stayed on the bus!"

*

Before the end of 1963 there was a mini parked at the bottom of our entry, with 402B0P on the registration plate. A notice of demolition was also put on every house in the grove, with the evacuation to new premises in Kings Norton due to commence on the first of July, 1964.

Twenty eight
1965

Daisy and Vera at the end of the grove were the first to leave, followed by Erick a few weeks later. Our house was the last to be evacuated, and on April 15th the day came when we had to leave too.

With Lizzie and Sean helping, we travelled back and forth to our new house in Kings Norton, transporting everything that could go in the cars. Anything we couldn't move we left in the garden for the rag and bone man.

We had put the last of the things in the Mini, and were walking from room to room for the last time. This damp old house had been our home since we were born; and every room had a story to tell. Such as Pat's and I, bouncing up and down on our steel spring beds, laughing as each spring made a different Boingging sound. And Lizzie shouting down to mom, 'MOM, they're in the bedroom being stupid again, tell them before I hit them!' And mom playing on the piano singing, 'My old man come follow the band,' while the piano bounced up and down on the rotten floorboards. And the Christmas's we had, sitting in front of the roaring fire, listening to mom humming to the carols on the wireless, while dad made our Christmas breakfast of bacon and eggs in the scullery.

In this house we were boys in short trousers, living in the glow of its gas lamps. We had witnessed the transition of gas being replaced by electricity; and our battery powered wireless made redundant. Our first ever television sat on the shelf in the corner of the living room.

All through the years this house had seen us grow into young men. It had watched Lizzie, growing into a beautiful caring woman, then becoming wife and a mother living in Erdington. It had welcomed her back every Saturday, popping in to see mom and dad; and watched over her daughter, playing on the floor we played on.

"Are you ready, Jay, the workmen are waiting to board up the house?"

"Yeah, I'm ready!" I looked behind one more time, then walked outside. "Have you got the key, Pat's?"

"What for?!"

"To lock the door!"

"We don't need to now, Jay!"

It was the slowest we'd ever walked to the gate, and as I closed the gate gently behind me, it was hard to swallow the lump in my throat.

Mom and dad said to never look back, and always look forward. Our past ended when we left Edward Road in the mini; to continue in a new build in Kings Norton.

*

I closed the album, and gently slid it back on top of the wardrobe. It would be many years before its memories were written in a book - for others to share.

The end

Gas lamps
And
Long trousers

Other books by the author on Amazon

THE GIRL WHO COULD HEAR THE STARS

ESMERELDA
The flower Princess

GORE

AMELIA

Printed in Great Britain
by Amazon